THE
HISTORY OF
COSTA RICA

ADVISORY BOARD

THE
HISTORY OF
COSTA RICA

Monica A. Rankin

The Greenwood Histories of the Modern Nations
Frank W. Thackeray and John E. Findling, Series Editors

 GREENWOOD

AN IMPRINT OF ABC-CLIO, LLC
Santa Barbara, California • Denver, Colorado • Oxford, England

Library of Congress Cataloging-in-Publication Data

Rankin, Monica A., 1972–
  The history of Costa Rica / Monica A. Rankin.
     pages cm. — (The Greenwood histories of the modern nations)
  Includes bibliographical references and index.
     ISBN 978–0–313–37944–4 (hardcopy : alk. paper) — ISBN 978–0–313–37945–1 (ebook)
1. Costa Rica—History. I. Title.
F1546.R36   2012
972.86—dc23   2011053292

ISBN: 978–0–313–37944–4
EISBN: 978–0–313–37945–1

16 15 14 13 12   1 2 3 4 5

This book is also available on the World Wide Web as an eBook.
Visit www.abc-clio.com for details.

Greenwood
An Imprint of ABC-CLIO, LLC

ABC-CLIO, LLC
130 Cremona Drive, P.O. Box 1911
Santa Barbara, California 93116-1911

This book is printed on acid-free paper ∞

Manufactured in the United States of America

To Brian
Pura Vida, *mi amor*

Contents

Series Foreword   ix

Preface   xiii

Timeline of Historical Events   xv

1   Introduction: *Pura Vida*   1

2   Colonial Costa Rica   15

3   Independence and the Early Nineteenth Century   35

4   Emergence of National Identity   51

5   The Consolidation of the Liberal State   65

6   The Banana Republic   79

7   The Social Welfare State and Civil War   95

8   The Cold War and the *Liberación* Era   113

9   State-Led Development and Debt   127

10   Contemporary Costa Rica   143

Notable People in the History of Costa Rica   161

Glossary   171

Bibliographic Essay   183

Index   191

Series Foreword

The Greenwood Histories of the Modern Nations series is intended to provide students and interested laypeople with up-to-date, concise, and analytical histories of many of the nations of the contemporary world. Not since the 1960s has there been a systematic attempt to publish a series of national histories, and as series editors, we believe that this series will prove to be a valuable contribution to our understanding of other countries in our increasingly interdependent world.

Some 40 years ago, at the end of the 1960s, the Cold War was an accepted reality of global politics. The process of decolonization was still in progress, the idea of a unified Europe with a single currency was unheard of, the United States was mired in a war in Vietnam, and the economic boom in Asia was still years in the future. Richard Nixon was president of the United States, Mao Tse-tung (not yet Mao Zedong) ruled China, Leonid Brezhnev guided the Soviet Union, and Harold Wilson was prime minister of the United Kingdom. Authoritarian dictators still controlled most of Latin America, the Middle East was reeling in the wake of the Six-Day War, and Shah Mohammad Reza Pahlavi was at the height of his power in Iran.

Since then, the Cold War has ended, the Soviet Union has vanished, leaving 15 independent republics in its wake, the advent of the computer age has radically transformed global communications, the rising demand for oil makes the Middle East still a dangerous flashpoint, and the rise of new economic powers like the People's Republic of China and India threatens to bring about a new world order. All of these developments have had a dramatic impact on the recent history of every nation of the world.

For this series, which was launched in 1998, we first selected nations whose political, economic, and socio-cultural affairs marked them as among the most important of our time. For each nation, we found an author who was recognized as a specialist in the history of that nation. These authors worked cooperatively with us and with Greenwood Press to produce volumes that reflected current research on their nations and that are interesting and informative to their readers. In the first decade of the series, more than 40 volumes were published, and as of 2008, some are moving into second editions.

The success of the series has encouraged us to broaden our scope to include additional nations, whose histories have had significant effects on their regions, if not on the entire world. In addition, geopolitical changes have elevated other nations into positions of greater importance in world affairs and, so, we have chosen to include them in this series as well. The importance of a series such as this cannot be underestimated. As a superpower whose influence is felt all over the world, the United States can claim a "special" relationship with almost every other nation. Yet many Americans know very little about the histories of nations with which the United States relates. How did they get to be the way they are? What kind of political systems have evolved there? What kind of influence do they have on their own regions? What are the dominant political, religious, and cultural forces that move their leaders? These and many other questions are answered in the volumes of this series.

The authors who contribute to this series write comprehensive histories of their nations, dating back, in some instances, to prehistoric times. Each of them, however, has devoted a significant portion of their book to events of the past 40 years because the modern era has contributed the most to contemporary issues that have an impact on U.S. policy. Authors make every effort to be as up-to-date as possible so that readers can benefit from discussion and analysis of recent events.

In addition to the historical narrative, each volume contains an introductory chapter giving an overview of that country's geography, political institutions, economic structure, and cultural attributes. This is meant to give readers a snapshot of the nation as it exists in the contemporary world. Each history also includes supplementary information following the narrative, which may include a timeline that represents a succinct chronology of the nation's historical evolution, biographical sketches of the nation's most important historical figures, and a glossary of important terms or concepts that are usually expressed in a foreign language. Finally, each author prepares a comprehensive bibliography for readers who wish to pursue the subject further.

Readers of these volumes will find them fascinating and well written. More importantly, they will come away with a better understanding of the contemporary world and the nations that comprise it. As series editors, we hope that this series will contribute to a heightened sense of global understanding as we move through the early years of the twenty-first century.

Frank W. Thackeray and John E. Findling
Indiana University Southeast

Preface

I first ventured to Costa Rica in 1991 as a naïve college student from the Midwest, embarking on the grand adventure that was my summer study abroad in Central America. I had hoped the trip would fine-tune my Spanish language skills, having been told by numerous language experts that in order to *really* speak a foreign language one must experience complete language immersion. And indeed I left the land of the Ticos with more fluency than when I arrived. I managed to find my way around the capital city, order food at restaurants, haggle with vendors in the market, and complete most of my homework in a timely fashion. It was in San José that I had my first dream in Spanish and woke up feeling as though I had mastered the language. But my Costa Rican experience took me far beyond language acquisition as I absorbed the nuances of a beautiful culture and a captivating history. The pulse of the city, the rhythm of daily life with my host family, and the halcyon setting of the countryside on weekend excursions all combined to create a cultural experience that marked the beginning of my fascination with Latin America. My life changed in important ways that summer—June of 1991 marked my first steps on a path that eventually led to an academic career in Latin American studies. I also met my future husband that summer in San José. Eight years later we named our new puppy "Tica" as a statement of our affection for the delightful country that had brought us together. To this day he shares my appreciation for the land of *Pura Vida!* I hope this book imparts to its readers some of sense of what Costa Rican exceptionalism means to me.

I would like to express my gratitude to those individuals who have supported this project. Costa Rican historiography is a developing field—particularly for works published in English or available in the United States. My friend and colleague Thomas Leonard first introduced me to this project. Kyle Longley and Sterling Evans provided intellectual and moral support, and I relied heavily on their excellent scholarship in diplomatic and environmental history, respectively. Bill Beezley offered suggestions, critiques, and encouragement throughout the writing process. And although they are in different fields of study, Jessica Murphy and Cihan Muslu watched this project evolve from the very beginning and provided indispensable intellectual support. I would like to acknowledge the support staff at the McDermott Library at the University of Texas at Dallas for helping me to secure research materials and the editorial staff at ABC-CLIO for helping me see this project through completion. Dr. Roger Dowdy sponsored that initial study-abroad program in the summer of 1991, and he could not have imagined at the time the kinds of future intellectual pursuits the trip would inspire.

As always, I thank my husband Brian and my daughters Kyla and Shiloh for their unwavering support and encouragement.

Timeline of Historical Events

30,000–12,000 BCE	Asiatic nomads cross the Bering Strait in a mass migration to the American continents.
10,000–7000 BCE	First human inhabitants arrive in present-day Costa Rica during the Paleoindian period.
2000–300 BCE	Early Formative period begins and the first permanent settlements are established.
300 BCE–500 CE	Late Formative period.
500–800	Early Polychrome period.
800–1000	Middle Polychrome period.
1000–1500	Late Polychrome period; emergence of *cacicazgos*.
1502	Christopher Columbus lands along the Caribbean coast of Costa Rica and adopts the native name for the region— Cariay or Cariai.
1506	Diego de Nicuesa leads an expedition along the Caribbean coast of Costa Rica.

1508	*Patronato real* decreed by Pope Julius II establishing the Spanish Crown's royal patronage over the Catholic Church in the Americas.
1524	Founding of Villa Bruselas by Francisco Fernández de Córdoba.
1525–1600	European diseases decimate native population.
1527	Villa Bruselas is abandoned by the Spanish.
1540	Founding of Ciudad Badajoz.
	Arrival of Governor Rodrigo de Contreras, who becomes known for his cruelty to natives.
	Formation of the province of Nuevo Cartago y Costa Rica.
1542	Spanish Crown passes the New Laws, which call for humane treatment of natives and limit the *encomienda* system.
1543	Arrival of Governor Diego Gutiérrez y Toledo.
1544	Native uprising against the cruelties of Governor Gutiérrez y Toledo.
1564	Founding of Cartago, which becomes the provincial capital.
1565	Formation of the province of Costa Rica.
	Juan Vázquez de Coronado becomes the first governor of the province of Costa Rica and is known for his humane treatment of natives.
1568	Governor Perafán de Rivera arrives in Cartago and introduces the *encomienda* system.
	Costa Rica becomes part of the *audiencia* of Guatemala.
1590s	Emergence of Costa Rican mule trade.
1609	The *audiencia* of Guatemala becomes a captaincy general.
1635	Appearance of *La Negrita* or the Virgen de los Angeles near Cartago.
1660s	Emergence of cacao cultivation.
1709	Talamanca native uprising.

1710	Execution of Pablo Presbere as punishment for his role in the Talamanca uprising.
1722	Basilica of Our Lady of the Angels completed in Cartago.
1740s	Decline of Costa Rican cacao trade.
1759–1788	Bourbon reforms of the Spanish Crown intensify under Charles III.
1808	French monarch Napoleon Bonaparte invades Iberian Peninsula and forces the abdication of the Spanish king, eventually sparking independence movements in Latin America.
1810–1820s	Wars of independence waged throughout Spanish colonies in Latin America.
1812	Promulgation of the liberal Spanish Constitution of Cádiz, which called for dramatic reforms and greater equality for the Latin American colonies.
1814	Spanish monarch Ferdinand is restored to the throne after the defeat of Napoleon Bonaparte. He immediately abrogates the Constitution of 1812.
1821	Captain General Gabino Gaínza declares independence for the *audiencia* of Guatemala, which includes the province of Costa Rica.
	Central America is absorbed into the newly independent Mexican empire.
1823	Costa Rica breaks away from the Mexican empire.
	Mexican empire collapses.
	Formation of the United Provinces of Central America, made up of Costa Rica, Guatemala, El Salvador, Nicaragua, and Honduras.
	San José becomes the capital of Costa Rica.
1824	United Provinces constitution is promulgated, modeled after the Spanish Constitution of 1812.
	Juan Mora Fernández elected as the first president of the province of Costa Rica.
1825	Costa Rican government removes tithe on export crops.

	Manuel José Arce becomes the first president of the United Provinces of Central America.
1829	Costa Rican mint is established.
1830	First printing press arrives in Costa Rica.
1830s	Costa Rican merchants begin exporting small amounts of coffee.
1830s–1840s	Land reforms aimed at encouraging coffee cultivation are introduced.
1833	Costa Rica's first newspaper, *El Noticiero Universal*, is founded.
1834	*Ley de ambulancia* is passed calling for the administrative capital to rotate among Costa Rica's four principal cities.
1835	War of the League fought by Heredia, Alajuela, and Cartago against San José after *Ley de ambulancia* is abolished.
1838	Costa Rica withdraws from the United Provinces of Central America.
1840s–1930s	Costa Rica ruled by "coffee presidents."
1842	President Braulio Carrillo passes the Law of Foundations and Guarantees, naming himself executive for life and giving himself significant authority.
	Jocote Pact signed between Francisco Morazán and Vicente Villaseñor, leading to the eventual overthrow of Braulio Carrillo.
	Francisco Morazán overthrown and executed after less than six months in office.
1843	Universidad de Santo Tomás opened in San José.
1844	Constitution of 1844 promulgated, allowing for direct elections.
1846	Costa Rica's first major highway, between the port of Puntarenas and the Central Valley, is completed.
1848	Costa Rica declared a republic. A new constitution is promulgated, eliminating direct elections.
	Pacífica Fernández, wife of President José María Castro Madriz, designs the Costa Rican flag.

1850	Clayton-Bulwer Treaty between the United States and Great Britain.
	Costa Rican government launches a failed attempt to attract French colonies in southern Costa Rica.
1850s	Coffee exports dominate Costa Rican economy.
1851	Major earthquake strikes the Central Valley.
1852	Teatro Mora opens in San José.
1856	National Campaign against U.S. filibuster William Walker.
	Juan Santamaría becomes a national hero at the Battle of Rivas.
1856–1857	Cholera epidemic spreads throughout Costa Rica.
1859	Constitution of 1859 promulgated.
1860	Juan Rafael Mora—ousted one year earlier—executed by firing squad.
	William Walker executed in Honduras.
	Creation of Public Works Department within the Costa Rican government.
1862	First national census.
1865	Civil registry is established.
1867	Port of Limón opened to external trade.
1868	First telegraph line between San José and Cartago is built.
1869	First normal school for teacher training opens in San José.
	First system of indoor plumbing introduced in San José.
	Laws passed establishing free and obligatory public education, codified in the Constitution of 1869.
1870	Tomás Guardia Gutiérrez takes power.
1870–1889	Era of "the Olympians."
1870s–1920s	Wave of Afro-Caribbean migration to eastern Costa Rica.
1871	Constitution of 1871 promulgated.

	Costa Rican government signs a contract with Henry Meiggs for the construction of the nation's first railroad.
1877	Tomás Guardia passes Law on Individual Rights.
1881	Creation of Costa Rica's national archives.
1883	Soto-Keith contract.
1883	Minor Keith marries Christina María Fernández, daughter of former president José María Castro Madriz.
1884	Electric street lights installed in San José.
	Archbishop of San José and entire Jesuit order expelled from Costa Rica by liberal government.
1885	*Ley general de educación común* passed, establishing a national curriculum.
1888	National library established.
	Costa Rica adopts Civil Codes, which allow civil marriage and divorce.
	Catholic-run Universidad de Santo Tomás closed by liberal government.
1889	Opposition candidate wins presidential election, bringing an end to the era of "the Olympians."
1897	National Theater opens.
1899	United Fruit Company formed in merger between Minor Keith and Boston Fruit Company.
1903	United States backs Panamanian independence and secures an agreement to build a canal.
1910	Large earthquake in Cartago causes more than 700 deaths.
	Artisan's and Labourer's Union formed in Limón.
1914	Panama Canal completed.
1917	Military coup begins dictatorship of Federico Tinoco. United States announces policy of nonrecognition.
1919	Popular uprising overthrows Federico Tinoco.
1923	Formation of the Costa Rican Feminist League.
1924	Jorge Volio Jiménez forms the Reformist Party.

1928	Banana Massacre on United Fruit Company plantation in Ciénaga, Colombia.
1930s	United Fruit Company expands banana cultivation to the Pacific coast.
1931	Creation of Costa Rica's first Communist Party.
1934	Great Banana Strike in Limón involving 10,000 workers.
1940	University of Costa Rica founded.
	Center for the Study of National Problems founded.
1941	Publication of *Mamita Yunai*.
	Costa Rica declares war on the Axis powers following the Japanese attack on Pearl Harbor.
1942	Nazi submarines sink *San Pablo* cargo ship docked at the Port of Limón.
	José Figueres arrested and sent into exile.
	Introduction of Social Guarantees by President Rafael Angel Calderón Guardia.
1943	Communist Party changes its name to the People's Vanguard Party.
1945	Social Democratic Party founded.
1948	War of National Liberation and formation of the Second Republic.
	Abolition of Costa Rica's standing army.
	Formation of the U.N. Economic Commission for Latin America and the Caribbean.
1949	Adoption of the Constitution of 1949.
	Universal adult suffrage enacted, including women and people of color.
1950s–1970s	Import substitution industrialization serves as Costa Rica's economic development framework.
1951	National Liberation Party founded.
1953	Women vote for the first time in national elections.
	José Figueres elected president.

1954	Creation of National Fisheries Plan and the National Institute for Housing and Urban Development.
	Jacobo Arbenz, left-leaning president of Guatemala, is overthrown in a U.S.-backed coup after he attempts to expropriate United Fruit Company lands.
	Costa Rica boycotts the Tenth International Conference of American States in Caracas to protest the dictatorship of Marcos Pérez Jiménez.
1955	Teodoro Picado, Jr., launches a failed attempt to overthrow José Figueres by leading an invading force from Nicaragua.
	Institute of Costa Rican Tourism (ICT) founded.
1956	Wildlife Conservation Law passed.
	Mexican film *Pura Vida!* debuts in Costa Rica, eventually giving rise to a national motto.
1957	Costa Rica proposes arms reduction in Latin America through the Organization of Latin American States.
1959	Cuban Revolution.
1960	Creation of the Central American Common Market.
1961	U.S. President John F. Kennedy introduces the Alliance for Progress as an aid program for Latin America.
1962	Costa Rica joins the Central American Common Market.
1968	Creation of the Center for the Promotion of Exports and Investments (CENPRO).
	Eruption of Mt. Arenal volcano.
1969	Soccer War between Honduras and El Salvador.
	Forestry Law is passed.
1970s–1980s	Civil wars in neighboring Central American nations.
1972	Creation of the Costa Rican Development Corporation (CODESA).
1973	Oil shock caused by manipulation of production and supply of oil among OPEC countries.
1974	Ratification of the Convention on International Trade in Endangered Species.

1976	Ratification of the Convention for the Protection of Flora, Fauna, and Places of Natural Scenic Beauty in the Countries of the Americas.
1977	Creation of the National Parks Service.
	Social Christian Unity Party is founded.
1980s	"Lost decade," marking economic stagnation in Latin America.
1981	Costa Rica defaults on foreign debt.
	Export Processing Zone and Industrial Parks Law establishes free trade zones.
1982	Costa Rica accepts nearly $100 million in aid from the International Monetary Fund and begins imposing austerity measures.
	Creation of the Costa Rican Coalition of Development Initiatives (CINDE).
1982–1989	Costa Rica receives more than $1 billion in aid from the United States.
	U.S. backed *contras* wage war in Nicaragua in an attempt to bring down leftist Sandinista government.
1983	Caribbean Basin Initiative (CBI) created by United States to offer aid to Central America and prevent revolutions.
1983–1985	Contadora Group attempts to mediate Central American conflict.
1984	Efforts to privatize CODESA begin.
1985	Costa Rica receives $11 in military aid from the United States.
	Tourism Investment Incentives Law is passed.
1986	Reagan administration withholds aid to Costa Rica after President Oscar Arias publicly opposes *contras*.
	Oscar Arias sponsors peace talks with other Central American leaders.
1987	Esquipulas II Peace Accord is reached to bring an end to Central American civil wars.
	Oscar Arias wins Nobel Peace Prize for his role in pursuing Central American peace.

1991	Magnitude 7.5 earthquake strikes Limón.
1997	Intel Corporation opens major microchip manufacturing plant in Heredia.
2002	Because of declining voter participation, Costa Rica is forced to hold a run-off presidential election.
2004	Former president Miguel Angel Rodríguez resigns as secretary-general of the OAS over corruption allegations.
2006	Oscar Arias elected president again after a constitutional amendment changes the law on term limits.
2007	Central American Free Trade Agreement (CAFTA-DR) narrowly approved by Costa Rican voters.
2010	Laura Chinchilla elected as Costa Rica's first female president.

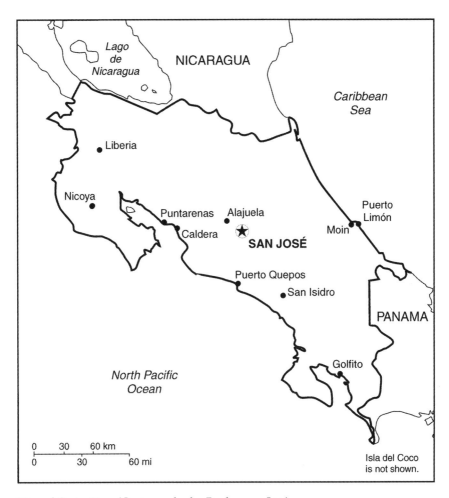

Map of Costa Rica. (Cartography by Bookcomp, Inc.)

1

Introduction: *Pura Vida*

In 1956, a Mexican film debuted in Costa Rica. The comedy, directed by Gilberto Martínez Solares, tells the tale of a clumsy yet likeable main character who—despite his near-constant blunders—maintains a positive attitude that is represented by his use of the phrase that also serves as the title of the film. The phrase becomes his optimistic response to life's obstacles and his own failures, and he delivers the line in such a cheerful manner that a small number of Costa Ricans began emulating his attitude by using the phrase in daily conversations. The phrase that was introduced to Costa Rica in 1956 had become so widely used by the 1970s that it is now considered part of Costa Rican national identity. The name of the Mexican film that gave rise to a uniquely Costa Rican national mantra: *Pura Vida!*

Since 1956, the expression *pura vida* has come to epitomize the character of the Costa Rican nation. *Pura vida* translates literally to "pure life," but its meaning in colloquial usage varies widely. It is commonly expressed as a form of salutation and as a parting remark, similar to the way *aloha* is used in Hawaii. Additionally, it is frequently used as a general affirmative response, an expression of positive feeling, and a term of friendship. But the phrase resonates even more deeply with

many Costa Ricans who use it to express a relaxed and peaceful outlook on life. *Pura vida* provides a useful trope through which we can
examine the Central American country that has earned a reputation
for economic stability, long-standing political freedoms, and an
advanced system of social justice, particularly when compared to the
experiences of its Latin American neighbors. Costa Ricans embrace
the expression as a reflection of the nation's own sense of exceptionalism—as a symbol of the national character that sets it apart from its
Latin American neighbors. While some may challenge the notion of
Costa Rican exceptionalism, many more will affirm that the motto
Pura Vida is a fitting one to describe the unique national identity that
has emerged in Costa Rica over the course of its history.

GEOGRAPHY

Located in the heart of the Central American isthmus, Costa Rica
measures slightly less than 32,000 square miles (roughly 51,000 square
kilometers), making it approximately the size of the state of West
Virginia.[1] Abundant rivers crisscross the nation, providing fresh water
for irrigation, industry, and domestic use. Costa Rica shares a border
to the north with Nicaragua and to the southeast with Panama. One
of the largest rivers, the San Juan, marks the northern border with
Nicaragua and is fed by two other main rivers, the San Carlos and
the Sarapiqui. Boundary disputes and disagreement over navigation
rights on the San Juan River generated significant conflict between
Costa Rica and Nicaragua, particularly in the decades following
independence in the nineteenth century. The smaller Sixoala River
forms part of the border with Panama in the southeast.

Costa Rica's 800 miles (1,290 kilometers) of coastline include boundaries marked by both the Caribbean Sea and the Pacific Ocean. The
Pacific coastline is roughly three times the length of the Caribbean
coast. Its topography is rugged and hilly, and Pacific coastal rivers
are largely unnavigable. But the Pacific coast is host to two major pen-
insulas—the Nicoya to the north and the Osa to the south. Puerto Cal-
dera and Puntarenas are two main ports that operate along the Pacific
coast. They serve industrial shipping needs and are also ports of call
for some tourist cruise lines. The Caribbean coast has a smoother
topography with inviting and well-developed beaches, making it an
ideal setting for the luxury beach resorts that have been developed in
recent years. The rivers in this region are more navigable, and 14 major
river systems empty into the Caribbean Sea. The thriving tourism
industry has taken advantage of impressive whitewater rapids along

many of these rivers to market Costa Rica as a favorite destination for adventure vacationers. Puerto Limón is the nation's primary Caribbean port. Its strategic location as the main exit point for Costa Rica's agricultural export sector in the late nineteenth and early twentieth centuries facilitated the growth of the city, which now boasts a population of roughly 60,000. U.S.-based railroad and tropical fruit companies recruited large numbers of Afro-Caribbean migrants workers to the region, many of whom have remained in Limón and have given the city a unique cultural flair.

Costa Rica enjoys a varied topography, with a combination of coastal plains and mountainous zones, that is ideal for certain types of agriculture. The relatively small landmass that makes up the nation is generally divided into four geographical areas based on location, climate, and topography. The Northwest Peninsula includes the Nicoya Peninsula that juts out prominently into the Pacific Ocean from Costa Rica's northwestern coast. The North Central Plains region borders Nicaragua, and many areas of the plains have been cleared for livestock. The region also contains lush rainforests, which have made some areas of the North Central Plains popular destinations for the nation's many ecotourists. The Tropical Lowlands occupy the Caribbean and Pacific coastlines, where climate and soil conditions allowed the emergence of a thriving banana industry in the late nineteenth and early twentieth centuries. The Central Valley is nestled in the mountain ranges that divide the coastal regions. Costa Rica's largest cities are located there, and the Central Valley has historically been the hub of political and economic activity, at least since the beginning of the colonial period.

Costa Rica's climate is mainly tropical and subtropical, with a characteristic warm and dry season from December through April and a rainy season from May through November each year. Costa Ricans refer to the dry months as "summer" because the lack of rainfall tends to be accompanied by warm, sunny weather. The rainy season is generally cooler and therefore is referred to as "winter" in Costa Rica. During the rainy season some areas of Costa Rica experience near-daily tropical downpours while other areas receive more prolonged bouts of steady rain. The average annual rainfall is between 80 and 160 inches for the country as a whole.

Temperatures vary by region more than by season. Coastal areas are the warmest with average annual temperature ranges around 80 degrees Fahrenheit. Due to their altitude, the highland regions are much cooler with average annual temperatures between 40 and 50 degrees Fahrenheit. The Central Valley is generally known for its temperate climate. Rainfall also varies by region with the Caribbean coast generally receiving more rain than the Pacific coast. As a result of differences in cloud cover, rainfall, and other climatological factors, the Pacific coast is often warmer on average than the eastern coast. Costa Rica's tropical and subtropical climate supports a system of rainforests and one of the most diverse ecosystems in the world. In recent decades the government has taken important steps to protect tropical vegetation and to cultivate an ecotourism industry. Roughly 25 percent of the nation's territory today is set aside as forest reserves, national parks, or some other protected-area designation.

A series of mountain ranges bisects Costa Rica's coastal topography, with four main cordillera chains descending the length of the country and making up the Continental Divide through Central America. The Talamanca Mountain Range is located in the south and stretches across the border into Panama. It houses Chirripó Mountain—which is Costa Rica's highest peak at 12,450 feet (approximately 3,800 meters)—as well as the Cerros de Escazú, which form part of the border of the Central Valley. The Talamanca Mountain Range is the largest cordillera in Costa Rica, and its difficult terrain has meant that much of the range remains unexplored. The Guanacaste Mountain Range is located in the north, stretching westward toward the Nicoya Peninsula and resting close to the Nicaragua border. It is home to a number of national parks and nature preserves. The Tilarán Mountain Range and the Central Mountain Range are more centrally located, just north of the Central Valley.

The dramatic presence of Costa Rica's many mountain ranges is due to the active shifting of two tectonic plates—the Cocos Plate on the Pacific side and the Caribbean Plate to the east. The Cocos Plate is gradually compressing underneath the Caribbean Plate, which results in significant volcanic and seismic activity in Costa Rica. Indeed, its dozens of active volcanoes situate Costa Rica as part of the Pacific Ring of Fire. Volcanic activity occurs regularly throughout the mountainous zone, drawing a number of tourists to Costa Rica each year. Four major volcanoes are located in the Central Mountain Range: Poas, Irazú, Turrialba, and Barva. All four are situated in protected national park land, and they are surrounded by spectacular forests. They are the highest volcanoes in Costa Rica, and all have been active but not destructive in recent decades with the exception of Barva, which has not been active for hundreds of years. Arenal, the nation's most active volcano, is located in the Tilarán Mountain Range. It was considered inactive prior to the 1960s, but a major eruption occurred on July 29, 1968, and the crater has been regularly belching out lava,

Ash cloud created by the eruption of Mt. Arenal, July 29, 1968. (AP Photo)

ash, and boulders ever since. Arenal has become a major tourist attraction with its impressive eruptions that were occurring almost nightly until late in 2010. Nevertheless, dangerous eruptions are not common, although a major eruption occurred at the Irazú volcano in 1963, after which ash and debris rained over San José and other areas of the Central Valley for two years.

Such high levels of tectonic activity also make Costa Rica home to an extensive network of fault lines that produce regular seismic movement, ranging in strength from minor tremors to more powerful and destructive earthquakes. Seismic activity has long played a prominent role in the nation's history. Cartago—a principal colonial city in the Central Valley—suffered severe damage due to temblors throughout the colonial period and the nineteenth century. In fact, a major tourist attraction there is the ruins of the Parish of Santiago Apóstol Church. The church was leveled by a major quake in 1910, which claimed more than 700 lives, but city residents left the ruins of the church structure in place. It is now part of a city park in the historic center of downtown Cartago. In 1991 a magnitude 7.5 quake struck near Limón, destroying much of the surrounding infrastructure and resulting in substantial casualties. Costa Rica may experience as many as 1,000 mild tremors each year, but most go unnoticed by the population.

PEOPLE

Costa Ricans refer to themselves as "Ticos" (or "Ticas" in the female form), and the colloquialism has become yet another expression of a Costa Rican sense of national exceptionalism. While the origin of the moniker is uncertain, a commonly held belief is that it came about because of Costa Ricans' tendency to add the suffix -*tico* instead of -*ito* to the end of nouns. Appending the suffix -*ito* to the end of words makes them diminutive in Spanish, and it is also an expression of affection. Costa Ricans' unique use of the suffix -*tico* sets them apart from the rest of Latin America, and many Ticos believe the practice eventually evolved into the charming sobriquet reserved exclusively for native Costa Ricans. The use of the word *Tico* to describe all things Costa Rican is recognized throughout the country and indeed around the world. Numerous Costa Rican businesses use the word *Tico* in their names, and the word is frequently used as an adjective to describe "something from Costa Rica."

According to the 2011 Costa Rican census, of the roughly 4.5 million Ticos inhabiting the nation, nearly two-thirds reside in the Central Valley, or *Meseta Central*. This includes the approximately 1.4 million people who live in San José, the nation's capital. In contrast to many other regions of Latin America, the country's population is relatively ethnically homogenous. This is due in part to the comparatively small indigenous population that resided in the region in the pre-Columbian era. When the Spanish arrived in the sixteenth century, they found small, scattered native villages, which were difficult to conquer and resistant to Spanish control. Many of the villagers fled into the surrounding highlands, and small villages remained outside the Spanish system throughout the colonial period. The expansion of capitalist agriculture through the cultivation of coffee, and later tropical fruits, eventually encroached on Indian lands in the nineteenth and twentieth centuries. Miscegenation between European settlers and the local indigenous population did occur, and today approximately 94 percent of Costa Ricans are classified ethnically as mestizo. But the preponderance of the nation's European racial and cultural heritage is still evident today as most Costa Rican mestizos categorize themselves racially and ethnically as white. Only about 1 percent of the population is classified as Indian, and most of them live as subsistence farmers on specially designated Indian reserves.

This serves in stark contrast to neighboring Guatemala, where roughly 40 percent of the population is classified as Indian.

The prevalence of European heritage in Costa Rica belies the fact that the nation was host to significant waves of immigration at various times throughout its history. A small influx of African slaves arrived during the colonial period, but their numbers were quite small, and most were assimilated into the European and mestizo population by the beginning of the nineteenth century. A more significant wave of Afro-Caribbean migration occurred between 1870 and 1920 to fill the need for laborers in the construction of the nation's first railroad and later on coastal banana plantations. Chinese, German, Italian, and Nicaraguan workers also migrated to Costa Rica in the late nineteenth and early twentieth centuries, but they were outnumbered by the West Indians from Jamaica, St. Kitts, Barbados, and Trinidad. Migrant workers settled primarily along the Caribbean coast, where a thriving banana plantation economy was emerging. During that time, nearly 25 percent of Costa Rica's population growth was due to immigration. Immigrants' labor was vital in developing the nation's transportation infrastructure and expanding its economic base, but their presence was often the source of intense racial conflict. A series of laws was passed in the early twentieth century that aimed to prevent West Indian migrants in particular from relocating to the Central Valley and the Pacific coast. Those laws were later repealed, and descendants of the original Afro-Caribbean laborers were free to relocate to other areas of the country. But the impact of such discriminatory practices is still evident today as most of the black population in Costa Rica remains concentrated in Limón and the surrounding provinces along the eastern coast.

With a relatively high life expectancy and a relatively low infant mortality rate, Costa Rica ranks high according to common measures of overall health and standard of living. Its population grows at a manageable 1.3 percent per year, and the national government has historically devoted considerable resources to social services. Costa Ricans have ready access to health care and social security, and many outside observers credit those programs in explaining the nation's relatively high standard of living. Costa Ricans take pride in the nation's tradition of high-quality education programs, and approximately 95 percent of the adult population is literate.

ECONOMY

Historically, Costa Rica's economy developed as one based on agricultural production. The nation's biodiversity, topography, and moderate climate allow for the cultivation of a variety of foodstuffs. Early European colonists learned early that despite the name *Costa Rica* (rich coast), the region yielded few precious metals or other mineral resources. Colonial settlements emerged around privately and publicly owned landed estates, and Costa Ricans experimented with a number of agricultural products prior to the nineteenth century. After achieving independence from Spain, Costa Rican landowners began cultivating coffee, which became the nation's first commodity export product. A national coffee elite emerged, controlling politics for many decades in the last half of the nineteenth century. By the end of the century U.S. entrepreneurs—led by railroad magnate Minor Keith—had secured lucrative land contracts and were developing a new industry in banana cultivation. Keith created the United Fruit Company (UFC), and he expanded his business venture to include most of Central America and significant holdings in northern South America as well. As the original "banana republic," Costa Rica saw a dramatic expansion of its export economy through the cultivation of bananas and other UFC activities.

While the advent of the banana industry brought some benefit to Costa Rica, the fact that U.S. business interests dominated the new export sector became a source of contention over time. Workers argued that UFC's labor practices were exploitative while national leaders grew concerned that the economy was growing dependent on a foreign entity. In the last half of the twentieth century, new economic models were put into place that aimed to develop an industrial sector and to create a new level of economic self-sufficiency for the nation. Those models were labeled import substitution industrialization, and over time the push to industrialize proved enormously costly to the national government. Like other Latin American nations, Costa Rica suffered a severe debt crisis in the 1980s, and in exchange for foreign aid packages from the United States and the International Monetary Fund national leaders were forced to impose a number of economic reform measures that effectively dismantled the industrialization schemes of the preceding decades.

In the final years of the twentieth century, Costa Ricans turned increasingly to neoliberal economic models, which emphasize trade liberalization policies and the creation of a favorable climate for foreign investments. Costa Rica continues to be an agricultural producer, but it has also diversified its economic base as well. Technical manufacturing firms have opened operations in free trade zones near port cities and in the Central Valley. Costa Rica's service sector has expanded significantly as well, a trend aided by the existence of a highly skilled and educated workforce. Notable growth has occurred in the tourism industry, with large luxury beach resorts and adventure and ecotourist facilities opening throughout the country in recent decades. Costa Rica's reputation for peace and stability has made the country an attractive option for international travelers. High school and college students also look to Costa Rica as a favorite destination for study abroad programs that focus on language and culture.

POLITICAL SYSTEM

Costa Ricans have long embraced their political system as evidence of Costa Rican exceptionalism. Over time, the nation has gained a reputation as a defender of democracy and as a symbol of political stability. To be sure, Costa Rica suffered its share of instability and conflict, particularly in the decades immediately following independence. But the extreme violence and near-constant abrogation of governments that plagued many other regions of Latin America did not afflict Costa Rica. Brief struggles emerged in the immediate aftermath of independence as local leaders sought to sustain their authority through various power shifts. Costa Rica endured an attempted invasion by a private U.S. citizen acting as a mercenary, or filibuster, in the 1850s and several strongman dictators in the nineteenth century. A brief period of dictatorial rule returned in the 1920s, followed by a 44-day civil war in 1948, but the scale of political volatility was significantly less than the protracted and bloody insurrections that repeatedly occurred in the rest of Central America.

Costa Rica's government operates as a democratic republic under a constitution that was revised and rewritten in 1949. The three branches of government—executive (made up of the president and two vice presidents), legislative, and judiciary—offer a set of checks and balances, and power has changed hands peacefully since the governing document went into effect. Some consider the Supreme Electoral Tribunal to operate as a fourth branch of government. It oversees elections, campaigning, political party activities, and all other functions associated with the electoral process. All citizens ages 18 and older are permitted and required to vote, and Costa Rica has generally enjoyed an impressive rate of voter turnout. Costa Ricans have an aversion to allowing any one person or party to wield too much power, and the outgoing president is not allowed to run for immediate reelection—in fact a former president must wait eight years before running for president again. Voters have demonstrated their reluctance to allow one party to dominate by generally electing the presidential candidate from the opposition party in each election. In 2010 Costa Ricans flouted that trend and elected the nation's first female president, who had been vice president to the incumbent. Laura Chinchilla, who was 50 years old when she took office, was seen by many as a new generation and a fresh start in Costa Rican politics.

Administratively Costa Rica is divided into seven provinces: Alajuela, Cartago, Guanacaste, Heredia, Limón, Puntarenas, and San José. Representing the provinces in the national Legislative Assembly are 57 deputies who are selected by a combination of direct election and proportional representation. Deputies are not eligible for immediate reelection but may run for office again after sitting out one four-year term. Until recently Costa Rica had a fairly stable two-party system, but voter discontent in the 1990s allowed grassroots opposition parties to gain ground, and a new multiparty system has emerged. This type of system can be more cumbersome as it requires a large degree of cooperation and alliances across party lines.

CULTURE

As the motto *Pura Vida* suggests, Costa Rica's population maintains a carefree and optimistic attitude, and that spirit is often associated with a number of historical and contemporary characteristics that have defined national identity. Unlike the Central American nations surrounding it, Costa Rica boasts a relatively smooth and peaceful historical development, particularly in the twentieth century. Having dissolved its standing military in 1948, the country avoided much of the violence and political instability that plagued other Latin American nations in the context of the Cold War. Indeed, Costa Rica has been viewed as a stabilizing force in Central America, and former President Oscar Arias Sánchez (1986–1990, 2006–2010) was awarded the 1987 Nobel Peace Prize for his role in bringing an end to the bloody and violent armed conflicts that were raging in Guatemala and El Salvador as well as general political unrest in Honduras and Panama in the 1980s. His peace accords were widely popular and were viewed as a Central American solution to a Central American problem, allowing the region to resolve Cold War unrest without the domineering hand of the United States. Additionally, eliminating its military budget allowed Costa Rica to expand its expenditures for education and other social services significantly. Education spending stands at roughly 5 percent of gross domestic product (GDP), ranking Costa Rica 66th in the world. By comparison, the United States ranks 46th with 5.5 percent of GDP devoted to education. Such a strong emphasis on education in Costa Rica has produced an impressive literacy rate and has allowed the country to cultivate a large middle class of educated and highly skilled workers.

Costa Rica's Spanish heritage is evident in the predominance of the Roman Catholic religion. Indeed, the constitution of 1949 named Catholicism as Costa Rica's official religion, but it did not forbid other religions. Evangelical and other Protestant religions have gained ground in recent years, but more than three-quarters of Costa Ricans still consider themselves Catholic. Catholicism was an important presence during the Spanish conquest and the colonial period, and when the nation became independent in the nineteenth century Catholic leaders often played a prominent role in political and social developments. The Church controlled early education and was the keeper of vital statistics, such as births, marriages, and deaths, but by the end of the nineteenth century Liberal politicians had secularized many of the social functions the Church had fulfilled. Anticlericalism in Costa Rica was not as contentious as it was in other areas of Latin America, but conflict between church and government leaders did surface from time to time.

Even though Protestant denominations have made significant inroads into Costa Rica, the Catholic Church maintains a ubiquitous presence. Large colonial churches adorn the central plazas of large cities and small villages alike, and significant numbers of Costa Ricans attend mass regularly. Prayers are read at the start of each day in public schools, and many government offices have a small chapel or shrine for employees. One of Costa Rica's national symbols is the Virgen de los Angeles, or La Negrita, in honor of a stone figurine of the Virgin Mary discovered by a peasant girl in the seventeenth century. Small shrines to the Virgin are common throughout the country, and many Ticos visibly showcase their faith by displaying crucifixes and other religious replicas in their homes, cars, and places of business.

Other national symbols were created and reinforced by the national government starting in the nineteenth century. Costa Rica's most widely recognized national hero is Juan Santamaría, a lowly foot soldier who sacrificed himself to bring the Costa Rican army to victory against the invasion by U.S. filibuster William Walker in the 1850s. Statues to Juan Santamaría are prominently displayed throughout the country, and San José's international airport is named for him. The music that became Costa Rica's national anthem was written around the same time. Lyrics were added in 1903, and the anthem was officially adopted by the government in 1949. Costa Rica's flag features a wide horizontal red stripe through the middle surrounded by narrower white and blue stripes above and below. The national coat of arms is featured on the left side. Costa Rica adopted the color scheme in 1848, modeling the national symbol after the French flag in a statement of support for revolutionary activity in Europe. The nation celebrates its independence day on September 15, and a number of additional government holidays commemorate national heroes and religious occasions throughout the year.

Markers of Costa Rican culture further reflect the nation's rich history. Pre-Columbian civilizations produced a number of impressive artifacts, and recent excavations have generated new interest in early jade and gold figurines from Costa Rica's early inhabitants. As a colony, Costa Rica was generally poor and isolated from the power centers of the Spanish empire. Some remnants of the rich colonial heritage are visible in majestic churches and other historic architecture, but Costa Rica's colonial culture left fewer imprints than are evident in other areas of Latin America. Starting in the nineteenth century, buildings, artwork, and daily practices began to reflect historical trends that accompanied an emerging Costa Rican character. The income generated by the coffee industry allowed the elite to import markers of high culture from Europe, a common trend in the nineteenth century. Monuments and public buildings, such as the National Theater, often imitated European styles that were considered the hallmark of sophistication and modernization. In the early decades of the twentieth century, literature, art, and other cultural expressions began to reflect more nationalist themes as writers and painters sought to create a national style and rejected the informal imperialist tendencies associated with borrowing cultural signifiers from abroad.

Cultural expressions in Costa Rica often followed economic trends. In the early decades of the twentieth century, bucolic settings characterized many artistic works, and the role of the agricultural sector was prominently visible. One of Costa Rica's most well-known novels, *Mamita Yunai*, is set on a Caribbean banana plantation and describes the plight of exploited banana workers. In the last half of the twentieth century, writers and artists often looked to the urban middle class as a representation of Costa Rican culture, and in recent years, environmental issues have become a favorite topic. Other artists have resurrected a unique style of folk art to appeal to the growing number of foreign tourists. Charming folk dances, carved figurines, and the painted Costa Rican miniature oxcart tantalize tourists and satisfy their quest for quaint, local culture.

In the 1970s the Costa Rican government formed the Ministry of Culture, Youth, and Sports along with other national organizations to promote theater, music, and art. Government funding for artistic programs has been unreliable as the country experienced major economic crises in the 1980s, but the forum for promoting a national culture remains. Daily expressions of popular culture today reflect the strong influence of the United States and the rest of the world in Costa Rica. Movies and television are popular forms of daily entertainment, and most of them are produced in the United States or in neighboring Latin American countries. Sports offer another form of cultural expression, and *futból*, or soccer, is one of the most popular forms of recreation. Informal games pop up wherever a ball and makeshift field can be found. Professional leagues offer a source of common identity for fans, and the Costa Rican national team provides an important forum for national unity during World Cup series.

The notion of Tico exceptionalism exemplified in the expression *pura vida* is tied to a long history in which Costa Ricans have generally viewed themselves as distinct from their Latin American neighbors. It is a hard-won label that can belie the fact that the nation experienced its share of ups and downs during the era of Spanish colonial rule, the period of national consolidation in the nineteenth century, and the quest for political and economic stability in the twentieth century. But the fact remains that today Costa Rica enjoys a reputation as a stable and peaceful country. That reputation is illustrated by the fact that the small Central American nation has successfully attracted a diverse array of direct investments by foreign corporations and is a favorite destination for vacationers and student travelers. While there are some who question the validity of Costa Rican exceptionalism, the concept has come to define the way many Costa Ricans understand the nation's history. Costa Rica is peace. Costa Rica is democracy. Costa Rica is happiness. Costa Rica is *Pura Vida!*

NOTE

1. All facts and figures in the chapter are from the 2011 version of the Central Intelligence Agency's *World Fact Book*.

2

Colonial Costa Rica

THE TALAMANCA INSURRECTION

On July 4, 1710, Pablo Presbere, a native of the Suinse indigenous community, was paraded through the streets of Cartago in the Central Valley of Costa Rica and then publicly executed by Spanish colonial officials. His corpse was decapitated and the head placed on a high stake for public display. Presbere had been condemned to death for leading a native uprising against Spanish settlers and missionaries in the Talamanca region of southeastern Costa Rica. Indigenous insurgents had revolted as Spanish settlers attempted to extend colonial rule to the Talamanca region and to bring the people there under Spanish control. Rebels targeted symbols of Spanish authority, burning more than a dozen chapels and killing several missionaries and soldiers. The response by colonial officials was immediate and aggressive. More than 700 natives were captured along with Presbere, and the group of prisoners was marched for two weeks from Talamanca to the city of Cartago; 200 perished during the arduous journey. Presbere's execution was intended to serve as a testament to Spanish power as well as a warning to other local natives who might be tempted to resist colonial authority.

Despite the harsh punishment imposed on Presbere and his followers in 1710, the natives of the Talamanca region continued to resist Spanish attempts to colonize the area. More than two centuries after the first Europeans landed on the shores of Costa Rica, large pockets of native resistance thrived in many of the outlying areas, indicating precisely how tenuous the Spanish administrative presence in Costa Rica was. Indeed throughout the rest of the colonial period, natives in Talamanca and in other regions remained free from direct Spanish subordination. Their success can partially be explained by the distance and difficult topography separating the outlying region from centers of Spanish colonial authority in the Central Valley that allowed many natives to remain outside the official colonial sphere. But Talamancan autonomy was also due to an emerging sense of unity among local natives groups and a strong resolve to maintain a sense of independence. In his death, Pablo Presbere became a symbol of the natives' defiant spirit and their successful efforts to resist Spanish rule, and today he is recognized as one of the country's national heroes. But this incident illustrates more than just the recalcitrant nature of the local native population. It is a fitting example of the complexities that emerged in the Costa Rican province during the colonial period. Small, scattered indigenous communities proved difficult for the Spanish to conquer, and many of the peripheral regions—like Talamanca—remained isolated and detached from the colonial society that was emerging in the Central Valley.

PRE-COLUMBIAN PEOPLE

When the first Europeans arrived in the Americas in the late fifteenth century, they found a variety of native civilizations ranging from small, scattered tribes in outlying regions to large, sophisticated, and densely populated cities. Archaeological evidence indicates that Asiatic nomads crossed the Bering Strait between Asia and present-day Alaska between 30,000 and 12,000 BCE. As hunter-gatherer societies, many of those people migrated southward, arriving in present-day Costa Rica between 10,000 and 7000 BCE during an era known as the Paleoindian period. For several thousand years, Costa Rican natives remained nomadic and relied on hunting and gathering techniques for subsistence. The Early Formative period began in 2000 BCE when pre-Columbian peoples began making the shift away from the nomadic lifestyle to more permanent settlements based on rudimentary agriculture. During the Late Formative period from 300 BCE to 500 CE and the Middle Polychrome period from 500 to 1000 CE cultural differences among various regions in Costa Rica began to emerge. Spanish exploration in the region began at the end of the Late Polychrome period. By then, Costa Rica had become a site of cultural and economic interactions between local indigenous people and the pre-Columbian civilizations that inhabited both North and South America.

Estimates suggest that prior to the arrival of Europeans, approximately 400,000 indigenous people inhabited the region that today encompasses Costa Rica. Generally, archaeologists divide pre-Columbian Costa Rica into three distinct geographic and cultural areas. The Central Highlands and Atlantic Watershed zone encompasses the area stretching from the Central Valley to the Atlantic coast. The Greater Chiriquí-Diquís region is located along the southern Pacific coast. The Guanacaste-Nicoya area is located in the northwestern corner of present-day Costa Rica, bordering Nicaragua and the Pacific Ocean. Compared to other pre-Columbian civilizations in Mexico and South America, Costa Rican native communities were relatively small and dispersed, but their small size and lack of a centralized political organization made it difficult for the Spanish to bring these Central American indigenous populations under control. This was particularly true of native groups in the Central Highlands and Atlantic Watershed zone as well as the groups in the Greater Chiriquí-Diquís region.

The sparsely populated central and southern regions of Costa Rica were inhabited by Bribri, Cabecares, Cotos, Guaymí, Quepos, and Borucas, which were all subsets of the South American Chibcha group. These groups shared a number of common cultural traits with their South American progenitors. They were seminomadic, living in small settlements and subsisting on tubers, tree fruits, small animals, and fish. The architectural sites in these regions suggest additional South American influence, particularly in the form of large spherical stones found at burial sites and other locations. Central and southern Costa Rica lacked large organized native settlements and yielded little in the way of precious metals. Gold, jade, and other materials played a prominent role in religious rituals and were symbols of political and economic power, but the quantity and quality of precious metals and gems were much poorer than in other areas of the Americas.

Costa Rica's natural topography kept the southern portion of the isthmus relatively isolated from the large native societies that had emerged in Mesoamerica over many centuries. The area known as Mesoamerica (or Middle America) encompasses central and southern Mexico and extends southward to include present-day Guatemala,

Belize, El Salvador, Honduras, and Nicaragua in Central America. The pre-Columbian societies that occupied this area developed sophisticated systems of agriculture, astronomy, mathematics, and religion. As early as 1500 BCE, the Olmec civilization rose to prominence in central and southern Mexico. Their influence quickly spread throughout Mesoamerica and extended as far as the northern regions of Central America. The Olmecs built large cities, impressive architectural structures, and a complex political organization. The eventual decline of this civilization facilitated the rise of other Mesoamerican societies, and the Olmecs are often referred to as the "mother culture" in the region. The Teotihuacan, the Zapotecs, and the Maya were sophisticated civilizations that emerged throughout central and southern Mexico and Central America from 300 BCE to 650 CE. Influenced by the scientific and cultural advances of the Olmecs before them, these societies built cities that housed some of the largest populations in the world at that time. The Maya were in a state of decline by the time European explorers arrived in Central America, but a significant though dispersed population could be found throughout Central America.

While the formal Mayan empire did not extend as far south as Costa Rica, archeological evidence indicates that its informal reach did extend to the Nicoya region. Relatively large populations inhabited the northern Pacific region and parts of the Central Valley, where the influence of Mesoamerican civilizations was evident through commonalities in agriculture, diet, and religious beliefs. These included the Garabito, Pococí, Corobici, Orotina, Tomi, Chira, Guetar, and Chorotega societies. The largest and most organized of these peoples were the Corobici and the Chorotega, who were located in the Nicoya Peninsula in the north along the Pacific coast. Like the Maya and the Aztecs to the north, Costa Rican natives held religious beliefs that were based on a polytheistic pantheon and tied very closely to natural phenomena. Natives used the scarce amounts of gold available in the region to create religious relics, which were housed in specially designated temples. Religious ceremonies incorporated some human sacrifice, although this practice was relatively rare in comparison to other Mesoamerican civilizations. Like the Maya, the natives of northern Costa Rica revered corn and developed religious practices to ensure a fruitful harvest. Indeed the cultivation of corn and other agricultural products was an important part of daily life for native communities in the Nicoya Peninsula, and it facilitated the growth of organized and more densely populated villages.

Although pre-Columbian villages had earlier been organized into large confederations, by the beginning of the sixteenth century this political organization had broken down, and the Spanish were greeted by semiautonomous villages loosely organized into chieftainships, or *cazicazgos*. Each of these chieftainships was administered by a member of the local nobility known as a *cacique*, and each occupied a specific place within the regional hierarchy. *Caciques* generally inherited their authority through kinship ties, and their authority was legitimated through religious beliefs. Many native populations attributed divine and supernatural qualities to local leaders. Warfare, as a means of acquiring wealth, material goods, territory, and a slave labor force, was not uncommon among the chieftainships. As a result, a system of loose alliances had evolved among many of the main chieftainships in the northern regions. Spanish conquistadores sought to disrupt these alliances and subvert the system of *cacicazgos* that had kept a tenuous balance prior to their arrival.

SPANISH CONQUEST

The first Europeans arrived in present-day Costa Rica in 1502, when Christopher Columbus's fourth voyage landed on the Caribbean coast. Columbus, who famously assumed he had landed in India, also erroneously reported in his journal that the region held great caches of gold. The area, which is today the port city of Limón, was called "Cariari" or "Cariay" by the local native population. Columbus retained the name, and later conquistadores perpetuated the myth of the region's mining wealth by naming it "Costa Rica," or rich coast. The great irony of this nomenclature is that Spanish conquistadores, and later Spanish settlers, found very little mineral wealth, and throughout the colonial era Costa Rica gained a reputation as one of Spain's poorest overseas possessions.

Unlike other regions of the Americas, the Spanish conquest of Costa Rica was difficult and drawn out. After Columbus's initial landing in 1502, other explorers were drawn to the region by the promise of great riches. The first attempt at establishing a permanent Spanish presence in Costa Rica occurred in 1506 when the Crown dispatched Diego de Nicuesa to colonize the region. Nicuesa led an expedition to Central America but landed far south of his intended landing spot and was forced to travel northward over land from present-day Panama. He encountered hostile natives and unforgiving terrain as he struggled to lead his forces toward Limón. Nicuesa eventually abandoned his quest after losing more than half the members of his expedition. After Vasco Nuñez de Balboa discovered the Pacific Ocean in 1513, even more Spanish explorers arrived in Costa Rica, leading expeditions along both coasts.

It was not until 1524 that the next explorer attempted to establish another permanent settlement when Francisco Fernández de Córdoba founded Villa Bruselas along the Pacific coast. Although the town was abandoned after just three years, it served as a base of operations for the first formal attempts at conquest in Costa Rica. Spanish conquistadores raided neighboring native villages and sent captured Indians into forced labor. In fact, many natives were shipped to other Spanish settlements in the Caribbean and along the mainland to serve as slave laborers for the earliest conquistadores and settlers. Some Spanish leaders followed the example that had produced desired results in Mexico by allying themselves with native *caciques* and demanding the local leaders comply with onerous tribute and labor demands. Cooperation between *caciques* and conquistadores prevented the natives from mounting an organized and united resistance to the Spanish incursions, and it also quickly undermined the authority of local leaders. Many natives did resist, but their efforts were hampered by the introduction of European diseases against which natives had no immunity. Many of the Costa Rican indigenous people succumbed to smallpox, influenza, typhus, and other European illnesses, while others were captured and enslaved. By the 1550s, the native population in the Nicoya Peninsula had dropped by more than 75 percent, and by the end of the century it had fallen by more than 90 percent.

Because Costa Rican natives along the Caribbean coast and in the south were less unified politically and did not subscribe to the same strict system of *cacicazgo* that was dominant in the Nicoya Peninsula, the Spanish faced a more difficult conquest in those regions. Early attempts to explore the Caribbean coast in search of gold and other valuable resources eventually met considerable native resistance in the early decades of the sixteenth century. Furthermore, infighting among Spanish conquistadores undermined their ability to navigate unfamiliar territory, a difficult climate, and the increasingly hostile native people in the surrounding areas. For example, in 1540 Hernán Sánchez de Badajoz attempted to establish a permanent settlement to facilitate the conquest of the Caribbean coast. Ciudad Badajoz had only been in existence a few short months when Rodrigo de Contreras— the recently appointed governor of neighboring Nicaragua—arrived to challenge Sánchez de Badajoz for control over Spanish claims in the region. Contreras eventually placed his rival under arrest and dissolved Ciudad Badajoz. Instead of seeking an alliance with local native leaders, Contreras and others like him attempted to force the *caciques* of small surrounding villages into submission, inciting a violent response. Contreras eventually returned to Nicaragua where he gained a reputation for his cruelty to natives and became a target of Bishop Antonio de Valdivieso and Bartolomé de las Casas in their quest to compel the Spanish Crown to protect the native population of the Americas.

In an attempt to bring a sense of order to the region, in 1540 King Charles of Spain created a new administrative unit encompassing most of contemporary Costa Rica. The province of Nuevo Cartago y Costa Rica was to be administered by Diego Gutiérrez y Toledo, who arrived in 1543 and established two townships close to the Caribbean coast. Gutiérrez lasted only one year in his leadership position as his cruelty toward neighboring native people and his incessant quest for gold eventually led to a violent native uprising in which Gutiérrez and many of his men were killed. The Caribbean coast proved difficult for the Spanish to control until well into the seventeenth century. It was only after conquistadores managed to establish control over the Central Valley that the coastal regions in the east eventually also fell under Spanish dominance.

Even though Spanish attempts to rule Costa Rica began almost immediately in the early decades of the sixteenth century, the conquerors did not manage to establish a permanent settlement until the founding of Cartago in the 1560s. Located in the Central Valley, Cartago served as the capital of the Costa Rican province until 1823, when the administrative seat was moved to San José. Under the leadership of Juan Vásquez de Coronado, Cartago served as a base for expeditions of exploration and conquest in the surrounding areas. Vásquez de Coronado became known for his fairness and his humane treatment of the native population in surrounding areas. He encouraged Spanish settlers to move into the fertile valley surrounding the city of Cartago where they worked to develop an incipient agricultural sector. Having achieved impressive success in the Central Valley in just a few short years, Vásquez de Coronado departed for Spain in 1565 to receive the appointment as governor and *adelantado* (the king's representative in administrative, legislative, and judicial affairs) of Costa Rica by the Spanish Crown. But his ship disappeared on the return voyage, and Costa Rica was left without its leader.

The tenuous order that Vázquez de Coronado had achieved appeared to be threatened, particularly after a series of native uprisings nearly caused settlers to abandon Cartago entirely. But in 1568

Perafán de Rivera arrived to take over as governor, and his presence and policies brought a renewed sense of order. He immediately launched a series of counterattacks against the native uprisings in the regions surrounding Cartago. He also began targeting indigenous communities in the outlying areas in an attempt to bring the entire isthmus under control. But Spanish soldiers and settlers demanded greater compensation for participating in ventures against unruly natives in frontier areas, and the Spanish governor was forced to institute the system of labor distribution that was being employed in other areas under Spanish control. The *encomienda* system rewarded conquistadores by allowing them to exact labor and various forms of tribute from conquered natives.

As in Spain's other colonies, the Spanish use of the *encomienda* in Costa Rica attracted conquistadores and helped the Spanish consolidate control over the Central Valley by the end of the sixteenth century. Nevertheless, the application of *encomienda* grants in Costa Rica evolved quite differently compared to other colonies. In particular, Spanish settlers in Costa Rica demanded that natives within the *encomienda* system fall directly under their authority. This demand was a violation of the Spanish Crown's New Laws of 1542, which stipulated that only the Crown itself had direct authority over the native people. But conditions in Costa Rica were not the same as in other regions where the Spanish conquest had already been carried out. The lack of mineral resources attracted fewer conquistadores, and the dispersed nature of the native population made conquest more elusive on the Central American isthmus. As a result, Spanish officials allowed settlers to have direct authority over the native population and accepted this concession as a "necessary evil" of the realities of conquest in a difficult region.

In all of Latin America, exploration and military conquest was always accompanied by a spiritual conquest as well. Priests and missionaries accompanied conquistadors in the Americas from the first expeditions, and they were an important presence in Costa Rica as well. The Spanish Crown fervently believed it had a God-given duty to Christianize natives in the Americas, and evangelization became a motive as well as a tool of conquest. Franciscan friars established missions and helped to reorganize native communities into reconcentrated villages that allowed for greater control. Church objectives of converting natives to Catholicism and assisting in the conquest often came into conflict with traditional native religious beliefs, and the Christianizing mission was far from peaceful throughout much of the colonial era.

After 1570 the administration of Costa Rica became more systematic and more formalized. In 1568 Costa Rica became part of the *audiencia* of Guatemala—a recently formed judicial and geographic entity that remained in place throughout the colonial period. *Audiencia* districts were generally political units as well, known as captaincies general; and the *audiencia* of Guatemala formally became a captaincy general in the early seventeenth century. Costa Rica also fell within the jurisdiction of the larger viceroyalty of New Spain. While in theory local Costa Rican leaders answered to the president of the *audiencia* and to the viceroy of New Spain, distance, geographic impediments, and a local economy that yielded few riches kept Costa Rica relatively isolated from the rest of the Spanish empire. As a result, the local governor and the town council (*cabildo*) of Cartago had considerable authority over the province of Costa Rica throughout the colonial period.

THE COLONIAL ORDER

Despite its name meaning "rich coast" and contrary to the unremitting quest for riches by Spanish conquistadores, the colonial province of Costa Rica yielded little in precious metals or any other resources of value. The region attracted few colonists, and the mountainous regions surrounding the Central Valley provided natural protection for the scattered groups of Indians who continued to resist Spanish control. Eventually a diverse land tenure system emerged out of the original *encomienda* grants, particularly after the passage of the New Laws in 1542. Once a system of labor allocation that worked hand-in-hand with the promise of allowing Spanish settlers to become members of the landowning elite, the *encomienda* eventually became a form of tribute collection. Spaniards could acquire significant wealth by collecting tribute from natives within the *encomienda* system, and many of the earliest conquistadores and settlers took advantage of the tribute system to acquire wealth and a labor force for their landed estates. Nevertheless, the precipitous decline in the indigenous population meant that settlers arriving late to Costa Rica often found that local natives had already been distributed to the Spanish elite and the potential for becoming a member of the landowning noble class was limited for them. As a result, Costa Rican agriculture in the colonial period became characterized by various forms of production, largely dependent upon region and local population.

In the Central Valley, multiple forms of land tenure emerged simultaneously as Spanish control over the region was consolidated. The earliest conquistadores had been awarded large landed estates, but as the colonial period progressed smaller farms—known as *chacras*—predominated the agricultural system. These farms were often only able to support a single family and, despite their disdain for manual labor, Spanish colonists were forced to work the land themselves. Many *chacras* were public lands surrounding municipal areas that were rented out by local governments. Communal indigenous communities also coexisted with Spanish settlements in the Central Valley, although early settlers generally claimed the best lands for themselves, leaving native villages to struggle on less arable lands.

In the Nicoya Peninsula, larger landed estates—known as *haciendas*—grew out of the early *encomienda* system and were initially facilitated by a more concentrated indigenous population. *Hacendados* were generally those who had successfully made the transition from the labor *encomienda* system to the tribute *encomienda* system. They retained large land allocations and used wealth acquired from exacting tribute payments from surrounding native villages to purchase a slave labor force. Many *hacendados* also used their wealth to expand their landholdings, and a system of very large landed estates, or *latifundio*, took root in the northern regions of the Costa Rican province. Late in the colonial period, as the Spanish eventually established more firm control over the eastern portions of the province, plantation agriculture developed along the Caribbean coast. The emergence of plantation estates coincided with the cacao boom in Central America, but eventually plantations also began producing tobacco and other commodity products.

THE SPIRITUAL CONQUEST

As the Spanish extended their reach over the Americas and worked to consolidate control over the colonies, settlers recreated as much of their Spanish culture as possible in their new setting. They did this in part as an attempt to replicate the familiarities and comforts of home, but introducing Spanish culture was also a mechanism by which the newly arrived inhabitants aimed to dominate the remaining native population. The *encomienda* system, introduced both to appease conquistadores and to make effective use of native labor, was a close replication of the seigniorial system of land tenure that was in place in Europe. Other markers of European culture soon made their appearance as new crops and animals were incorporated into the emerging agricultural system. European livestock and crops, such as cattle, pigs, wheat, and sugarcane, thrived alongside agricultural goods that were native to the Americas. Spaniards introduced European standards of dress, and the Spanish language quickly became the dominant form of communication, even among disparate native tribes. In all of these instances, the ascendancy of Spanish cultural markers over those of the indigenous population served to placate Spanish settlers with the familiarities of home. But it also served as a method of control and a symbol of Spanish dominance over native culture.

The Spanish use of religion was no different. The earliest explorers and conquistadores had pursued their adventures, at least nominally, under the banner of a "just war." The Spanish Crown was staunchly Catholic, and in 1508 Pope Julius II sanctioned the *patronato real*, or royal patronage. This papal decree established a close and collaborative relationship between the Catholic Church and the Spanish Crown and effectively empowered the Spanish to carry out the conquest as a religious mission. As a result, members of the Church often accompanied expeditions to conquer areas of the Americas, and missionaries almost always arrived to newly conquered areas on the heels of conquistadores. The Church and the Crown worked in concert to quash native religious practices and to ensure that all of the Spanish Crown's new subjects converted to Catholicism. Despite these efforts, many native religious practices persisted, and some "conversions" were questionable at best as Spaniards often resorted to mass baptisms where many indigenous participants were unaware of the significance of the ceremony. Once converted, many natives often strayed back to their former religious practices, which were more familiar in times of enormous change. Furthermore, indigenous beliefs were generally polytheistic, allowing for the worship of multiple deities and requiring homage to the entire pantheon to maintain a balance according to a recognized hierarchy. Since native religions were closely tied to nature, disasters such as weather phenomena, diseases, earthquakes, and volcanic eruptions were often understood as a failure to worship a particular deity sufficiently. There was certainly room in the indigenous pantheon for Catholicism, and many natives attempted to supplement, but not replace, those previous religious practices with Spanish religious beliefs.

Some Spanish leaders confronted religious resistance violently, destroying relics of indigenous beliefs and resorting to physical punishment for natives found to be continuing their former religious practices. Others saw the need to accommodate native tendencies and tolerated a modest degree of indigenous influence in religious practices; and they considered the more conciliatory approach to be the most effective way of subverting indigenous religions. As a result, local traditions often emerged as a syncretic blend of

Catholicism with remnants of native religions. In Costa Rica, this syncretism was most evident in the appearance of the Virgen de los Angeles, who eventually became known as *La Negrita*, or the Black Madonna, and was eventually recognized as the patron saint of the nation.

According to legend, *La Negrita* was discovered in 1635 by a native peasant girl while she was washing clothes at the springs outside of Cartago. The virgin appeared as a small figurine carved out of black granite. The girl took the tiny statue home, but the next day she discovered that the virgin had mysteriously disappeared from her small hut and had reappeared at the spring where the girl originally found it. Church officials quickly determined that this Virgen de los Angeles wanted a chapel to be built on that spot in her honor. Similar to Mexico's Virgin of Guadalupe, Costa Rica's *La Negrita* is associated with the non-European population. The statue's dark color and the fact that she was discovered by an Indian girl appealed directly to the nonwhite population. While Spanish settlers initially maintained their devotion to the European styled image of the Virgin of Ujarrás, Indians, blacks, and those of mixed race descent looked to *La Negrita* as a close representation of their religious identity.

The Basilica of Our Lady of the Angels was completed in Cartago in 1722 to replace the modest structure that had been built to *La Negrita* in 1639. Throughout the seventeenth century, confraternities devoted to the Virgen de los Angeles emerged in Cartago. Membership in these brotherhoods was largely made up of black and mixed-race devotees in the earliest years, but by the eighteenth century the local Spanish population had started taking a more active role in festivities to honor *La Negrita*. By the 1780s, Church officials declared the Virgen de los Angeles to be the patron saint of the city of Cartago, and they sanctioned specific festivities to honor her. Those activities included an annual pilgrimage that relocated the Virgin's figurine from the basilica to the main cathedral in Cartago, where it was displayed for several weeks in a celebration known as *la Pasada*. Incorporating the cathedral into the local celebration was a clear sign that Catholic leaders had assimilated the local patron saint into mainstream Church practices. Over time, devotees from the surrounding areas began making pilgrimages to Cartago to honor the Virgin. The devotion to *La Negrita* grew, and shortly after independence she was officially named the patron saint of Costa Rica. Pilgrimages to Cartago continue to this day, and the Virgin is celebrated every August 2 when hundreds of thousands make the journey to the cathedral during *la Pasada* to honor Our Lady de los Angeles.

Basilica of Nuestra Señora de Los Angeles (Our Lady of the Angels) in Cartago is the site of pilgrimages to *La Negrita*, Costa Rica's patron saint. (© Jolanda Jolanda Pattijn | Dreamstime.com)

AGRICULTURE AND ECONOMY

Settlers in Costa Rica quickly discovered that the "rich coast" moniker was a false representation of the resources the region had to offer. Failing to uncover lucrative mining deposits and continually facing resistance from the scattered groups of local natives, Spaniards sought economic activities to sustain the colony. One of the first of these activities was cattle raising, which was introduced in the Central Valley and northern Pacific plains. Ranchers raised cattle primarily to sell the hides and to process tallow for use in candles and lubricants. The early livestock industry was inefficient and failed to bring a significant profit. A market for other agricultural goods began to emerge by the late sixteenth century, and in addition to production for local consumption, landholders in the Central Valley began to market surplus foodstuffs. Early agricultural activities included the production of onions, garlic, and corn in addition to pigs and hens, which were exported through Portobello in the Spanish Empire's tightly controlled trade network. With the development of these agricultural activities and due to the Spanish Crown's move away from its reliance on *encomienda* grants, land tenure in Costa Rica shifted to the *hacienda*, particularly in the Pacific northern region of Nicoya.

By the beginning of the seventeenth century, Costa Rica had firmly established its reputation as an outpost of the Spanish empire. Compared to Central Mexico and the northern Andes in South America—whose large native empires had been effectively brought under Spanish control and whose mountainous terrain yielded large deposits of mineral wealth—Costa Rica's modest agricultural economy was far less impressive, and the region attracted fewer Spanish settlers. Furthermore, the Spanish Crown devoted far more resources and administrative attention to the more profitable colonies in New Spain and Peru. As a result, few resources were available for the construction of cities and the development of an economic infrastructure to facilitate trade. Interior transit routes were often treacherous and poorly maintained, and government income was so sporadic that colonial officials were forced to rely on neighboring Nicaragua to supplement administrative expenses. Costa Ricans reacted to this reality by developing an early sense of autonomy and self-sufficiency that persisted throughout the colonial period and after.

In the early years of the seventeenth century, new economic activities began to emerge that would bolster Costa Rica's financial status and tie the region more directly to the outside world. Merchants to the south developed a demand for mules as a way to transport goods by land across the narrow Panamanian Isthmus. Mules bred in Nicaragua and Honduras were transported through Costa Rica, and some livestock regions in Costa Rica began breeding mules as well. The mule train brought some economic stability to Costa Rica, but its income potential was limited since mules could only be transported during the dry season each year. In the last half of the seventeenth century, cacao cultivation emerged as an important part of the Costa Rican economy. Cacao beans are the main ingredient in chocolate, and as the treat became more popular in Europe, demand for cacao fueled new economic activities in Costa Rica. In fact, cacao exports became Costa Rica's first commercial tie to the European markets. Cacao trees thrived in the tropical regions in the eastern part of the colony, and the proximity of Caribbean ports facilitated shipping.

As the cacao trade expanded, plantation agriculture emerged and began to dominate the tropical zones along the Caribbean coast. The Matina region became one of the most important cacao producing areas. Many of the lands in that region were newly acquired by Spanish settlers since small bands of recalcitrant natives also inhabited the Matina Valley. As the Spanish gained control over more fertile lands, new cacao plantations emerged and an urgent need for a reliable plantation labor supply also developed. Some planters attempted to fill their labor demands by forcing the local indigenous population into service. Others resorted to using African slave labor. Although slavery was not as prevalent in Costa Rica as it was in other areas of Latin America, it did constitute an important part of the colonial labor system. Reliable statistics for slave populations in colonial Costa Rica are lacking, but some studies indicate that census data throughout the colonial era consistently showed approximately 200 "pure blacks" in the province. While the black population remained constant, the "part-black" or mixed-race population (mulatto, *zambo*, and *pardo*) grew substantially, indicating that a small but steady stream of African slaves arrived in Costa Rica throughout the colonial period and that racial miscegenation was common. By the early nineteenth century, the "part-black" population of Costa Rica had reached nearly 9,000 and people of African descent accounted for 13 to 17 percent of the population in major cities such as San José, Ujarrás, and Alajuela. Mulattos and blacks made up more than 50 percent of the population in the west-coast city of Esparza.[1]

The institution of slavery in Costa Rica reflected the unique position the colony played in the Spanish Empire. While many inherent cruelties of the slave labor system were certainly a reality in Costa Rica, the nature of the economy and social system in the colonial outpost created a labor system that was distinct from many other areas of Latin America. Slaves' duties in colonial Costa Rica included laboring on cacao plantations, which tended to be relatively small in comparison to the large sugar and coffee plantations in Brazil and in the Caribbean. Cacao plantations were often managed by absentee owners, which meant the labor force operated with more autonomy and frequently under better working and living conditions than in other areas. Furthermore, manumission was not uncommon in Costa Rica, either through slaves purchasing their own freedom or by slave owners granting slaves their freedom in reward for good service or in a last will and testament. By the end of the colonial period, a prominent free black and mixed-race population had become a part of the Costa Rican demographic. Some free blacks and mulattos worked as overseers on plantations, while others worked in supervisory roles in the livestock industries along the northern Pacific coast. Racial and cultural assimilation was also quite common, and over time, many Costa Rican blacks and mulattos were racially and socially integrated through marriage with the white and mestizo population.

The cacao trade, supported by a small but prominent slave labor force, sustained the Costa Rican economy through the end of the seventeenth century, but after that the once-lucrative cacao sector experienced a precipitous decline as several factors conspired against it. As cacao plantations expanded further into the Matina region and other areas along the Caribbean coast, colonists increasingly encountered fierce resistance among the *zambos mosquitos*—a group made up of the interracial descendants of escaped African slaves and the indigenous population, who occupied the eastern portion of Costa Rica and Nicaragua. *Zambos* generally defied Spanish rule and operated autonomously as a pseudokingdom throughout the late seventeenth and much of the eighteenth centuries. They were formally recognized by the British, and they traded with English merchants in Jamaica, which helped to sustain them economically. To supply that trade, *zambos* carried out raids against Spanish establishments throughout Central America, including cacao plantations in Costa Rica. Cacao planters struggled to defend against these raids, and at one point colonial officials even attempted to reach a peace accord with the raiders in the interest of protecting local growers. Nevertheless, Costa Rican planters could not compete with cacao production in Venezuela and other colonies because of high transport costs, and by the middle of the eighteenth century Costa Rica's cacao trade was in decline.

SOCIAL STRUCTURE

As Costa Ricans experimented with new agricultural pursuits to meet the evolving needs of the colony, a system of power brokerage developed and became firmly rooted in the social structure. An elite class emerged, originating with the earliest conquistadores, whose descendants maintained close family linkages and passed down power and wealth from one generation to the next. These families tended to hail from the original *encomendero* class, and they controlled the largest landed estates in the Central Valley. Much of Costa Rica's modest colonial population resided in the Central Valley, creating a distinct sense of isolation for Costa Ricans. That isolation was exacerbated by the rugged mountainous terrain of the Central Valley and the lack of adequate roads and bridges connecting the interior region to the coast and to neighboring colonies. During the rainy season in particular, some mountain passageways were impassable even under ideal conditions and travel by land from Costa Rica to the seat of the *audiencia* government in neighboring Guatemala took several months. The arduous nature of that journey kept many colonial and Church officials from making regular trips to Costa Rica, and as a result inhabitants of the Central Valley were not immediately tuned in to the major developments in the Spanish Empire. Physical isolation, a lack of adequate communication, the relatively small size of the population, and evolving economic realities combined to create an ever-growing sense of autonomy and the beginning notions of a unique Costa Rican identity.

Some semblance of general Spanish culture was certainly evident. The Church played a prominent role in society and closely guarded morality and behavior. Gender relations operated under a patriarchal norm, particularly among the upper classes, and the Church played a vital role as regulator of marriage and domestic life, arbiter of disputes, and keeper of vital statistics through religious sacraments. As in other regions of the Spanish colonies, the Costa Rican population generally broke down into a social stratification based on race and ethnicity. The elite white families of pure European descent generally held the most privileged social, political, and economic positions while the population of color was often seen as socially inferior and worked in less prestigious professions. But these characteristics often played out with a specifically Costa Rican flair. Local religious practices often deviated from the precise structures of Catholic dogma to incorporate folk beliefs from the masses. The syncretic blend of popular and institutional rituals that emerged in the devotion to the Virgen de los Angeles is one of the most visible examples of this phenomenon, but the influence of local folk culture on religious practices was prominent throughout the colonial period.

The particularities of the Costa Rican economy also contributed to nuanced but important distinctions in the social structure. While the European elite controlled large estates and dominated the highest political and economic positions, Costa Rican society had already developed in a way that was far more egalitarian that in other Spanish colonies. Some early histories of Costa Rica perpetuated an exaggerated portrayal of a democratic, agrarian society dating back to its colonial origins, and while those early portrayals misrepresent the realities of colonial society, a somewhat equitable system did emerge in many areas of the colony. Since the Costa Rican economy had failed to produce a profitable commodity agricultural sector, elite landowners did not necessarily enjoy a standard of living comparable to colonial elites in Mexico or South America. Particularly as the cacao sector declined, many of the landed elite found it difficult to afford a large pool of laborers—either wage earners or slaves. In the last century of the colonial period, the sector of small agricultural peasants grew as *hacienda* production declined. The slave labor force also diminished through manumission. Many elite landowners worked their own lands just as the small subsistence peasant farmers did. Over time and especially among the masses, racial miscegenation produced a population that was largely a blend of indigenous, African, and European ethnicities. Nevertheless, despite miscegenation and a relatively egalitarian economic structure, discrimination based on ethnicity and socioeconomic position persisted. The old aristocratic colonial families centered around Cartago continued to dominate the elite class, and social privilege generally remained limited to those of white, Spanish ancestry.

The social trends that had emerged in the Costa Rican province by the eighteenth century were already evident in the early years of the colonial period. The earliest European explorers encountered a relatively small and dispersed native population compared to other areas of Latin America. The demographic realities of the region combined with a difficult topography and lack of mineral wealth attracted only small numbers of Spanish settlers, the majority of whom took up residence in the Central Valley. Scattered native dwellings, a lack of gold and silver, and little interest among Spanish conquistadores meant that the formal conquest period in Costa Rica was difficult and drawn out. Some of the earliest settlers in the Central Valley were the predecessors to the close-knit circle of elite landed aristocracy that came to dominate local political and social networks. But the landed elite existed side-by-side with small farmers and other poor Costa Ricans in the Central Valley as agriculture became the economic backbone of the colony.

Even though Costa Rica was part of a large and powerful empire, a clear sense of local autonomy and singularity evolved throughout the colonial period. Yielding little in the form of valuable natural resources, Costa Rica failed to capture the attention of the Spanish Crown, and a significant administrative presence did not emerge there. As a result, the Spanish Crown devoted few resources to the region and the local population often had to fend for itself. Even after centuries of colonial rule, many parts of Costa Rica remained "unconquered" as significant pockets of defiant native populations still persisted in the outlying regions outside of the Central Valley. The story of Pablo Presbere that opened this chapter is but one example of the continued resistance of Costa Rican natives as late as the eighteenth century. As the colonial period drew to a close, Costa Rica was a diverse region with a relatively self-sufficient European and mestizo population in the Central Valley but also with vast frontier lands in the surrounding countryside. Both the more settled central region and the unsettled frontier area would play an important role in the emergence of a new independent republic in the nineteenth century.

NOTE

1. Michael D. Olien, "Black and Part-Black Populations in Colonial Costa Rica: Ethnohistorical Resources and Problems," *Ethnohistory* 27, no. 1 (1980): 17–19.

3

Independence and the Early Nineteenth Century

THE JOCOTE PACT

On April 11, 1842, Honduran general Francisco Morazán signed the Jocote Pact with Costa Rican general Vicente Villaseñor. The Costa Rican military leader had been dispatched by the nation's president, Braulio Carrillo, to repel Morazán's invading force, but Villaseñor betrayed the president, whose regime had become increasingly dictatorial. Under the Pact of Jocote, Villaseñor joined forces with his would-be adversary and overthrew Carrillo. The agreement stipulated that Morazán would take over as head of the provincial government, and the Honduran liberal promised to institute a series of reforms for the good for the Costa Rican people. But almost immediately after Morazán took power, Costa Ricans rose up in opposition, and less than six months later he was executed by firing squad in San José. Morazán's downfall ultimately stemmed from rumors that he was planning to reintegrate Costa Rica into a federation with other Central American states.

The events surrounding Morazán's death unfolded less than two decades after Costa Rica achieved its independence from Spain, and the nation's strong reaction to Morazán illustrates both the volatility and the emerging sense of autonomy that characterized Costa Rica in the first years following independence. Making the transition to self-rule after being an ancillary part of a large overseas empire for more than 300 years proved to be a difficult task. Local Costa Rican leaders experimented with various forms of political organization after independence, leading the region to join the Mexican empire, to become part of a Central American federation, and ultimately to establish a separate and sovereign republic. New security and economic concerns created a sense of urgency for national and local leaders to bring stability to the region and to facilitate modernization. Costa Ricans endured many difficult decades as national leaders and ordinary citizens alike grappled with their new political, economic, and social realities. But throughout the trials that accompanied the process of nation formation, Costa Ricans' sense of autonomy and singularity remained constant.

ERA OF INDEPENDENCE

Costa Rica began the nineteenth century as it had spent the previous centuries—as a Spanish colony in the *audiencia* of Guatemala. But turmoil had been brewing within the Spanish Empire since the Bourbon royal line in Spain had inherited the throne from a long line of Hapsburg rulers in the early eighteenth century. Several Bourbon rulers had instituted major changes throughout the colonies, and those reforms intensified under the rule of Charles III (1759–1788). Bourbon reforms were generally designed to enhance the administrative and economic effectiveness of the colonies. New policies included such things as improved tax collection, a more streamlined administrative system, more open trade policies, the creation of tobacco monopolies, and a larger and ostensibly more professional military. With the exception of the tobacco monopoly, few of these new policies had a direct and immediate impact on Costa Ricans. But the residual effects of the Bourbon reforms helped to shape the region's path in the nineteenth century. Many of the reforms caused resentment throughout the Americas, particularly among the American-born colonial elite, and in some circles discussions of greater autonomy and even independence began to circulate.

Ideas about autonomy that had sparked in the late eighteenth century were fanned into full-fledged flames after the French monarch Napoleon Bonaparte forced the abdication of the Spanish king in

1808 and installed his own brother on the throne. Colonists throughout the Americas formed resistance *juntas* and declared their independence from French-controlled Spain. In many areas that initial
declaration of autonomy in opposition to the French quickly transformed into movements for complete independence and self-rule.
Some of those movements in the colonies took inspiration from events
in Spain, such as the promulgation of the liberal Constitution of Cádiz
in 1812, and independence leaders often modeled ideas about new
social and governing structures after the new progressive system laid
out in Spain. The constitution, which was drafted by Spanish and
American members of the resistance *juntas,* called for dramatic
changes in the political and social fabric of the Spanish empire by
introducing concepts such as equality, representative government,
and individual rights. The influence of the French Enlightenment
was evident in the document, and when Spanish monarch Ferdinand
VII was finally restored to the throne in 1814 and immediately abro-
gated the constitution, many colonists who already endorsed Enlightenment ideas moved to support independence even more fully.

While the fervor of independence was not as urgent in Costa Rica,
colonists there watched with keen interest as major rebellions erupted
to the north in Mexico and to the south in New Grenada (present-day
Venezuela). Those rebellions escalated into full-scale wars between
1810 and the 1820s, and one by one portions of Spain's colonial empire
broke away in attempts to form independent nations. The wars devastated many areas of the once-prosperous Spanish Empire as violent
battles and contagious diseases claimed lives, trade routes and local
production were disrupted, and the long-standing system of power
brokerage was called into question. And while the wars for independence that plagued other Spanish colonies for more than a decade
did not touch Costa Rica directly, other Central American colonies
did see minor insurrections, particularly in the early years of the
independence movement. Most of those were stifled fairly easily, but
they did serve as indications of new attitudes that were emerging
among some sectors of the population. Costa Rica did experience trade
disruptions and other peripheral effects of the wars, but it was not host
to the major battles and other destructive signs of war. Nevertheless, the
minor insurrections in Guatemala, Nicaragua, and San Salvador—in
addition to the major wars in Mexico and South America—did have
an impact on many Costa Ricans. Some feared the political and social
instability that challenging long-standing royal authority would surely
bring, while others embraced the new ideas ushered in by the Enlightenment and promoted by liberal independence leaders.

The first half of the nineteenth century was chaotic as all mainland colonies that had been under Spanish control secured independence by 1824 (Spain retained its Caribbean colonies until the end of the nineteenth century). Nevertheless, the future of this once large and prosperous colonial empire was uncertain as military and provincial leaders throughout the Americas experimented with various forms of political organization. Some former colonial provinces broke away almost immediately and formed autonomous republics. Others banded together in loose confederations based in part on the remnants of colonial administrative units. Costa Rica had been part of the *audiencia* of Guatemala, and the captain general, Gabino Gaínza, declared independence for the entire Central American province on September 15, 1821. At the same time, neighboring Mexico had secured its independence, and its leaders formed an empire that was extremely conservative in political orientation. Former independence leader Agustín Iturbide became Emperor Agustín I and set up a governing system that relied on monarchical rule and that maintained close ties with the Catholic Church. Since the viceroyalty of New Spain had encompassed all of Central America, Iturbide considered the regions to the south to be part of the newly formed Mexican empire. But some residents of those areas had other ideas, and minor revolts in Guatemala and San Salvador delayed consolidation for several months. By January 1822, a relative stability had been achieved, and all of Central America—including Costa Rica—was annexed to the Mexican empire.

UNITED PROVINCES OF CENTRAL AMERICA

The Mexican empire was the result of an incompatible relationship between Mexico's liberal, republican-oriented independence leaders and a cadre of conservative elites who hoped to shape an independent nation that would still retain much of its traditional colonial character. Those contradictory political philosophies were also evident in Costa Rica—and indeed throughout all of Central America—and the difficulties inherent in the Mexican empire manifested themselves at the local level as well. Political divisions were rife in the immediate aftermath of independence, and rifts quickly began to surface. Within the province of Costa Rica, local elites within the four main cities of San José, Alajuela, Heredia, and Cartago—the colonial capital—jockeyed for power and often disagreed over how to shape the region's future. Leaders in Heredia and Cartago tended to concur with the visions of Mexico's conservative elite, and they strongly supported joining the Mexican empire. Leaders in San José and Alajuela opposed the idea of empire and instead pushed for the formation of an independent nation with some form of republican government. Those disagreements culminated in a brief but significant civil war. At the battle of Ochomogo on April 5, 1823, monarchist supporters from Cartago were defeated by prorepublican forces from San José. While Costa Rican leaders clashed over their individual governing visions, political divisions also erupted in Mexico City as republican proponents clashed with the newly installed emperor. By 1823, the Mexican empire had collapsed while Costa Rica and other Central American provinces broke away.

In 1823, the provinces that today make up the nations of Costa Rica, Guatemala, El Salvador, Nicaragua, and Honduras joined together to form the United Provinces of Central America. The United Provinces was structured as a loosely organized federated republic with its capital in Guatemala City. Delegates from each of the provinces, under the leadership of José Cecilio del Valle of Honduras, drafted a new constitution, which was promulgated in 1824. It was a liberal document modeled largely after Spain's 1812 Constitution of Cádiz and the Constitution of the United States. It abolished slavery and established procedures for a limited electorate—effectively restricting suffrage to the wealthy and educated. It also protected the privileged position of the Catholic Church as the official religion while at the same time limiting its authority.

The governing document called for the constituent provinces to retain a large degree of autonomy and called for each to elect a provincial president to serve as a regional executive. Nevertheless, other provisions within the document countered the ostensible aims of maintaining provincial autonomy. The constitution established a central government, which included a president and a legislative body made up of representatives from each province. Because the legislature was designated according to proportional representation, the more populous province of Guatemala was allotted 40 percent of the initial 45 congressional seats, giving that region disproportionate influence in shaping policies in the central government and creating a system of distrust and rivalry that would ultimately prevent the United Provinces from establishing a strong, unified political presence.

THE EMERGENCE OF A NATIONAL GOVERNMENT

As the particulars of the new federation took shape in Guatemala City, Costa Rican elites made use of their new suffrage rights by electing Juan Mora Fernández as the first provincial president. A native of

San José, Mora Fernández was committed to liberal policies and had played a leading role in declaring Costa Rica's independence from Spain. He later helped to lead Costa Rica's withdrawal from the Mexican empire. By all accounts, Mora Fernández was a capable leader. He oversaw important developments in Costa Rica's early years as part of an independent nation, including the founding of the first printing press, the first mint, and an incipient system of social services such as health and education. Mora Fernández and his supporters relocated Costa Rica's capital from Cartago to San José, which had become the hub of the liberal elite in the early nineteenth century. Mora Fernández was reelected, but political friction among the four principal cities surfaced once again in 1830, and his second presidential term was defined by attempts to maintain peace in a volatile environment. Mora Fernández completed his second term in 1835, and his successor served only two years before resigning and turning over leadership to Braulio Carrillo Colina.

Carrillo's administration is generally recognized as the beginning of Costa Rica's liberal reform era of the nineteenth century. The new leader immediately began implementing policies intended to modernize the nation and make its economic and political systems more efficient. By passing the Law of Foundations and Guarantees, Carrillo was able to streamline government bureaucracy in a highly centralized system that gave the executive significant authority. Like many nineteenth-century liberal leaders throughout Latin America, the Costa Rican president believed a more authoritarian executive was necessary to bring a sense of order to the turmoil that was so prevalent in the decades following independence. He reformed civil and criminal codes within the judicial system and increased government revenue by restructuring government monopolies on alcohol and tobacco. Taken collectively, these policies helped to solidify the power of the state and gave Carrillo the legitimacy necessary for carrying out some basic liberal reforms. Such reforms included the introduction of a system of land privatization that targeted communal municipal lands and distributed them to small farmers. Carrillo also implemented reforms intended to improve government efficiency and strengthen the economy. These included paying off government debt and curtailing corruption in government offices.

With constant turmoil throughout Central America and increasing infighting among Costa Rica's major cities, Braulio Carrillo understood that his authority was tenuous and that he faced the threat of overthrow by the region's more conservative political forces. In an attempt to strengthen his own administration while weakening his would-be adversaries, Carrillo reformed the nation's armed forces. He implemented policies that augmented local security forces, enhanced the national militia, and created a modern urban police force for San José. And to keep potential opponents in check, Carrillo diminished the presence of armed forces in select areas around the country.

Carrillo's rule also was not without its problems. He inherited a cumbersome administrative system whereby the seat of the executive rotated among the four principal cities. The previous administration had created the process through the Ley de la Ambulancia in an attempt to maintain a balance among the four cities and to appease local elites. Carrillo abolished the system shortly after taking office, provoking a brief but formidable uprising by Heredia, Alajuela, and Cartago against the government in San José. The armed conflict between these major cities became known as the War of the League. Carrillo's forces quashed the rebellion with relative ease, but the new president reacted to the threat by becoming increasingly dictatorial. He seized the property of those who had fought against him, and many of his adversaries fled into exile. Carrillo further enhanced the power of the executive, and he solidified the position of San José as the principal administrative center.

By the end of his first term, Carrillo's autocratic tendencies had taken firm root. He passed antivagrancy laws to bring more order to society and enacted policies intended to strengthen the state at the expense of the Catholic Church and municipal governments. In 1839, Carrillo ran for reelection and was defeated by Manuel Aguilar, but Aguilar was ousted by a coup just one year later, which brought Carrillo back to power. He suspended the constitution in 1841 and declared himself absolute ruler for life. He continued ruling as a dictator until he was eventually overthrown in 1842.

THE DISSOLUTION OF THE UNITED PROVINCES

Carrillo is perhaps best remembered for his role in facilitating Costa Rica's secession from the United Provinces of Central America. The federation had faced numerous challenges from its inception, not the least of which stemmed from fears and suspicions that the more populous province of Guatemala was positioned to dominate the central government. Furthermore, many leaders in the provinces jealously guarded the notion of local autonomy while acknowledging the need for a larger and more unified federated republic that could potentially offer greater economic stability and political security than any of the five provinces could achieve alone. The governing structure of the

United Provinces and the attitudes of local elites created irreconcilable contradictions between the quest for autonomy and the need for unity. But the most serious challenge to the United Provinces manifested in escalating discord between governing elites who disagreed over the political future of the region. Conservative elites throughout Central America sought to maintain many of the systems that had been in place during the colonial period, including protecting the power of the Catholic Church and strengthening the role of the central government. Liberal leaders believed that the antiquated systems of the colonial period must be cast off in order for the federation to progress. They favored policies to diminish the power of the Church. Many promoted land reform decrees aimed at stripping the Church and other communal entities of landholdings and redistributing those lands to create a population of private property owners. Liberals also promoted economic policies that favored relatively free trade and the development of commodity agriculture products for export.

In 1825 Manuel José Arce of El Salvador became the United Provinces' first president as the result of a disputed election. Although Arce was initially elected as a liberal, he quickly lost the support of liberal elites as he catered to the interests of powerful conservatives in Guatemala. His relationship with the Guatemalan traditional elite further antagonized the regionalists in Costa Rica and caused even greater distrust for the central government in Guatemala. Many feared that Guatemala's larger population and proximity to the governing institutions of the United Provinces would allow the province to dominate federation policy, and Arce's presidency did little to assuage those fears. Shortly after taking office, Arce saw political unity disintegrate as the United Provinces descended into a three-year civil war. That conflict came to an end only after Honduran liberal leader Francisco Morazán drove Arce from power and was elected as the new president of the United Provinces in 1829. Morazán forced many of his conservative rivals into exile and initiated an aggressive liberal reform platform. Guatemala, which had been a hotbed of conservative politics, became host to a number of revolts as local liberal leaders took control there and pushed through their own reforms.

While the United Provinces' decade-long series of revolts had little direct impact on Costa Rica, the indirect consequences of such turmoil were significant. The push for local autonomy seemed all the more warranted as neighboring provinces erupted in revolt and the delicate balance of power within the loose confederation became increasingly tenuous. In his efforts to instill a sense of stability and order in Costa Rica, Braulio Carrillo convened a special delegation to determine the region's future path. In 1838, he declared Costa Rica an independent and sovereign nation. The United Provinces of Central America quickly disintegrated as Honduras and Nicaragua broke away and declared their sovereignty at the same time. Within the next year, the failed experiment to form a Central American federation had come to an end.

Costa Rica continued to feel the effects of its participation in the United Provinces many years later. Carrillo's dictatorship became increasingly repressive in the early 1840s as he suspended many personal liberties and attempted to impose morality codes on the population. He passed decrees outlawing vagrancy and vice while attempting to instill the values of hard work among the people. Carrillo continued to justify those measures by insisting that they were necessary for the advancement and modernization of the nation, but the liberal elite rallied as he restricted individual freedoms and suspended the constitution. After spending a brief period in exile in South America, the former liberal president of the United Provinces, Francisco Morazán, returned to Central America, put together a small force, and launched an invasion from the Pacific coast. Morazán appealed to Costa Ricans who had grown disillusioned with Carrillo's dictatorial regime and promised to liberate them from his repression. Indeed, many of the Costa Rican dictator's enemies offered support to Morazán and saw his arrival as an opportunity to rid the nation of an increasingly autocratic regime.

Carrillo sent his trusted military leader Vicente Villaseñor—who had fought with him in the War of the League—to repel Morazán's invasion. But instead of engaging Morazán in battle, Villaseñor betrayed Carrillo and negotiated an alliance with the former leader of the United Provinces. In the Jocote Pact—the story of which opened this chapter—Villaseñor joined forces with Morazán in an attempt to oust the Carrillo dictatorship. The agreement stipulated that a representative assembly would be convened to restore a more democratic system to Costa Rica and that Morazán would serve as the provisional leader of the Central American nation. The Villaseñor-Morazán alliance quickly defeated Carrillo and forced the dictator to flee the country. Initially many Costa Ricans welcomed Morazán enthusiastically, especially as the new leader dismantled the authoritarian system of his predecessor and reinstated individual liberties. He implemented a new taxation system in an attempt to solidify the government's fiscal position. Morazán also instituted a system of compulsory military service as a way to buttress the nation's military defenses, but he maintained an inner circle of El Salvadoran security forces, which served as a reminder that Costa Rica was being led by an outsider. Soon after taking power, he began making attempts to reconstitute a Central American federation, and his support among the Costa Rican people quickly faded. A few short months after Morazán entered San José a revolt erupted against him led by General Antonio Pinto. Morazán and his supporters fought against the uprising for several days before fleeing to Cartago. He and several loyal military leaders—including Vicente Villaseñor—were eventually captured. They were transferred back to San José where they were publicly executed in September 1842.

THE EMERGENCE OF COFFEE

The political consolidation of Costa Rica as an independent nation-state in the late 1830s coincided with a series of economic transformations that would have long-term repercussions for the rest of the century. Since the end of the colonial period, elite merchants and planters in the Central Valley had been experimenting with new enterprises to bolster the economy and to increase their own personal profits. But colonial entrepreneurs and large landowners failed to develop a cash crop or other major industry that would expand the region's trade and strengthen its internal commercial sector. After independence, various entrepreneurs attempted to establish viable industries through mining and the cultivation of brazilwood, which was valued as a natural dye. Nevertheless, they quickly found Costa Rica's natural resources to be limited, and these industries faltered.

The impetus to establish an income-generating export industry became all the more urgent because many Costa Rican leaders were influenced by liberal political and economic ideals. Liberal ideology stressed the need to leave behind the antiquated traditions of the past and to move the nation forward toward a prosperous future. To do this, many proponents of liberalism advocated the creation of a land tenure system that favored individual private property owners, who—because their economic well-being was tied to land ownership—would also become responsible and productive citizens. From an economic perspective liberal leaders generally favored dismantling many of the restrictive trade policies that had defined colonial mercantilism. They attempted to structure national economies that were tied to the global market—often through the production and export of agricultural commodity cash crops.

Many of the economic and political elites in the former Spanish colonies found liberalism appealing as they sought to stabilize and fortify new nations after independence, and Costa Rican leaders were no different. The commercial limitations imposed by the Spanish Crown under the colonial system had impeded economic growth substantially in Costa Rica, and local leaders were eager to support policies that would promote commercial expansion. But while other Latin America nations endured decades of political strife as civil wars and other crises erupted when political conservatives pushed back against liberal measures, Costa Ricans escaped much of that turmoil. As a colony, Costa Rica had been far removed from the traditional centers of Spanish imperial authority. And the elite conservative power brokers within the colonial system—namely the Church, the military, and high-ranking members of the royal bureaucracy—were largely absent from daily life in colonial Costa Rica. As a result, liberalism took hold relatively easily and quite quickly among Costa Rican leaders in the decades following independence, as evidenced by the policies and reforms enacted by Braulio Carrillo. That liberal impulse carried over into economic policy as well. Failing to establish a strong export industry through mining or other local production, farmers and merchants began experimenting with other products.

In the 1830s, merchants began exporting small amounts of coffee, first to South America and later to the European market. Costa Rican topography and climatological conditions were well suited for the production of coffee, and worldwide demand for the product was quite strong. The cultivation of this commodity crop expanded quickly, aided by liberal government policies that promoted the export of coffee and offered incentives for its cultivation. By 1850 coffee exports dominated the Costa Rican economy and a system of power brokerage between coffee elites and the peasant class emerged.

The Costa Rican government encouraged and facilitated the emergence of the coffee industry through land policies and economic incentives. Throughout the colonial period and immediately after independence the majority of Costa Rica's population lived in the Central Valley. The fertile lands of that region were ideally suited to coffee cultivation, but individuals did not own most of the land as private property. Instead, municipal governments rented large tracts of communal land—known as *tierra de legua*—to users in a land tenure system left over from the colonial period. In unoccupied or frontier regions, large swaths of public land—known as *terrenos baldíos* or *tierras públicas*—were available for cultivation.

Beginning as early as the 1820s, municipal leaders of San José sought to dismantle what they perceived to be the antiquated systems of the colonial period and replace them with more liberal policies designed to promote growth, modernization, and progress. The land tenure system was one of their targets as liberal leaders argued that public or communal land holdings impeded growth and that individual private-property owners were better suited to maximize the profitability of agricultural lands. Therefore, San José municipal leaders implemented land privatization policies that allowed farmers to acquire public lands at little to no cost. Soon other major cities adopted similar policies, and by the 1830s national laws were passed that expanded and strengthened liberal land reform. The government also offered other incentives such as free coffee seedlings and assistance in surveying lands. In 1825 the government removed the tithe on export crops, and in later years it offered subsidies to coffee farmers.

Particularly in the early phases of the emergence of the coffee industry, many government policies favored small land holdings over large *haciendas*. In fact, in many areas of the country more than 90 percent of coffee estates were less than 50 *manzanas*, or roughly 86 acres.[1] In other areas of Latin America, market pressures often threatened the viability of small land holdings. Inheritance practices often subdivided estates that were too small to yield a profitable harvest. Many peasant farmers sold out to land speculators, particularly as the price for property in prime areas rose steadily. Those same pressures existed for Costa Rican coffee farmers, and some consolidation of coffee lands into large estates did occur. But the government's preference for small farmers persisted, and as land in the Central Valley became more valuable government leaders passed laws extending land distribution policies to outlying areas of the country. By the 1840s the government was facilitating the settlement of *terrenos baldíos* in frontier regions outside of the Central Valley. Legislation was also passed that limited the amount of land that any one individual could acquire.

As a result of these government initiatives an intricate system of small farms that coexisted with larger estates emerged as the backbone of the coffee industry. And even though the elite planter class financed the earliest exports of coffee, small farmers and peasants participated in the supply of the coffee crop, particularly as demand for coffee grew. Furthermore, the labor force in the coffee industry was generally made up of relatives and other members of individual households rather than wage laborers working in forced labor or other exploitative systems. The growing market and healthy demand for coffee beans resulted in expanding access to credit for coffee growers, and by the end of the 1840s small family farms and large estates operated side-by-side to increase coffee cultivation more than 12-fold over the output at the beginning of the decade. Because the coffee sector relied on small farmers to produce a significant portion of the raw beans, a more egalitarian and less exploitative system of commercial agriculture emerged in Costa Rica compared to other countries where agricultural production was dominated by the landed elite. As a result, the elites found themselves in a system where they needed to work in cooperation with the nonelites to advance coffee's economic potential. A unique symbiosis developed that allowed small farmers to participate in significant ways in the global coffee trade.

Nevertheless, despite the strong position initially held by small farmers in Costa Rica's foray into capitalist agriculture, the wealthy, landed aristocracy still controlled important pieces of the coffee industry, including transportation, processing, and credit. Furthermore, as coffee demand increased, landowners saw a concomitant appreciation in the value of their lands. The privatization of communal lands and the emergence of *latifundio*—large landed estates in the hands of a few—took place only gradually in Costa Rica, but it did occur. As landed elites in the coffee industry acquired more territory and became more involved in the economy, their political influence expanded as well. The "coffee elites" or *cafetaleros* became an important force in the Costa Rican political system over the course of the nineteenth century as political power, economic decision making, and even the presidency itself generally passed within a small group of elite families with shared economic interests.

CULTURAL DEVELOPMENTS

Economic growth, precipitated by coffee exports, brought a measurable increase in general prosperity and the standard of living, particularly in San José and other major cities. By the 1850s, impressive levels of progress were visible in urban areas as a preference for European styles of architecture, entertainment, food, and various other forms of material culture became clear. In 1852 the Teatro Mora opened as San José's first public theater. It featured the finest classic European plays and musical performances. Public works projects brought paved streets, improved drainage, and streetlights to major cities, and in 1869 the nation's first system of indoor plumbing was installed in San José. Education flourished, particularly among the elite, as the printing press ensured that adequate books were available. Furthermore, as more coffee was exported, Costa Ricans began importing a number of consumer goods from abroad. Iron stoves, glass windows, and other so-called luxury goods improved the standard of living for many of the urban elite.

The impact of the coffee economy was not limited to the cities. Developing an internal transportation infrastructure became a priority and the elite formed private economic societies to ensure such projects were realized. Costa Rica's first major highway connecting the Central Valley to the Pacific port of Puntarenas was completed in 1846. Construction of rail lines to the Caribbean coast began in 1871, and construction of a Pacific rail line was underway by 1883. New transportation lines facilitated not only the shipping of the coffee crop but also the migration of the Costa Rican population. People often relocated in response to new economic realities. Peasants from the Central Valley, many of whom were squeezed off their lands due to rising property values, began relocating to other agricultural regions of the country. Those who migrated southward generally cultivated alternate agricultural products such as beans, corn, potatoes, and other vegetables to meet the food demands of the coffee-growing population in the Central Valley. Food production in the south also helped to feed the slowly growing urban population. Migrants to the northern Guanacaste region provided meat for the national market as well.

The first half of the nineteenth century became a time of enormous change for Costa Rica. The region that had evolved as a colonial backwater over more than three centuries of Spanish imperial rule was suddenly faced with the prospect of nationhood and self-rule. Spain's mainland colonies broke away from the empire between 1810 and 1824, which produced enormous change and political instability throughout the region. Costa Rica was initially absorbed into the newly formed Mexican empire, only to pull away a few years later and establish a loose federation with other Central American nations. But that experiment was also short lived; the federation of Central America nations dissolved into smaller nation-states. At the same time, Costa Ricans had to contend with local wars between major cities and coups to oust political leaders.

Despite those challenges Costa Ricans laid important political, economic, and social foundations in the first half of the nineteenth century that helped to bring stability and growth in later decades. Small farmers and large hacienda owners alike discovered the lucrative industry of coffee cultivation, which made the nation relevant in the emerging system of global trade. A profitable economic sector combined with a clearer political direction paved the way for important social and cultural developments. These were most prominently visible in the growth of major cities, the advent of an incipient educational system, and the development of transportation infrastructure through-out the country. By the 1840s and 1850s, the colonial backwater that had characterized Costa Rica in the sixteenth through eighteenth centu-ries had given way to an independent nation searching for a path to progress.

NOTE

1. James Mahoney, *The Legacies of Liberalism: Path Dependence and Political Regimes in Central America* (Baltimore, MD: Johns Hopkins University Press, 2001), 145.

4

Emergence of National Identity

THE CREATION OF A NATIONAL HERO

On April 11, 1856, the Costa Rican military faced off against the invading force of filibuster William Walker. Pinned down by rifle fire, commanders feared that the battle would quickly be lost as casualties mounted and enemy troops continued to gain ground. Suddenly, Juan Santamaría—a simple day laborer–turned–foot soldier—grabbed a nearby torch and ran full-charge into a hail of bullets to set fire to the main structure where the enemy had holed up. Eyewitnesses and other participants credited this act of bravery for turning the tide of the Battle of Rivas in favor of Costa Rica—for allowing the hastily assembled national military to salvage victory from the jaws of defeat as Walker's larger and better-equipped force descended upon Central America to claim territory for the United States. But Juan Santamaría did not live to see Walker's defeat and eventual execution. The young soldier had barely reached the *mesón* and touched his torch to the eaves when he was struck down by enemy fire. His lifeless body slumped to the ground as the flames of the inferno he had started lapped at his head and eventually consumed his corpse in a dramatic blaze. As Juan Santamaría died, the image of a national hero was born—and with it a more cohesive sense of nationalism that became fundamental to an emerging sense of Costa Rican identity in the last half of the nineteenth century.

In the years following the Battle of Rivas, Juan Santamaría's legacy reached legendary proportions, precipitated by the efforts of the liberal government to craft a national hero that encompassed notions of patriotism and the character of the nation. By the middle of the nineteenth century, Costa Rica was going through an era of national consolidation that was in part facilitated by the wealth and relative economic stability created by the coffee industry. Particularly after the uncertainties of the independence period and Costa Rica's participation in the failed experiment of the United Provinces of Central America, Costa Rican elites consciously pursued political institutions that would promote the expansion of economic prosperity and national vitality. Juan Santamaría came to epitomize the process of national consolidation in the late nineteenth century as the future vision crafted by the coffee elite included not only a liberal set of political and social principles but also the cultivation of patriotic and nationalistic sentiments to foster a cohesive and unified sense of the nation.

LIBERALISM AND COFFEE POLITICS

Many new Latin American nations witnessed the emergence of competing political parties in the nineteenth century based on diverging views of the region's colonial past and its potential for progress in the future. Conservative leaders arose in areas that were home to a strong Spanish presence during the colonial period and where traditional institutions of power—such as the Church and the landed aristocracy—dominated. Liberals throughout Latin America generally challenged the traditions and dominance of colonial institutions, positing that progress could best be achieved by casting off the regressive and backward practices of the past. Costa Rica's isolation and relative sense of autonomy during the colonial period meant that the region did not attract the staunchly traditionalist Spanish elite, who instead tended to settle in long-standing viceregal centers like Mexico and Peru. Additionally, Costa Rica remained out of the reach of the Catholic hierarchy, and even though Catholicism was the dominant religion in Costa Rica, it did not permeate daily life and the political influence of the Church was not as strong as in other areas of Latin America. As a result, by the 1840s, liberalism had emerged as the preferred political and economic ideology among most of the nation's *cafetaleros*.

Liberalism was already evident in the policies and positions of Costa Rica's early national leaders. But in the last half of the nineteenth century, the wealthiest of the elite coffee families formed a veritable ruling oligarchy. Under several successive administrations, many of the tenets of nineteenth-century liberalism became formalized in the nation's political reality through the passage of reform laws, the enforcement of market-oriented economic policies, and the promulgation of constitutions. Indeed, Costa Rica witnessed the enactment of two constitutions in the 1840s alone. The first of these came about in 1844, partially in response to the autocratic system implemented by the earlier administration of Braulio Carrillo. Enacted during the administration of José María Alfaro Zamora, the Constitution of 1844 was heavily influence by the Enlightenment ideas that had circulated prior to the wars for independence. It allowed for direct popular election, albeit with a severely restricted electorate as literacy, property, and gender limitations were spelled out in the document. The Constitution of 1844 also prioritized education following the establishment of the Universidad de Santo Tomás one year earlier, and it protected basic individual liberties, such as freedom of expression and freedom of association. A new constitution was created in 1848, replacing the 1844 document. The Constitution of 1848 maintained some of the foundations established in its predecessor but eliminated the system of direct elections, did away with the national senate, and further restricted the electorate. The constitution also formally declared the nation to be the Republic of Costa Rica, and Pacífica Fernández, wife of then president José María Castro Madriz, created a design that was adopted in 1906 as the national flag. In keeping with the Enlightenment influence, the blue, red, and white horizontal stripes on Costa Rica's flag were specifically modeled after the French design.

A paradox in Costa Rican liberalism appeared in the machinations of electoral politics. While many liberal leaders espoused the virtues of the social and economic aspects of the liberal agenda in both their words and their actions, presidential succession was often dictated by military might. More often than not, new presidents rose to power as the result of a military coup backed by different factions within the coffee elite. These "coffee presidents" dominated the national scene until the 1930s, but contrary to the authoritarian means by which they attained power, most ruled in a manner that upheld and even strengthened the nation's emerging liberal tendencies.

The first of these coffee presidents was Juan Rafael Mora, who was Castro Madriz's vice president and rose to the presidency when his predecessor was forced to resign. Once in office, Mora restricted the electorate even further and began working to strengthen his executive power against possible opposition in the national Congress. The despotic way in which he became president created significant discontent among the nonelite population, and that discontent continued as Mora instituted a system of land reform that dismantled the communally held properties that had traditionally been controlled by the rural peasantry and then offered them for sale to private owners. Much of that land was purchased by the wealthy *cafetaleros*, and many of Mora's economic policies benefited the coffee elite. He devoted national funds to improve the road between Cartago and Puntarenas in an effort to facilitate trade, and he manipulated the composition of Congress to create an alliance system for his benefit within the national legislative body.

Mora's presidency was controversial, but he did enact policies that were intended to benefit the nation as a whole. He created new hospitals in Puntarenas and San José, and he promoted public health policies in an attempt to eradicate smallpox and other communicable diseases. Mora oversaw the reconstruction of public infrastructure following a major earthquake in 1851 and initiated a system of urban planning in the capital city of San José. Diplomatically, Mora secured formal recognition of Costa Rica's sovereignty from Spain, and he finalized a treaty establishing a more defined boundary between Costa Rica and neighboring Nicaragua.

CANAL ISSUES

It was during Mora's presidency that Costa Rica became intricately involved in global politics as merchants, filibusters, and national leaders from Western Europe and the United States turned their attention to Central America. Attracted by the region's resources and also by its strategic location as a transit point between the Atlantic and Pacific Oceans, foreigners resorted to trickery and even the use of force in their dealings with each other and with Central American leaders in a virtual chess match to position themselves for economic and strategic gain.

As leaders in world trade, the United States, Great Britain, and even France became keenly interested in the Central American region immediately after independence. The area produced some desired natural resources, but more importantly it offered a potential transit point for trade between the Atlantic and Pacific Oceans. Throughout the first half of the nineteenth century the United States and its European trade rivals had periodically considered the possibility of building a trans-isthmian canal to facilitate trade and transport across the relatively narrow stretch of land in Central America. Of several potential locations for such a project, one of the favorites was a transit route along the San Juan River. The river runs more than 100 miles along the Costa Rica–Nicaragua border from the Caribbean coast to Lake Nicaragua, which is a large body of water that sits in southwestern Nicaragua. The lake's western shore lies just 12 miles from the Pacific coast across a narrow strip of land known as the Isthmus of Rivas. The area was already a popular transport route, as ships would travel by river to the lake. From there goods were unloaded and transported by land to awaiting vessels at Pacific ports. Interested investors eyed the Isthmus of Rivas as a sensible location to build an artificial canal so that vessels could cross from one ocean to the other without having to incur the expense and the delay of offloading goods to be shipped over land.

Because the region was already suitable for shipping and because it was attracting so much interest from potential canal investors, the San Juan River quickly became the subject of a lengthy and at times contentious border dispute between Costa Rica and Nicaragua. The river itself was generally accepted as the demarcating boundary between the two nations. But navigation rights on the river and the way the boundary should be marked through the Isthmus of Rivas were strongly disputed. During the colonial period, the Guanacaste region, which encompassed the San Juan River, fell within the boundaries of the province of Nicaragua. After the United Provinces of Central America formed, Costa Rica annexed Guanacaste along with the neighboring Nicoya region. When the United Provinces dissolved, Costa Rica maintained its claim over Guanacaste and Nicoya. In the subsequent decades, Nicaragua and Costa Rica engaged in a near-constant dispute over Guanacaste as well as navigation rights on the San Juan River.

While the official boundary between Nicaragua and Costa Rica remained in dispute, foreign powers demonstrated strong interest in the San Juan River and the Guanacaste region as well. The United States and British governments both eyed the region as the favored location to build a canal, and each wanted to ensure it had reliable access to any future canal. U.S. leaders attempted to negotiate directly with Nicaragua throughout the 1840s while the British strengthened their claims in British Honduras (present-day Belize) and along the Mosquito Coast. U.S. and British leaders eventually agreed to the Clayton-Bulwer Treaty in 1850, whereby both countries would jointly control any canal across Central America.

The French also maintained a strong interest in Central America, and they reacted with concern at the passage of the Clayton-Bulwer Treaty. French leaders launched negotiations with President Mora of Costa Rica for colonization and transit rights in the southern portion of the country. Mora went so far as to approve a colonization plan in 1850 that had been put forward by French promoter Gabriel Lafond du Lurcy in the Dulce Gulf region along the Costa Rica–Panama border. After several years, only a few hundred French colonists had relocated, and the plan fizzled.

Canal politics in Central America seemed to stall in the 1850s, particularly after the signing of the Clayton-Bulwer Treaty. Although leaders in the United States, Great Britain, and France were keenly interested in canal transit across Central America, none of those major powers had the resources or knowledge to carry out such a monumental project at the time. But the fact that Central America was attracting such intense attention at the time was indicative of several developing trends. By the middle of the nineteenth century, global trade was driving economic expansion around the world. Commercial networks connected the Americas with Europe and Asia, and the new nations of Latin America participated in those networks in important ways. Business leaders and politicians alike in the United States and Western Europe understood the importance of Central America both in terms of trade and in terms of transit routes. Despite the fact that a trans-isthmian canal did not exist until the Panama Canal was completed in 1914, canal politics were a driving force behind many diplomatic episodes in Costa Rica, and in all of Central America, in the last half of the nineteenth century.

WALKER AND FILIBUSTERS

A more serious global incursion into Costa Rica emerged in 1855 with the filibustering expeditions of William Walker. Walker was a lawyer and journalist from the United States who abandoned his career in 1853 to lead missions for territorial conquest in northern Mexico and later in Central America. Walker's filibustering adventures were characteristic of the nineteenth-century U.S. notion of Manifest Destiny. This was a belief that the United States had a God-given mission to acquire territory throughout the Western Hemisphere and to civilize the people there by imposing U.S. political, social, and religious institutions, which proponents of Manifest Destiny thought to be far superior. People "in need of civilizing" were often of mixed-raced descent, and Manifest Destiny often materialized

William Walker, U.S. filibuster, was defeated by Rafael Mora and the Costa Rican army in the 1856 National Campaign. (Library of Congress)

with a highly racial component. The implication was that "white" U.S. traditions were superior to the "uncivilized" ways of the mixed races and people of color.

The U.S. government formally instituted Manifest Destiny by forcing Mexico to cede nearly half of its national territory at the conclusion of the U.S.-Mexican War in 1848. It also encouraged white settlers to migrate westward onto lands that had once been (and sometimes still were) inhabited by Native Americans. Some private citizens, William Walker among them, relied on extralegal strategies to pursue their own form of Manifest Destiny through expeditions for territorial acquisition known as filibusters. While Walker and others like him acted on their own accord and their undertakings were not officially sanctioned by the U.S. government, filibusters' actions were often quite popular, and they received a large degree of support from national leaders, businessmen, and the U.S. general public. In fact, Walker's first failed filibuster attempt to invade and colonize the northwestern Mexican states of Sonora and Baja California landed him in a U.S. jail. He stood trial for breaking neutrality laws, but his actions were so popular that he was easily acquitted.

In 1855, Walker turned his sights to Central America. Political infighting in Nicaragua had created a crisis between the rival Liberal Party and the Legitimists, or Conservative Party. After years of near-constant civil war, the Liberals sought assistance from Walker, hoping to bolster their fighting force. In exchange for payment—and at the invitation of the Liberal Nicaraguan president—Walker arrived in Central America with approximately 300 armed men. In less than six months Walker had defeated the Legitimist stronghold in Granada, and he continued to expand his influence over internal affairs in Nicaragua. He eventually pushed southward toward the Costa Rican border.

Costa Ricans and other neighboring Central Americans watched Walker's endeavors with great concern. The possibility of constructing a trans-isthmian transit route through the San Juan River along the Nicaraguan and Costa Rican border initially compelled Walker to attempt to collaborate peacefully with Costa Rican president Rafael Mora. But Mora and other Central American leaders approached Walker cautiously. Many feared that Walker intended to create a large empire throughout all of Central America with institutionalized slavery, similar to the U.S. south. The arrival of white "colonists" from the United States seemed to confirm those fears, and the reticence of the U.S. government to curtail Walker's activities led many Costa Ricans to conclude that the eventual annexation of Central America to the United States was a foregone conclusion.

Mora also saw Walker's invasion as an opportunity for Costa Rica to strengthen its position in the Guanacaste region. And he feared that Walker's presence would give the United States an advantage in negotiations for the construction of a trans-isthmian canal. Indeed, Walker had used the promise of investment opportunities in a canal project to lure more U.S. settlers to Nicaragua. Mora worked with the British, whose leaders also wanted to prevent the United States from gaining a stronghold in the debate. He arranged to receive military aid from the British as he worked to fortify Costa Rica's defenses while carefully monitoring Walker's actions in Nicaragua.

Ultimately, Mora did not wait for Walker's forces to act. He quickly assembled an army, marking the first military mobilization of Costa Rican troops in the young nation's history. The president appealed to an incipient but growing sense of nationalism, calling on all patriots to resist the incursion by foreign invaders in Nicaragua. Mora insisted that Walker was in the process of enslaving the country's neighbors to the north and that Costa Ricans would surely be next. Indeed, Walker's close connections with the southern, slave-holding elite in the United States suggest that those fears may not have been far fetched. Mora recruited a force of 9,000, and in March 1856 he led his soldiers north to attack the filibusters in what became known as the National Campaign.

The first encounter between Mora's forces and the filibusters took place at the Hacienda Santa Rosa in the Guanacaste province on March 20. Several hundred of Walker's troops were caught by surprise and driven from Santa Rosa. They retreated to the town of Rivas further to the north, and Mora continued his advance. On April 11 the two sides faced off in a major confrontation that has become known as the Battle of Rivas. It was in this battle, after a long day of fighting and after seeing numerous casualties on each side, that Juan Santamaría sacrificed himself in an act of bravery that handed victory to Mora and the Costa Ricans.

Mora's celebration following the battle of Rivas was short lived. Because numerous dead bodies were not buried properly, a major cholera epidemic broke out in Rivas following the battle. As Costa Rican soldiers returned home, the disease spread throughout the country, killing more than 10,000 and debilitating the nation. For his part, Mora continued to pursue Walker and the remaining filibusters with a small number of Costa Rican soldiers. He also worked to form a coalition with neighboring Central American nations in an effort to drive Walker's forces out of the region.

Walker and the filibusters fled further north into the interior of Nicaragua. They fortified themselves in Granada, and in June 1856, Walker manipulated national elections to secure the presidency. He continued to expand his military and began enacting "reforms," such as legalizing slavery and creating a forced labor system for many of the nation's peons. He declared English the official language of Nicaragua and instituted a system of land reform that allowed him to appropriate properties held by his opposition. Additionally, Walker used his new political clout in Nicaragua to curry favor with economic backers in the United States. Specifically, two of Cornelius Vanderbilt's partners in the Accessory Transit Company—Charles Morgan and

Cornelius Garrison—began negotiating independently with Walker for exclusive transit rights through the San Juan River. Citing a legal technicality, Walker revoked Vanderbilt's transit contract and granted exclusive concessions to Morgan and Garrison. Vanderbilt reacted by closing down the Accessory Transit Company and moving all of his trans-isthmian shipping south to Panama. And he was so incensed by Walker's and his partners' duplicity that he began supplying arms to Mora's forces as they continued to strike against the filibusters. As Walker moved to strengthen his position, the coalition of Central American forces led by Mora and armed by Vanderbilt launched an attack against Granada. Walker eventually escaped to the United States, but in 1860 he returned to Central America in an attempt to claim territory once again. He was captured in Honduras and executed by firing squad in 1860.

The aftermath of the Walker episode in Costa Rica was significant. Liberal presidents in subsequent years seized upon the story of Juan Santamaría, and by the end of the century the collective memory of the brave soldier turned him into a national hero and an image of national unity. Monuments were erected in his honor and April 11, the date of his death, officially became a national holiday. The memory of one ordinary soldier's heroic death in the face of an invasion by a formidable foreign army was precisely what the young nation needed to reinforce a sense of national character and to fuel a growing sense of patriotism.

The fate of President Mora was not so fortunate. He had successfully rallied the nation together to confront the impending threat of Walker's invasion, and he used the momentum from his military stance in Guanacaste to negotiate the Cañas-Jerez Treaty to settle the border dispute with Nicaragua in Costa Rica's favor. The treaty established the San Juan River as the formal border between the two nations and granted Costa Rica the right to free navigation on the river. But perhaps the most significant aspect of the treaty was the provision that prohibited Nicaragua from negotiating a canal treaty in the region without the approval of Costa Rica. Despite these accomplishments, Mora's popularity with the Costa Rican people plummeted. Many blamed him for the cholera outbreak that ravaged the nation on the heels of the National Campaign. Furthermore, the military endeavor was costly, and the economic impact of waging war took its toll in the form of a recession. Already losing support among the population, Mora sealed his fate by attempting to diminish *cafetalero* economic influence through the establishment of a national bank. In 1859 the coffee elites, who felt threatened by Mora's policies, ousted him from the presidency and force him into exile. One year later Mora returned and attempted to effect his own coup. He was captured and executed by firing squad on September 30, 1860.

NATIONAL CONSOLIDATION AND THE *CAFETALERO* ELITE

The aftermath of the National Campaign and the Mora era was marked by a process of national consolidation and attempts to strengthen the liberal state. Mora's successor, José María Montealegre Fernández, oversaw the implementation of yet another constitution in 1859. The new governing document attempted to correct problems inherent in earlier constitutions and prevent political corruption by restoring the bicameral legislature. It also reduced the presidential term to three years with no consecutive reelection. The constitution aimed to mitigate the tendency to resort to military coups that had developed among the regional cohorts of the coffee elite. It protected the supremacy of constitutional processes and reinforced the authority of civilian command over the military.

Montealegre's administration brought much-needed calm and a sense of stability to Costa Rica after the turmoil of William Walker's invasion. He came from an elite *cafetalero* family and used his economic influence to solidify his political legitimacy. Montealegre prioritized economic and political stability, and he successfully renegotiated large foreign debts the nation had incurred during the National Campaign. He promoted the liberal notion that expanding the production of coffee and other commodity exports would benefit the national economy and attempted to attract European immigrants to establish new coffee "colonies" throughout the country. He also carried out the first national census in 1862 as a strategy to allow the Costa Rican state to understand its population and govern more effectively.

Montealegre was known as a progressive minded leader, and many of his policies reflect his liberal inclinations. He backed reforms that were designed both to improve public well-being and to foster a sense of national identity. Montealegre created a Public Works Department in his administration in 1860 as a step toward improving the nation's infrastructure and access to basic services. Public works projects were intended to improve health, facilitate trade, and generally improve citizens' lives, but they also served to highlight the presence of the national government on a day-to-day basis. Montealegre reformed the postal service and instituted a system of using adhesive stamps—an act that was intended not only to generate income but also to extend the presence of the government even more in the daily lives of Costa Ricans since those stamps often showcased the symbols of the nation.

Montealegre served out his term and handed over power to his successor, Jesús Jiménez Zamora, in a relatively smooth and democratic political process. Jiménez continued many of the progressive policies of his predecessor and pushed those policies even further by firmly defending the notion of a military subordinate to civilian control. When, just a few short months into his presidency, Congress attempted to limit his authority over the military, Jiménez responded by dissolving Congress and calling for new elections. The move defied political notions of liberalism tied to democracy, but Jiménez defended his actions as a necessary strategy to modernize politics by removing the influence of the military. He also staunchly defended Costa Rican sovereignty and autonomy in his diplomatic dealings with Central American neighbors. When El Salvador's ex-president, Gerardo Barrios, fled into exile in Costa Rica, Jiménez rejected the demands by other Central American leaders to expel the former military strongman. As a result Guatemala, El Salvador, Nicaragua, and Honduras severed diplomatic ties with Costa Rica temporarily—a move that only strengthened Jiménez's resolve.

Jiménez carried out his liberal impulse in social policies and in implementing economic reforms. He firmly believed in the need to make primary education free and obligatory for the population, and he expanded government education programs substantially during his administration. He backed the construction of primary and secondary schools and created the first normal school for teacher training, which opened in 1869. To provide necessary infrastructure and promote the growth of coffee trade, Jiménez expanded the nation's system of internal roadways and attempted to build the first highway connecting Cartago and the Atlantic coast. He viewed many of the nation's economic structures as remnants of an inefficient colonial past, and in an effort to stimulate economic growth, he ended the government monopoly in the tobacco industry and encouraged the expansion of private enterprise. Jiménez is largely credited with bringing a sense of order to Costa Rica's public finances, which contributed to a growing economy in the late nineteenth century.

Jiménez also completed his three-year term and handed over power in a democratic election to his successor, José María Castro Madriz, who had served as president once before from 1847 to 1849 but was overthrown in one of the young nation's many nineteenth-century barracks coups. His two presidencies fittingly bookend two decades of political consolidation by the *cafetalero* elite defined by attempts to create a national identity. Castro Madriz was the one who declared Costa Rica a sovereign republic in 1848, and he decreed September 15 a national holiday to commemorate independence from Spain. During his second administration, Castro Madriz continued the efforts initiated by earlier leaders to promote progress and modernize the nation. He opened the port of Limón to exterior trade and funded the construction of the first telegraph line between Cartago and San José. Castro Madriz was seen as a progressive liberal on social issues as he staunchly defended the freedom of the press and became a vocal advocate for women's education. Nevertheless, just two years into the Castro Madriz administration, Jiménez returned and overthrew the elected president in a military coup, in a continuation of the cycle of barracks coups and coffee politics.

The early decades of Costa Rica's liberal republic gave rise to inconsistencies and contradictions in the nation's social and political development. Political leaders touted the theoretical advantages of a forward-looking liberal ideology that favored democratic representation, yet they limited the electorate and often seized power through military coups. They defended individual liberties and steadfastly promoted public education while restricting political participation and reinforcing a governing system that favored a small and powerful oligarchy of *cafetaleros*. Large landowners dominated the political system but still supported development policies that allowed peasants and small farmers to play a prominent role in the nation's export economy.

In the midst of this political and economic paradox, the newly formed republic began to foster a sense of national identity through the creation of national holidays, patriotic heroes, and public symbols that reinforced the presence of the state. As a testament to the emerging sense of nationalism, President Mora recruited an inexperienced, rag-tag volunteer army to confront the threat of invasion by U.S. filibusters in the National Campaign of 1856. The army's eventual victory in the campaign was implausible. Mora's almost immediate fall from power and ensuing execution are yet another fitting example of the inconsistencies inherent in Costa Rica's early national history.

Despite the appearance of contradictions and instability, important foundations for future growth emerged in the middle decades of the nineteenth century. The coffee industry propelled an economic expansion that promoted migration into outlying rural areas, spurred the growth of cities, and funded new infrastructure projects to facilitate transportation and communication. Liberals' emphasis on education and public health created a more literate and robust population while reinforcing the presence of the state in people's daily lives. And, significantly, the paradoxical nature of early national development in Costa Rica contributed to the sense of autonomy and exceptionalism that was already present, reinforcing those notions as vital components of an emerging national identity.

5

The Consolidation of the Liberal State

HENRI FRANÇOIS PITTIER

In 1887 an unassuming Swiss scientist relocated from Europe to San José. Henri François Pittier had signed a contract with Costa Rican president Bernardo Soto, whose administration had recently revamped the public education system and opened two new secondary schools in the nation's capital. Following the lead of President Jesús Jiménez in the 1860s and President Tomás Guardia Gutiérrez in the 1870s, Soto recruited foreign professors to fill the ranks of the faculty at the new schools. But Pittier did more than simply work as a teacher in San José. Immediately after arriving in the Central American capital, he began urging government officials to establish a meteorological institute and observatory. Pittier insisted that the collection of accurate climatological, atmospheric, and terrestrial data would be indispensable to a nation so reliant on its agricultural economy, and that by investing in the advancement of scientific knowledge the Costa Rican government would facilitate national progress. Furthermore, his promise to produce an official map of the entire republic piqued the interest of government leaders who had for decades grappled with border disputes with neighboring countries and negotiated with foreign interests intent on constructing a trans-isthmian canal.

In 1889 Pittier became the first director of the National Physical-Geographic Institute (Instituto Físico-Geográfico Nacional de Costa Rica, or IFGN). The institute was founded during the era of "the Olympians," a boastful term self-ascribed by Presidents Guardia, Próspero Fernández, and Soto to describe and promote their staunch political liberalism. The timing of the creation of the IFGN was no coincidence. It illustrates important trends that defined Costa Rican society in the late nineteenth century: namely, the Olympians were motivated by ideas of modernization and progress, and they saw pub-lic education and science as the foundation of their modernizing mis-sion. They envisioned an educational system that would generate responsible and productive citizens; those citizens, educated in sci-ence and other technological matters, would lead the nation into the future.

While Costa Rica's Olympians prioritized modernity and trum-peted the values of nineteenth-century liberalism—such as equality, freedom, and representation—they were also haunted by the potential for chaos and instability. Following the era of barracks coups in the 1850s and 1860s, Olympians took a more authoritarian approach to governing. But they generally justified their strong-arm tactics as a necessary strategy in the interest of maintaining order and strengthen-ing government legitimacy.

THE END OF BARRACKS COUPS

Jesús Jiménez, whose presidency rounded out the 1860s, hailed from a cohort of coffee elites in and around Cartago. Following the trend of factional conflict that had characterized earlier decades of the nineteenth century, Jiménez faced intense opposition from the clans of the coffee elite led by the Montealegre family, which was based in the city of San José and which was connected to the former president José María Montealegre. Jiménez attempted to stymie potential sedition against his administration by reforming and restruc-turing the highest levels of military command, thereby removing indi-viduals loyal to his opposition and diminishing the risk of yet another barracks coup. Shortly after taking power for the second time, Jiménez ousted Máximo Blanco and Lorenzo Salazar, two high-ranking mili-tary leaders and allies of the Montealgres, from their military positions. He hoped such a move would prevent his rivals from initiating yet another barracks coup, but the Montealegres sought a new alliance—this time with Guanacaste native Tomás Guardia Gutiérrez. The Montealegre family schemed with Guardia to orchestrate what they expected to be another barracks coup, expecting the military commander to force Jiménez from power and then hand over the presidency to one of the members of the influential family. But Guardia surprised everyone by refusing to turn over power. With the support of his military allies, Guardia pressured the interim president, Bruno Carranza, to resign after just a few short months and maneuvered his political influence to have Congress name him president in August 1870. For the next 12 years, Guardia ruled outright or behind the scenes and worked to transform Costa Rica into his vision of a progressive and modern society.

Guardia was the first high-ranking military leader who served an extended term as head of state in Costa Rica, and he proved to be an adept leader with a keen understanding of the political currents of the late nineteenth century. Although he ruled as a dictator, Guardia derived a large degree of support from the masses, thereby escaping the suffocating political influence traditionally wielded by the elite classes. Having a broader base of political support also allowed Guardia to evade the contentious rivalries of the *cafetaleros* that had been the source of so many elite-backed military coups in the past, and under his leadership the long trend of barracks coups came to an end. Guardia immediately understood the need to professionalize the military and to separate the national military from the political sector. He increased military spending drastically in an attempt to eradicate corruption and boost morale. Furthermore, Guardia refocused military objectives to target external threats, effectively turning commanders' attention away from internal politics. Guardia solidified military reforms by enacting new training techniques, building new facilities, raising salaries, and writing new military codes. During his administration, the Costa Rican military underwent a transformation as the previous connections between the *cafetaleros* and the armed forces effectively disappeared.

THE CONSOLIDATION OF LIBERALISM

Despite political struggles and the continuation of barracks coups during the 1860s, the national government did manage to strengthen its position, and an even more thorough platform of liberal policy became evident. Costa Rican leaders continued to concern themselves with economic progress and expanding Costa Rica's position in global trade. Government leaders devoted new resources to expanding the national transportation and communications infrastructure in an effort to facilitate trade. Furthermore, a new constitution came into effect in 1869. This new document expanded the electorate by lowering the voting age to 21. It also bolstered local authority by giving municipal governments a greater voice in the political system. Local governments could now propose constitutional reforms. Political participation had been expanding and strengthening over the course of the 1860s, and the constitutional changes enacted in 1869 further reinforced the move toward a more inclusive electorate.

Jiménez, for his part, had backed the construction of several schools, and in 1869 he declared a system of free and obligatory primary education; the Constitution of 1869 formalized a system of state-funded public education. Although implementing such a program with any efficacy would not be achieved until well into the twentieth century, Jiménez's emphasis on education certainly reflects a common ideological belief held by many liberal leaders at that time—namely that a strong, productive, and responsible population relied on an adequate system of education provided primarily by the state. The liberal emphasis on education as a civilizing function for the lower classes would become part of official policy in subsequent decades.

The liberal impulse that became evident in the 1860s was further entrenched in the 1870s. Starting with the presidency of Tomás Guardia and continuing with his successors Próspero Fernández (1882–1885) and Bernardo Soto (1885–1889), many of the characteristics of Costa Rica's modern political system were put into place. Guardia, Fernández, and Soto collectively became known as the Olympians because of the bold and aggressive nature of their liberal reform platform. The Olympians' liberalism followed a trend that had become standard among many Latin American governments in the late nineteenth century. Many believed that three centuries of colonial rule had left the region in an underdeveloped state—a condition that was made worse by decades of political instability following independence. As a result, liberal leaders concluded that aggressive, state-driven reform was necessary to correct the inherent problems inherited from colonial rule.

Liberals in Costa Rica—and indeed throughout Latin America—identified numerous weaknesses in the political, economic, and social structures that made up the young nation. Of paramount importance to the Olympians was strengthening the power of the state over other influential corporate institutions such as the Church, indigenous communities, and the network of conservative aristocracy. Throughout Spanish colonial rule, various corporations—or formal groups with rights and responsibilities defined by law—had held privileged positions in society. Protections and guarantees conferred by the Spanish Crown had allowed these institutions to acquire considerable wealth, power, and social prestige, and by the end of the colonial period the Catholic Church and associated *cofradías* were among the wealthiest and largest property holders in Latin America. In Costa Rica, early reform policies under Braulio Carrillo had targeted much of that wealth, but late nineteenth-century liberal leaders also perceived the social and cultural influence of corporate institutions as contrary to their attempts to consolidate control in a strong, centralized state.

THE OLYMPIANS

Guardia and his liberal cohort labeled themselves the "priests of progress," and they launched a vigorous campaign to create a modern society by strengthening the state and using government authority to promote a prescribed notion of progress. Favored within the inner circle of the governing elite was a small group of young, like-minded intellectuals, scientists, and political reformers. They publicly spoke of the need to "civilize" the nation's masses, and they generally valued education as one of the most important ways to achieve that goal. In this way, reforms reflected the influence of positivism, which was prevalent throughout Latin American in the late nineteenth century. Positivists privileged progress and scientific knowledge over tradition and the status quo. In Costa Rica and elsewhere, liberals sought to promote a vision of progress that encompassed material goods, cultural trends, and economic growth. Guardia firmly advocated free trade and the development of a capitalist agricultural export sector as a way to promote and expand the nation's economy. He favored the coffee sector as the lifeblood of the Costa Rican economy, but he also introduced a more rigorous tax system that allowed the government to benefit more fully from coffee profits. Government revenue tripled during the 12 years of Guardia's rule, and the dictator used the expanding treasury to strengthen the role of the state. He enlarged the public sector, creating new layers of bureaucracy that expanded the functions of the national government. Tax revenue was funneled to social projects such as education, public health, and transportation. Guardia also funded modernizing infrastructure projects: paving streets, installing electricity and plumbing, modernizing highways and ports, and constructing new public buildings.

CONSTITUTION AND LIBERAL REFORM

Despite the recent passage of the Constitution of 1869, one of Guardia's most significant undertakings as president was to craft a new governing document that would more closely reflect the ideals of his liberal political platform. The Constitution of 1871 was the result of those efforts. Although the document was suspended several times in the late nineteenth century and went through several revisions, its basic framework remained as the nation's governing system until it was replaced in 1949. The 1871 constitution maintained the same suffrage specifications as the Constitution of 1869, but it strengthened the role of the executive over the electoral process. Open suffrage existed in theory, but the executive's ability to supervise voting, tally election results, and approve voter rolls gave the ruling party enormous power and allowed a considerable degree of electoral fraud.

The Constitution of 1871 continued the three branches of government and the unicameral legislature that had been in place for most of the century, requiring the approval of both the executive and the legislative branches for new laws. Despite that structure, the new constitution reflected Guardia's intent to strengthen the power of the state by consolidating the authority of the executive. It limited the length of time Congress was to be in session, and it allowed the president to convene a Permanent Commission and to call extraordinary sessions of the Congress for emergency measures. Through these functions, the executive retained considerable oversight of the congressional agenda. Furthermore, the constitution gave the president the authority to suspend the constitution and to limit individual liberties; presidents used these powers with regularity throughout the rest of the nineteenth century.

Guardia, and particularly the Olympians who succeeded him, implemented a liberal reform platform that included a number of social and cultural measures. Like the political reforms contained in the Constitution of 1871, the social and cultural changes instituted by these leaders aimed to strengthen the role of the state and to promote progress and modernization. Many of the reforms were intended to promote a "civilizing" mission toward the lower classes. Educational programs were designed to lift the lower classes out of an underdeveloped state, and the Olympians went to great length to expand the educational reforms introduced in the 1860s.

Despite earlier liberal efforts to reform education, by the 1880s most instruction was still controlled by the Catholic Church and was locally organized around municipalities. Few state-run schools existed, and the national government had little control over curriculum. Educational opportunities for women were inconsistent throughout the country, and even though universal public education had been mandated in reform laws, the role of the state in the education of its citizenry was still quite limited. In 1885, major state-led reforms to education began to take root as Bernardo Soto took office and passed the *Ley general de educación común*. The law mandated primary schooling for both boys and girls, established a national curriculum for primary education, and organized classrooms to allow for age-specific instruction. The new education law specifically targeted the Catholic Church by mandating that the national government—not the Church or local governments—have jurisdiction over curriculum and the implementation of a public education system. Soto's administration also closed the Universidad de Santo Tomás, which had been the nation's main institution of higher education and was closely tied to the Catholic Church.

In order to meet the new demands in primary education, the government opened the Colegio Superior de Señoritas, which served as a normal school for girls and offered scholarships to train female teachers. By the late decades of the nineteenth century, liberal governments throughout Latin America had concluded that women were best suited to educate young people. Many liberals firmly believed that women were inherently more nurturing and that men's natural abilities were best utilized in other professions such as politics, business, and agriculture. Female teachers also demanded a significantly lower salary than male teachers, which was a convincing trait as nineteenth-century governments struggled to implement public education programs with limited budgets. Costa Rican liberals followed these trends and targeted women to fill the ranks in the teaching profession. Over several decades, the Colegio attracted the daughters of middle- and working-class families, primarily from urban areas. Over time, the normal school gained a reputation as an institution that empowered women, and it was an organizing site of incipient feminist consciousness into the twentieth century.

Closely following the tenets of the liberal and positivist ideologies of the nineteenth century, Costa Rican leaders aimed to supplant the authority of priests and local Church leaders by training young women and promoting a state-approved curriculum through primary education. They envisioned a public education system that would train productive and responsible citizens and promote the tenets of the liberal ideology. Costa Rican leaders also hoped that a system of public education with a state-mandated curriculum would help to engender future generations of scientists and technical experts to help promote national progress along the precepts of positivism. Soto's government actively recruited European scientists to relocate to Costa Rica and to help build a modern, science-oriented educational curriculum. It was that recruiting effort that brought the Swiss scientist Henri François Pittier, whose story opened this chapter, to San José. At Pittier's urging, government leaders expanded the reach of science and the positivist ideology beyond the classroom. The creation of the IFGN demonstrates that government leaders embraced the use of scientific knowledge as a way to strengthen the nation's economic and political systems.

Other cultural reforms intended to "civilize" the nation took aim at "barbaric" practices. Tomás Guardia reformed the penal system by building new prisons, focusing on rehabilitation, and abolishing capital punishment. At the popular level, cockfighting and other recreational activities that were considered backward by the liberal elite were banned. Leaders discouraged personal vices such as excessive drinking and gambling. They viewed prostitution as a public health concern, a threat to the sanctity of the family as the backbone of society, and an obstacle to promoting nationalism and racial homogeneity. This was particularly true in the Central Valley region where women were encouraged to form nuclear families through legal marriages, while the reality for women in port cities and other regions of the periphery was quite different. Liberals also attempted to curb folk practices such as the use of traditional medicines. And in a continuation of the nation-building atmosphere that was evident in the 1850s, national leaders promoted the secular figure of Juan Santamaría over the religious icon of the Virgen de Los Angeles in an effort to create a unifying national symbol that would privilege the state over the Church. The state's campaign to create a national hero out of Juan Santamaría is also an illustration of the liberal government's emphasis on patriotism as a way to strengthen the nation.

The Catholic Church felt a particularly strong impact as the Olympians imposed liberal reforms. In an attempt to curb the influence of the Church and to privilege the power of the state, liberals instituted a system of civil registry for births, deaths, and marriages. Such a policy gave the government greater oversight of the population and attempted to replace the Church's traditional authority by replacing sacraments with a state-sponsored process. Combined with earlier reforms that divested the Church of much of its land and the ongoing showdown over educational policies, liberal reforms implemented by the Olympians left Church leaders feeling threatened by government policies. Monsignor Bernard August Thiel, Archbishop of San José, publicly opposed such measures, leading to growing animosity between the Church and the liberal government. In 1884, the archbishop and the entire Jesuit order were expelled from Costa Rica in a culmination of anticlerical moves on the part of the liberal government. After that, reforms aimed at secularizing society and strengthening the state over the Church continued in earnest. In 1888, Costa Rican leaders formally approved civil marriage and divorce, and reforms to Civil Codes codified aspects of family law that aimed to give the government greater control over household relations.

While Church leaders decried liberal reforms as anticlerical, the Olympians promoted them as modernizing and necessary to bring about progress for the nation. Government leaders publicly advocated the importance of protecting individualism over the well-being of institutions such as the Church. In 1877, Tomás Guardia passed the Law on Individual Rights, which codified many personal liberties similar to the Bill of Rights to the U.S. Constitution. Guardia's law called for freedom of religion, freedom of expression, rights to privacy, and freedom of movement. It also established a number of legal protections within the judicial system. Collectively, the measures contained in the Law on Individual Rights represent the liberal agenda to promote individualism. But despite this apparent attempt by a Costa Rican government to protect basic personal liberties, the Olympians' record for implementing such policies was certainly problematic.

RAILROAD POLITICS

A central tenet of nineteenth-century liberal thought was the primacy of a capitalist agricultural export sector as the basis for economic growth. Most Latin American nations had been pursuing such a model for decades, and they expanded their export trade substantially with the help of foreign capital coming from private investors in the United States and Europe. Costa Rica's economic development in the nineteenth century took a different path in the early phases. A capitalist agricultural export sector emerged with the rapid expansion of the coffee industry, but the coffee economy was largely controlled by domestic interests, in a shared venture between *cafetaleros* and small farmers. Coffee exports had dominated the national economy, had generated substantial income, and had facilitated impressive economic growth. But the Olympians and other leaders in the late nineteenth century envisioned an even larger export market supported by modern system of transportation and communication.

One of Tomás Guardia's highest priorities in the 1870s was developing and modernizing the nation's internal infrastructure to support the capitalist agricultural export economy he envisioned. He devoted government funds to improving Costa Rica's network of internal roadways, but further expansion of the export market proved elusive as jungles separating the Central Valley from the Atlantic coast remained impassable. For decades, coffee exporters had been shipping their product over land to Puntarenas on the Pacific coast; from there boats transported coffee shipments around the tip of South America and eventually on to the final destination in Europe. The journey was long, and transport costs were high. Since the principal export market for Costa Rica coffee was in Europe, domestic producers and government leaders alike had been searching for an effective way to export directly from Costa Rica's Atlantic coast.

In 1871 Guardia signed a contract with Henry Meiggs for the construction of a railroad line connecting San José to the Atlantic coast. Since the 1850s, government leaders in Costa Rica had been pursuing opportunities to improve internal transportation by building rail lines. A number of foreign engineers and investors had conducted initial investigations into such projects, but they almost all quickly gave up for lack of funds or as a result of the daunting physical terrain. Henry Meiggs was a railroad tycoon from New York, and he became known for his ability to conquer the rugged, mountainous Andean terrain of South America after overseeing the construction of hundreds of miles of railroad lines in Chile and Peru. Meiggs sent his nephew, Henry Meiggs Keith, to Costa Rica to spearhead the negotiations with Guardia's government. The Costa Rican leader envisioned a modern rail line connecting San José and the coffee-producing regions of the Central Valley with the Port of Limón to facilitate the export of the nation's main capitalist agricultural product to the markets in Europe. Meiggs and his nephew secured a contract to complete the project over a period of three years for a price of £1.6 million.

In order to meet such a large financial obligation, Guardia was forced to borrow £1 million from British banks with the intention of using government revenue for the balance. But the financing arrangements were questionable from the start. British bankers manipulated negotiations to secure terms that included exorbitant interest rates and that earmarked the majority of the loans as commissions. As a result, considerably less money was available for the construction project, and the Costa Rican government was quickly burdened with large debt obligations. The rugged terrain of the mountains surrounding the Central Valley delayed the project considerably, and the lack of funds meant that progress slowed to a crawl at times. Committed to completing the mass infrastructure project, the Guardia administration borrowed even more money in 1872 under equally adverse terms as the original loan. A mere 18 months after signing the contract, the rail line was nowhere near completion, and the Costa Rican government owed £3.4 million in foreign loans—of which it only had received £1.3 million to allot toward the project.

Henry Meiggs Keith was soon joined on the project by his three brothers. As construction slowly proceeded, Keith's negotiations with the Guardia administration became increasingly tense. Construction problems and difficulties securing financing brought continuous delays, and by 1873 only 33 kilometers of rail line had been completed even though the Costa Rican government had continued to make regular payments to the Keith organization. Eventually, the Guardia administration defaulted on its debt to the British and cancelled its contract with Henry Meiggs Keith. The unfinished railroad project was placed temporarily under government control, and it stalled for many years as the government was saddled with onerous debt obligations and few resources to increase national income.

Keith died of dysentery shortly after the termination of the contract, but his brother Minor Cooper Keith had established himself as a businessman in Limón and remained in Costa Rica. In the coming years, government leaders negotiated small contracts with Minor Keith to complete small sections of the rail lines. Keith made a name for himself and managed to start building a small fortune by exporting bananas from the Port of Limón. In 1883 the administration of Próspero Fernández approached Minor Keith hoping to secure an agreement that would guarantee the completion of the railroad and relieve the nation's foreign debt burden at the same time. Bernardo Soto, serving as Fernández's secretary of state, worked out a new deal with Keith. The Soto-Keith Contract gave the U.S. entrepreneur the power to renegotiate Costa Rica's European debt on President Fernández's behalf. Keith absorbed much of the financial risk of continuing the railroad construction venture, and in exchange the Fernández government granted him direct control over the administration of the rail lines. In addition Minor Keith received a 99-year lease on 800,000 acres of property in the Caribbean lowlands—a grant that amounted to roughly 7 percent of Costa Rica's national territory.

The Keith-Soto Contract rejuvenated the railroad project in Costa Rica as new money and renewed energy poured in to the endeavor. Keith benefited enormously from the new contract, and he quickly became one of the wealthiest and most powerful individuals in Costa

Rica. Nevertheless, Keith's company also struggled at times as tropical disease and rugged terrain escalated the costs for completing the project. Keith also faced difficulties in securing enough laborers to toil in such treacherous conditions. Thousands of workers died in the initial phases of the construction project alone. Keith eventually recruited West Indian laborers to supplement his labor force. Those immigrants stayed in Costa Rica long after the railroad project was completed. Most became workers on banana plantations that sprang up along the Atlantic coast, and their presence added a new racial dynamic to Costa Rican social relations.

While many new nations in Latin America had opened themselves to foreign investment quite early in the nineteenth century, Costa Rica had managed to avoid that trend for quite some time. But the liberal impulse for developing a capitalist agricultural export market eventually compelled the nation's leaders to seek economic backing from foreign investors in an effort to create the internal infrastructure necessary to integrate the country more fully into the global economy. Costa Rica's relationship with Minor Keith marked the beginning of an era of economic development heavily influenced by foreign involvement. Indeed, the liberal vision of Costa Rican progress in the late nineteenth century could not have foreseen the extent to which Minor Keith and other foreign investors would come to dominate the national economy.

THE 1889 ELECTION

The impact of Costa Rica's liberal reforms was visible in social and economic developments throughout the 1870s and 1880s. But the full extent of the nation's political transformation only became evident in the 1889 elections. Tomás Guardia and the Olympians who succeeded him had promoted democratic freedom and individual liberties as the vanguard of their reform agenda. The electorate had expanded, even though it was not yet universal since literacy and income requirements limited the vote to the elite and women were still prohibited from political participation. Guardia's Law on Individual Rights combined with the power of liberal rhetoric encouraged the formation of a political and civic consciousness. Additionally, the era of the Olympians brought the formation of the nation's first political parties in an effort to expand popular support. Liberals formalized their political platform through the Liberal Progressive Party (Partido Liberal Progresista) while conservative opposition formed the Constitutional Democratic Party (Partido Constitucional Democrático). Both parties were initially a reflection of elite political interests, but they also encouraged popular participation in ways not previously seen in Costa Rican politics.

Despite the appearance of equality and reform, a high level of corruption remained in the political system, and those in power often resorted to fraud and chicanery to ensure the opposition did not gain a foothold. The Olympians maintained power throughout the liberal era in part by manipulating the electoral system and therefore found themselves unprepared for the conservative backlash that surfaced in the 1889 elections. Supporters of the Catholic Church and other conservative leaders appealed to a constituency that was already suspicious of liberal reforms—particularly those reforms that aimed to remove the Church from the national curriculum and that exercised greater government oversight in family affairs. The Constitutional Democratic Party garnered enough popular support to secure the election of conservative José Joaquín Rodríguez Zeledón over the Liberal Progressive Party candidate, Ascención Esquivel. Liberals initially resorted to the usual underhanded strategies to prevent conservatives from taking power. But when a crowd of more than 10,000 rose in protest in San José, liberals were forced to step down in favor of an interim president on November 7, 1889. Six months later, Rodríguez assumed the presidency, and the 1889 election became known as a watershed moment in the emergence of a democratic political system in Costa Rica.

For the next three decades, Costa Rica experienced an era of relative stability in national politics. Brief moments of crisis erupted—Rodríguez dissolved Congress in 1892, and his successor Rafael Yglesias Castro attempted to amend the constitution to allow himself to run for a third term. But power changed hands between and among competing political parties, and each president completed his term peacefully until 1917. The late nineteenth and early twentieth centuries marked an era of political consolidation that was made possible in part by an expanding economy, which funded tangible signs of social progress. The state continued to devote considerable funding to public education and modern infrastructure appeared in major urban centers. Rodríguez introduced the nation's first telephone lines, while Yglesias focused on public health and sanitation programs. By the end of the century, the railroad connecting the Atlantic and Pacific coasts had been completed, a national theater had been built, and electricity had been introduced in most major metropolitan areas.

Despite the measurable gains made in material progress in the late nineteenth century, Costa Rican development came at a price.

The National Theater opened in San Jose in 1897. It represents an era of economic and social progress in the late nineteenth century. (Library of Congress)

The liberal preference for agricultural commodity export growth had paved the way for foreign investors to penetrate the national economy, and the presence of foreign influence would come to dominate much of the nation's history into the twentieth century. Minor Keith's contract in 1883 brought much-needed closure to the problematic construction of the Atlantic coast railway. The expansion of transportation lines benefited Costa Rican exporters, to be sure. But few could anticipate the juggernaut that would eventually emerge in the Costa Rican agricultural sector as Keith and his partners created a Central American banana empire.

6

The Banana Republic

ONE HUNDRED YEARS OF SOLITUDE

In Gabriel García Marquez's classic novel *One Hundred Years of Solitude*, the multigenerational Buenaventura family provides a lens through which the literary giant examines a century of Colombian history in the fictional jungle village of Macondo. One of the most riveting accounts in the novel is Marquez's portrayal of a labor strike on a U.S.-owned banana plantation that eventually results in the massacre of 3,000 peasant workers after the military opens fire on the unarmed crowd. The corpses of those workers are transported by the new rail line to be dumped in the ocean; and as the bodies disappear, so too does the fictional town's collective memory of the horrific event. Marquez's literary account was inspired by the 1928 Banana Massacre in the town of Ciénaga, Colombia, when the national military opened fire on striking banana plantation workers in order to protect the interests of the U.S.-based United Fruit Company. In the novel, the Banana Company brings ruin to the town of Macondo in the form of political repression, economic imperialism, and environmental devastation. Marquez includes the fictional Banana Company in his novel to make a specific critique about the very real activities of the United Fruit Company throughout Latin America.

Even though Marquez's tale takes place in Colombia, numerous parallels can be drawn to the history of the United Fruit Company in Costa Rica. The U.S.-based company got its start in Costa Rica, and it quickly grew to play a dominant role in the Central American export economy. And just as the train erases the grisly evidence of the Banana Company massacre in Marquez's novel, the real United Fruit Company originated and developed hand-in-hand with the railroad in Costa Rica. In the late nineteenth and early twentieth centuries, bananas and railroads came to symbolize modernity, economic growth, and progress in Costa Rica. And the company expanded quickly as a result of a close relationship between its owner, Minor Keith, and the Costa Rican government. Furthermore, the conditions under which the United Fruit Company emerged allowed it to expand very quickly into other areas of Latin America. As the corporation became more powerful, it also became a symbol of the exploitative nature of the capitalist agricultural export economy that dominated Costa Rica and the rest of Latin America. Labor reform movements of the early twentieth century surfaced in response to a growing set of social anxieties that surrounded the export agricultural sector and the expansion of the labor force. Often those reform movements targeted foreign corporations like the United Fruit Company. And while a "banana massacre" like the scene depicted in *One Hundred Years of Solitude* never took place in Costa Rica, the nation did play host to a serious labor dispute between peasant workers and the United Fruit Company in 1934. The Great Banana Strike involved 10,000 workers and was one of the largest labor stoppages in Latin America targeting a U.S. company. It also inspired Costa Rica's own literary response as one of the leaders of the strike, Carlos Luis Fallas, wrote *Mamita Yunai*, which chronicles the struggles of peasant workers on Costa Rica's banana plantations.

UNITED FRUIT COMPANY

In the late nineteenth and early twentieth centuries, the cultivation and export of bananas became a thriving economic sector in Costa Rica. The emergence of the banana industry coincided closely with the completion of the railway connecting the Central Valley with the Caribbean Coast. Even while construction of the railroad was ongoing, U.S. entrepreneur Minor Keith was already dabbling in a number of business ventures related to the export market. Bananas had caught his interest, and Keith purchased a batch of rootstalks for experimental plantings. He quickly found that bananas grew well in Costa Rica's semitropical climate. He exported part of his crop to a growing market in the United States and also used his banana crop to feed local railroad construction workers as the major infrastructure project was being completed. When the Costa Rican government granted him 800,000 acres of fertile land as part of his 1883 contract to finish the railroad, Keith expanded his network of banana planta- tions considerably. Once the remainder of the track was finally com- pleted, Keith owned the controlling share of the rail line and had taken on enormous debt obligations to bring the project to completion. When coffee freight and passenger transport failed to provide suffi- cient income, Keith filled out shipments by expanding banana trans- ports. He formed the Tropical Trading and Transport Company to coordinate his business activities in both the shipping industry and in the harvesting of bananas.

The Caribbean lowlands of Costa Rica proved ideal for the mass cul- tivation of bananas. The tropical fruit requires a warm climate and adequate rainfall with sufficient drainage to avoid swamp-like condi- tions. The port of Limón and surrounding areas receive 5 to 10 inches of rainfall per month and enjoy an average temperature of around 80 degrees Fahrenheit. The region boasts an extensive network of small rivers, streams, and other tributaries that yield fertile soil with sufficient drainage for the banana crop. But completion of the railroad combined with Keith's investment in steamship transport was particularly impor- tant in facilitating the expansion of the banana industry. Because cut bananas ripen very quickly, a rapid system of transport was essential for exporting the crop. The completed rail line allowed cut bananas to arrive at the port within 24 hours of harvest. Once there, Keith's steam- ship line carried the cargo to the United States.

The banana industry found a healthy market in the United States, and consumer demand quickly grew. After 1902 the export market expanded to include Canada and the United Kingdom. As banana exports increased, so too did Keith's landholdings, which allowed the businessman to expand production considerably. By 1890, the rail- road that was originally built to provide more cost-effective transport for the coffee crop was shipping bananas for export almost exclu- sively. Also by the 1890s, Keith's banana plantations were more valu- able than his rail line in terms of net worth and income. The American entrepreneur naturally turned his focus to the cultivation and export of tropical fruits, and he used his local transportation network to facilitate the growth of his export activities.

Keith quickly became one of the most influential men in Costa Rica. He built a powerful network of allies within the Costa Rican government by marrying Cristina María Fernández—daughter of former president José María Castro Madriz—in 1883. The nepotistic nature of Costa Rica's governing elite also meant that Keith's wife was the niece of President Próspero Fernández and cousin of Bernardo Soto Alfaro, who served in Fernández's cabinet and eventually became president in his own right from 1885 to 1889. Soto was also responsible for negotiating the railroad contract that awarded Keith control over the rail line along with hundreds of thousands of acres of agricultural land in 1883. Keith's wealth, power, and influence increased substantially throughout the 1890s.

Keith eventually extended his activities into Colombia, establishing plantations along the Caribbean Coast and founding the Colombian Land Company. In 1897, he purchased a 50 percent share of the Snyder Banana Company, which had already established a large operation in neighboring Panama. These expansions allowed Keith to dominate banana cultivation and shipping throughout Central America. Then in 1899, he merged his Costa Rica–based Tropical Trading and Transport Company with the Boston Fruit Company, which was formed by Andrew Preston and Lorenzo Baker in 1885 and had grown to control much of the banana industry in the Caribbean. The merger of the two powerful companies resulted in the formation of the United Fruit Company (UFC), and this U.S. corporation became one of the largest landowners in Latin America in the early twentieth century. The UFC expanded almost immediately into Honduras and Guatemala. Through negotiations with the Guatemalan government, UFC eventually controlled much of the nation's communication infrastructure and was responsible for highway and railroad networks. United Fruit eventually purchased the Guatemalan railroad and formed the International Railways of Central America in an effort to create one interconnected rail network. As UFC's landholdings and economic activities expanded in Latin America, company executives looked to the U.S. government to help protect their business interests abroad. The company's dominant economic position within Latin America and its persuasive position in U.S. government circles allowed it to wield enormous influence over Latin American policy.

The emergence of the banana industry had a profound impact on the physical, economic, and social landscape of Costa Rica. United

A United Fruit Company banana plantation in the early twentieth century. (Library of Congress)

Fruit Company found that virgin lands yielded the best banana crop, and in many regions a given plot could produce profitably for only five to eight years. By 1910 Panama disease, a soil condition that attacks bananas through the root system and causes the plant to wilt and rot, had begun to spread throughout United Fruit landholdings. Once the disease took hold, infected lands were incapable of producing a crop for many years. As a result, UFC regularly abandoned old lands in favor of new ones, and at any given point only a small fraction of the company's landholdings was being used for agricultural production. The nature of banana cultivation and the introduction of Panama disease meant that local growers could not compete with the United Fruit Company. Minor Keith had been granted control over 800,000 acres of fertile lands in his 1883 railroad contract, which gave the UFC access to sufficient virgin land to sustain a relatively short cultivate-and-abandon strategy. Local growers did not have that luxury. By 1926 the UFC had abandoned nearly 30,000 acres of banana lands in the Caribbean lowlands of Costa Rica. In later years, other soil afflictions caused the company to shift its operations to other regions of the country. But despite the vagaries of banana cultivation, the

United Fruit Company remained an important force in Costa Rica throughout much of the twentieth century.

Even as the United Fruit Company set up operations in Costa Rica and banana cultivation came to predominate the export market, local growers and foreign investors alike branched out to produce other commodity products. Cattle ranching developed in the northern Guanacaste region and in the Reventazón and Turrialba Valleys to the east of the Central Valley. In those areas large agricultural estates emerged, employing wage laborers in contrast with the small and medium-sized farms that played such a fundamental role in the nineteenth-century coffee sector. In Guanacaste the expansion of the cattle industry was facilitated by new logging operations. Hardwood exporters cleared lands that were later used for grazing. Throughout Costa Rica, foreign interests invested in sugar and cacao production as well as in mining activities. And while those industries attracted a number of foreign capitalists, many cacao and mining operations were controlled by companies with links to Minor Keith—further evidence of the U.S. entrepreneur's influence in the Costa Rican economy.

The development of these new commercial enterprises had a significant effect on Costa Rica. They served to diversify the economy to some extent and mitigated the power of the traditional *cafetalero* elite. Indeed, these new economic activities served as a backdrop to a political culture that was shifting away from the coffee clans that had controlled elections for much of the nineteenth century, and a system of greater popular participation began to emerge. But the changing economic climate did little to lessen Costa Rica's reliance on commodity exports as the foundation for economic growth. That model would eventually be challenged only after the onset of the Great Depression in 1929.

LABOR ISSUES IN THE BANANA INDUSTRY

With the labor demands created by new industries, the nature of Costa Rica's coastal population changed considerably, first with the construction of the railroad and then with the rise of the United Fruit Company. When Keith's family started construction of the rail line in 1873, the Costa Rican population was relatively small and generally concentrated in the Central Valley. A scarcity of laborers along the Caribbean coast compelled Keith to import foreign workers from China, Italy, and the Caribbean—particularly from Jamaica, St. Kitts, Barbados, Trinidad, and other British colonial possessions—to complete the railroad project, and many of those workers remained in

Costa Rica, becoming laborers in the banana industry. In particular, a large influx of Afro-Caribbean laborers proved crucial to the completion of the railroad and later the expansion of the banana industry. Keith and other UFC executives concluded that the West Indians' familiarity with tropical conditions and their expertise in banana cultivation made them ideal workers in the emerging economic sector. And while the Costa Rican government eventually passed legislation prohibiting new Chinese immigration, black workers from the Caribbean continued to migrate to Costa Rica, and West Indians quickly constituted a majority within the banana industry labor force.

Despite the large number of Afro-Caribbean laborers and the indispensable role they played in the banana industry, most of those workers endured deplorable working and living conditions on UFC plantations and faced pervasive racial discrimination in Costa Rican society. Costa Ricans thought of themselves as highly racially homogenized by the turn of the century, and the influx of black workers along the coast elicited a strong reaction among many in the Central Valley. Politicians attempted to pass laws that would isolate the black population along the coast by prohibiting them from settling in the Central Valley. They also considered outlawing interracial marriages in an attempt to preserve a stronger European character of Costa Rica's mestizo heritage.

Labor abuses on coastal plantations added to the plight of West Indian workers. Many of them were recruited to Costa Rica's banana industry with the promise of high wages and good living conditions, only to find a system of abuse and exploitation when they arrived. Laborers faced low wages, unsafe and unsanitary living and working conditions, and an exploitative system of payment in credit at company-owned commissaries in lieu of currency. Workers were often issued coupons that were only redeemable at the company store, where prices for basic goods were significantly higher than at other establishments. Most Afro-Caribbean workers had no contract and therefore had no legal recourse to challenge the abuses of their employer. Further aggravating the situation was the fact that the United Fruit Company continued to recruit large numbers of Afro-Caribbean workers in an attempt to glut the labor market and keep wages low. Veteran workers often complained that excessive and indiscriminate recruitment of additional workers weakened the position of laborers already on UFC plantations and undermined their ability to demand better working conditions.

Over time a sense of community emerged among black West Indian workers, and they eventually formed the Limón Workers' Federation

(Federación de Trabajadores de Limón). In a number of instances they resorted to collective action to push for change on UFC plantations. Minor work stoppages occurred in Limón in 1908 and 1909 as black laborers protested a series of layoffs and demanded compensation for unpaid back wages. The United Fruit Company used several strategies to break strikes, including hiring nonblack workers for higher wages and calling in the police to arrest striking workers. In some instances the UFC acquiesced to some labor demands while at other times the company broke the strikes without granting any concessions. In an era of growing labor consciousness worldwide, the emergence of working-class action in Costa Rica's banana enclaves was a significant development.

The modest workers' activism that began surfacing in 1908 and 1909 was a sign of a growing sense of strife that would culminate in significant labor unrest in Limón in 1910. In July of that year the Artisan's and Labourer's Union formed in an attempt to pressure the United Fruit Company into raising wages. The union also aimed to end the wide-scale recruitment of new West Indian migrants to UFC plantations. A new batch of laborers arrived in Limón later that year with no contracts, and they found the wretched living and working conditions and low wages to contradict the promises made to them before their arrival. Veteran workers, sensing an opportunity to pressure the United Fruit Company, fueled the unrest by intimidating the new arrivals with tales of mistreatment. The new workers rose up in protest, and riots broke out in Limón as the UFC called in the military to diffuse the unrest. When the Artisan's and Laborer's Union backed the workers, thousands more poured into the streets, and violent clashes erupted between workers and military troops. It was only through the intervention of the British Consul that the uprising abated. The Consul collected a list of worker demands and acted as mediator to end the dispute.

The British Foreign Office continued to play an active role in mediating labor disputes for West Indian workers in the coming years. Additional strikes occurred after the outbreak of World War I when wages were frozen while prices for goods at the company store continued to increase. One particularly effective work stoppage in 1918 involved a core of highly skilled UFC laborers whose expertise was difficult to replace. After two workers were killed in clashes with the police, strikers retaliated and attempted to pressure the company by blocking shipments, destroying fields, and even setting fire to the company store. Once again, British diplomatic officials intervened and convinced the UFC executives to implement a modest wage increase. But even as worker consciousness was on the rise in the early decades of the twentieth century, the company became increasingly intransigent and unwilling to compromise. A culture of labor exploitation remained on Costa Rican banana plantations, and workers sought new strategies to remedy those injustices.

One important consequence of the spate of strikes in the early twentieth century was a gradual diminishing of Afro-Caribbeans' political isolation within a larger Costa Rican labor movement. In 1921 the Limón Workers' Federation entered into an alliance with the San José based General Workers' Confederation (Confederación General de Trabajadores, or CGT). The CGT brought a sense of legitimacy to the small organization of West Indian banana workers. Experienced labor leaders in San José helped to incorporate Limón workers more fully into a national labor movement and began to erase the sense of foreign isolation among the Afro-Caribbean workers on U.S.-owned banana plantations along the coast. Throughout the next decade, in fact, Costa Ricans and Nicaraguans began migrating to Limón and surrounding areas looking for work in the banana industry. As more Hispanics assimilated with Afro-Caribbean workers in these banana enclaves, a cohesive sense of class identity emerged to override racial and cultural differences.

THE RISE OF ANTI-IMPERIALISM

The rapid rise of the banana industry and the United Fruit Company meant that by the turn of the century foreign interests dominated much of the Costa Rican economy. Foreign involvement certainly had its benefits—it facilitated the completion of the railroad, it brought much-needed diversification to the Costa Rican economy, and it generated some expansion of state revenue. But foreign influence over the economy—epitomized by the activities of the United Fruit Company—quickly drew a number of critics. Up-and-coming politicians began to point to the special concessions earlier governments had given to the UFC that allowed the company to export much of its profits and escape tax burdens within Costa Rica. They also denounced the disproportionate influence the company held over national affairs. Labor leaders rebuked foreign corporations for exploiting national workers. And a small but growing number of activists questioned the environmental consequences of UFC land usage practices, particularly as soil infestations began to penetrate once-fertile agricultural lands.

In the early twentieth century a wave of anti-imperialist sentiment began to emerge among Costa Rica's liberal oligarchy. Those leaders often reflected back to the National Campaign of 1856 when Costa Ricans found themselves the object of the expansionist aims of the United States. The war against U.S. filibuster William Walker and the championing of a national hero in the figure of Juan Santamaría had been part of a larger campaign of fostering a sense of patriotism and national identity by the liberal governments of the late nineteenth century. While the threat of individual filibuster activities had abated considerably, other signs of the expansionist aims of the United States were very much evident by the beginning of the twentieth century— particularly as Costa Ricans took stock of U.S. activities in surrounding areas. In 1898 the United States became involved in ousting Spain from its colonial possessions in the Caribbean. Spain's defeat in the Spanish-American War demonstrated the growing military reach of the United States and established a new pseudoimperialist U.S. hegemony over Puerto Rico and Cuba—with the former becoming a U.S. protectorate and the latter attaining independence only after surrendering much of its autonomy to the United States. In 1903 U.S. president Theodore Roosevelt encouraged separatist tendencies in Panama—previously a province of Colombia—after the Colombian government rejected the terms of a treaty that would have allowed the United States to build and operate a canal across the isthmus. When the Colombian government repudiated the U.S. proposal, Roosevelt backed the movement for Panamanian independence by sending naval forces to head off the Colombian military. Once Panama's independence had been secured, the new government approved a canal treaty that gave the United States considerable authority in Panama.

U.S. hegemony in the Caribbean and in Panama was reinforced by the construction of military bases in the canal zone, in Puerto Rico, and at Guantanamo Bay in Cuba. Costa Ricans found themselves concerned once again about U.S. expansionist plans in Latin America. Those concerns seemed validated when U.S. president William Howard Taft sent a military expedition to overthrow Nicaraguan President José Santos Zelaya in 1909. U.S. troops remained in Nicaragua until 1933. Witnessing a lengthy military occupation in Nicaragua to the north and a buildup of a U.S. military presence in Panama to the south, Costa Ricans began to sense that the circle of U.S. influence was quickly surrounding and closing in on the small nation. That feeling was exacerbated by the extent to which U.S. interests controlled economic activity along Costa Rica's Caribbean coast. Railroad transport, port facilities, and the cultivation of the newest commodity export crop all fell under the purview of Minor Keith and the United Fruit

Company. The economic component of U.S. dominance in Costa Rica elicited a strong response from the nation's leaders.

Ricardo Jiménez Oreamuno—son of former president Jesús Jiménez—was a lawyer and politician who served as president of Costa Rica on three separate occasions between 1910 and 1936. He became a vocal opponent of the economic power of the United Fruit Company, and he used that position to advocate for a sense of nationalism that he couched in terms of anti-imperialism. Many of Costa Rica's coffee elites sought to diversify their agrarian pursuits by expanding into the fruit industry, but they found themselves unable to compete with the United Fruit Company's dominant position. Jiménez capitalized on their discontent and used it to create a nationalist narrative that became an important part of the nation's twentieth-century experiences. While serving in the Costa Rican Congress, Jiménez assailed the United Fruit Company as a foreign, imperialist entity that exploited the nation's resources for its own profit while bringing little benefit to the nation as a whole. Jiménez and other leaders compared the activities of the United Fruit Company to William Walker's invasion decades earlier and warned that the company's dominant position in the Costa Rican economy was tantamount to a complete loss of national sovereignty. One of Jiménez's objectives as a lawmaker was to introduce a fiscal system that included a significant tax obligation for the banana industry. In the early decades of the twentieth century the issue of taxation, and particularly the debate over the extent to which the wealthy should be taxed, became a volatile political topic.

Workers often picked up on the anti-imperialist rhetoric being employed by political leaders and incorporated those sentiments into the labor movement. Increasingly labor groups outlined their positions in terms of foreign companies acting against national interests. By the 1910s a growing intellectual sector had adopted anti-imperialist rhetoric as well. The arguments tying labor issues to anti-imperialism were limited in scope in the early years, but they did serve as a foundation for a stronger movement that emerged in the 1930s.

THE TINOCO DICTATORSHIP

Costa Rican democracy in the late nineteenth and early twentieth centuries was not perfect, but the trend of barracks coups had come to an end, and the nation enjoyed a sustained period of relative political stability. From the 1870s until 1917 the Costa Rican presidency changed hands peacefully, and although the nature of electoral politics and elite factionalism was problematic, Costa Rica became known as one of the greatest stalwarts of democratic principles in Latin America. The nation's reputation as a bedrock of political cohesion was strengthened abroad by the conspicuous presence of Minor Keith and the United Fruit Company. And those political and economic traditions worked in tandem to attract additional foreign interest and investment in Costa Rica. Nevertheless, after decades of relative political stability and smooth transitions of power, Costa Rican democracy was threatened with a sudden military coup and the rise of a new dictator.

The first cracks in Costa Rica's ostensibly strong political foundations appeared in the presidential election of 1914 when none of the candidates from the nation's three competing political parties won an absolute majority. The responsibility for resolving the disputed election fell to the Costa Rican Congress, where leaders from the leading Partido Republicano Nacional (National Republican Party, or PRN) and the Duranista Party formed an alliance. The resulting agreement placed Alfredo González Flores in the presidency, but because of the problematic way he assumed power, González faced a number of challenges to his legitimacy. Discontent with his administration was further exacerbated when it became clear that the new president intended to pursue a progressive, reformist agenda. He introduced an export tax on coffee, raising the ire of many local elites. He also instituted a graduated income tax whereby the wealthy were to pay a larger share of the tax burden, which further alienated the upper classes. As opposition to the González administration mounted, the beleaguered president responded by restricting freedom of speech and censuring the press.

On January 17, 1917, González's own minister of war, Federico Tinoco—along with his brother José Joaquín Tinoco—carried out a military coup and drove the president from power. Federico Tinoco enjoyed some support, particularly among the elite and the leaders of the main political parties. He was related to the Keith family and, although such allegations were never proven, U.S. leaders harbored strong suspicions that high-ranking executives of the United Fruit Company had helped to facilitate the coup d'etat. Tinoco also curried favor with British investors and maintained strong connections to the Costa Rica Oil Corporation. The former minister of war–turned-politician rallied his supporters and won the presidency in a special election on April 2, 1917.

The early support base that Tinoco managed to create began to disintegrate within the first year, and much like his predecessor, Tinoco responded to dissent by becoming increasingly dictatorial. He named his brother as minister of war to ensure the support of the military. He also expanded the nonmilitary secret police and clamped down on the press. Furthermore, Tinoco faced considerable opposition abroad, particularly from U.S. president Woodrow Wilson, who made the protection of U.S.-styled democratic principles abroad one of his greatest foreign policy priorities. He took office in 1913 in the midst of revolutionary turmoil in neighboring Mexico and a violent civil war in Nicaragua. Wilson attempted to thwart revolution in those two countries by withholding recognition of leaders who rose to power through nondemocratic means. He reacted to the Tinoco coup by extending his policy of nonrecognition to Costa Rica.

Despite advice to the contrary from top officials within the state department, President Wilson pressured Costa Rica for nearly three years in an effort to force Tinoco to step down and to reinforce a democratic tradition in the Central American nation. Tinoco attempted to win U.S. recognition by pledging Costa Rica's allegiance to the Allied powers in World War I, all the while vilifying the United States for its intrusive policies and inciting a nationalist posture among Costa Ricans by labeling U.S. nonrecognition as imperialist. In the end, Wilson's policies did put financial pressure on the Tinoco government, but it was the dictator's waning support among Costa Ricans that eventually brought down his regime. In fact, grassroots opposition began in San José when women teachers and high school students led a series of marches to protest his repressive tactics. Some of those women joined more widespread feminist movements in subsequent years as popular activism began to take root in the collective consciousness of many urban female professionals. Former members of the González administration who had fled into exile in neighboring Nicaragua and El Salvador seized the opportunity to launch an offensive against the Tinoco dictatorship in May of 1919. Led by Julio Acosta García, the opposition quickly gained widespread popular support. Tinoco clung to power throughout the summer months, but when his brother was killed in August 1919 the defeated dictator fled into exile in Jamaica. Julio Acosta was elected president a few months later.

CULTURAL AND SOCIAL CHANGES IN THE 1920s

With the expanding export economy and the evolving political system as a backdrop, Costa Rican society underwent a profound transformation in the early decades of the twentieth century. Liberal social policies that had promoted modernization and progress in the nineteenth century had given rise to a highly literate population with a strong national consciousness. By the 1920s political participation was on the rise with the working class and the poor playing an ever-important role. In 1924 those underrepresented sectors of society found a collective voice with the founding of the Reformist Party by Catholic priest, scholar, and politician Jorge Volio Jiménez. Volio ran as the new party's presidential candidate that same year, putting forth an aggressive reform platform that included populist measures such as government protection for labor rights and state funding for basic social welfare programs. Volio failed to win the presidency, but the reformist politicians made enough inroads to be able to demand that their agenda be taken up by the incoming administration of Ricardo Jiménez, who had won his second presidential term. Jiménez invited a number of reformists into his administration, and in an effort to address new populist pressures the president passed legislation establishing a secret ballot in Costa Rican elections.

Volio's Reformist Party was short lived—it had effectively dissolved by 1936—but its influence in the Jiménez administration was a portent of other populist achievements yet to come. A clear popular consciousness was emerging among the working class and the poor. Individuals who had been overlooked and left out of the political and social system in earlier decades began to demand a voice. The populist platform often required an expansion of the state's presence in social welfare. By 1930, the Costa Rican government had created a Ministry of Public Health and a Ministry of Labor to provide direct oversight of many populist demands. Government-funded hospitals, prisons, and asylums appeared in the early decades of the twentieth century, and aggressive public health campaigns evolved to eradicate malnutrition and common communicable diseases. The efforts and objectives of the early reformists were later reflected in the creation of Costa Rica's first communist political party in 1931.

The 1920s also saw the rise of a new national and group consciousness among Costa Rican women. Inspired by the role female teachers had played in molding a sense of civic awareness in young people and eventually acting to bring down the Tinoco dictatorship, other Costa Rica women embraced new public roles and mobilized for social justice. Religious and philanthropic women's groups organized to support government programs to combat poverty and to promote sanitation and public health, particularly for children. The Liga Feminista (Costa Rican Feminist League) was formed in 1923 and became a forum through which women demanded greater equality in the workplace as well as in the political arena. Paramount to its efforts was an initiative to secure female suffrage in 1925. And while those efforts were unsuccessful until decades later, the actions of the Liga and other activists indicate that women were increasingly making themselves a part of the national conversation.

The early decades of the twentieth century also brought developments in recreation and entertainment as new technologies became more widely available. Economic growth precipitated by agricultural export industries and the expanding urban working class paved the way for the construction of cinemas and the proliferation of radio. Many entertainment and news programs broadcast on these new forms of media were initially imported from abroad, but locally produced programming quickly made its debut. The national theater played host to renowned entertainers from around the world, while the successful nation-building projects of the late nineteenth century were visible in museums, libraries, and monuments throughout major urban areas. But alongside those markers of progress existed other more seedy consequences of rapid urban growth. Drinking and prostitution were prevalent in San José and other large cities. The use of opium and other narcotics became a problematic habit for many urban inhabitants, and Costa Rica made its foray into the early world of drug trafficking by becoming a transit point in the opium trade.

Gabriel García Marquez's fictional account of the labor strife surrounding the U.S.-owned Banana Company in his novel *One Hundred Years of Solitude* is set in Colombia but was intended to make a statement about the role that multinationals—like the United Fruit Company—have played throughout Latin America in the twentieth century. Marquez's literary expression is particularly meaningful for Costa Rica because the UFC's long and fateful history began in the small Central American nation as U.S. investor Minor Keith secured large land grants as part of his contract to complete Costa Rica's first railroad. The emergence of the banana industry transformed Costa Rica, bringing an influx of cash as Keith and the United Fruit Company developed a capitalist agricultural export economy that quickly supplanted the coffee industry as the base of the national economy. A new political elite appeared as Keith married into a prominent political family, effectively giving him enormous influence over a new generation of leaders who favored positivist economic and social policies and who privileged the notion of modernization by opening the economy to vast amounts of foreign investment. The demographic landscape of Costa Rica changed as well as banana producers attracted large waves of Afro-Caribbean migrant workers to the Gulf coast banana enclaves. The arrival of new workers complicated Costa Rica's racial experiences in the early twentieth century, and discriminatory practices and attitudes surfaced as a result of those rapid changes. At the same time, signs of a collective worker consciousness began to emerge, and nascent union movements rose up to challenge the UFC's labor practices.

Despite the economic growth and relative prosperity created by the banana industry, the dominant presence of the United Fruit Company also generated antagonism among some Costa Ricans who supported a growing anti-imperialist movement. Standing up to foreign influence—and specifically U.S. hegemony—took on new urgency when the administration of U.S. president Woodrow Wilson withheld recognition of Federico Tinoco's presidency. Tinoco, who had risen to power by military coup, effectively ruled as a dictator. He quickly lost support among the Costa Rican people, and it was a grassroots opposition movement—not U.S. diplomatic pressure—that eventually brought an end to the Tinoco dictatorship. All of these developments helped to generate a growing national consciousness among many groups who had previously been ignored by national leaders. Women, workers, and activist reformers began to articulate a populist agenda that would gain traction in the coming decades.

7

The Social Welfare State and Civil War

THE SAN PABLO INCIDENT

On July 2, 1942, what started as a normal, quiet evening in the port of Limón turned into a violent and deadly reminder that the Americas had been pulled into a major world war. As dockworkers unloaded cargo from the *San Pablo*—a United Fruit Company vessel docked at the Caribbean port—an Axis submarine torpedo glided through the water and struck the *San Pablo*'s hull. Dramatic explosions lit up the night sky, and the UFC cargo ship sank quickly, killing 24 men and grimly reminding Costa Ricans of the role they had committed to by joining the Allied cause in World War II.

Costa Ricans were appropriately and understandably shaken by the sinking of the *San Pablo*, but few could have foreseen on that warm summer's evening the full extent to which the incident would affect the nation's future. Government leaders came under fire for failing to protect the small but strategically important nation. Indeed, the port of Limón was under a mandated blackout decree, but local officials had failed to enforce the edict, and in the moments leading up to the attack the lights of the dock shone brightly. The administration belatedly instituted measures to secure the Atlantic coast, including rounding up residents in the region of German and Italian descent. But the fear and anger among many Costa Ricans was not subdued. Two days after the attack, demonstrations organized by the United Committee of Anti-Totalitarian Associations descended upon the capital. Led by Communist Party representatives and other social activists, the public rally aimed to call attention to the perceived fifth-column threat and to admonish the government for its failure to prevent the attack. But the demonstrations quickly spun out of control, and a crowd of 20,000 erupted into riots and looting, targeting the properties of German and Italian residents.

The aftermath of the riots was significant. As Costa Ricans took stock of the deplorable actions of rioters and the damage inflicted upon properties in the capital city, many blamed Communist Party leaders while others directed their ire toward the government. Critics of the former included members of the virulently anticommunist Centro para el Estudio de los Problemas Nacionales (Center for the Study of National Problems, also known as El Centro or CEPN); José Figueres Ferrer—an outspoken social activist and critic of the administration of President Rafael Angel Calderón Guardia—led the criticism against the latter. Figueres, who eventually earned the nickname "Don Pepe," took his criticism to the airwaves and gave a radio address on July 8 accusing the Calderón government of ineptitude and malfeasance for failing to protect the nation against Axis aggression and for mishandling the riots of July 4. Before he could finish his diatribe, however, police stormed into the radio station and placed Figueres under arrest. Calderón accused Figueres of being a Nazi sympathizer and sent him into exile in Mexico.

The San Pablo incident and its aftermath illustrate a number of important aspects of the political and social climate of Costa Rica in the 1940s. The nation had become a firm ally of the United States in World War II and struggled with the realities of life during wartime. But new social and political movements had also surfaced in Costa Rica as a result of an expanding electorate, growing social awareness, and the economic fallout of the Great Depression. Conflicting visions of the government's role in such a dynamic time created the tensions visible between Calderón and Figueres. The expulsion of Figueres from the nation gave rise to a new crusade that would challenge the traditional political power structures in Costa Rica and that would eventually culminate in the War of National Liberation in 1948.

THE EMERGENCE OF "TICO-COMMUNISM"

The onset of a worldwide economic depression in 1929 brought profound changes to nations participating in the global economy, and Costa Rica was no exception. Demand for tropical fruits and coffee plummeted as nations around the world found themselves in the grip of economic decline. The nation that had relied so strongly on the export of commodity agricultural products to generate national revenue for nearly a century now saw export earnings fall by more than 50 percent by 1932. And as exports decreased, so too did revenue generated by export taxes. As a result, the government ran a sizeable deficit until 1936. Furthermore, a decline in exports and the concomitant reduction in revenue meant that Costa Ricans' purchasing power also diminished. Imports fell by 75 percent in the first three years of the Great Depression.[1]

The impact of these macroeconomic indicators on people's daily lives was significant. Unemployment increased and wages fell as industries struggled to absorb the fiscal shock of the global collapse. As the well-being of workers came under attack, the organized labor movement gained momentum. In 1931, the Costa Rican Communist Party was founded with Manuel Mora Valverde as its leader. Costa Rica's version of the Communist Party was not as extreme as those in other areas of the world. Instead Mora and other labor leaders advocated moderate reform based on issues of social justice, and they generally aimed at improving workers' lives. This brand of communism became known as "Tico-Communism," but, particularly in its earliest years, the Costa Rican capitalist elite feared even this moderate version of communism just as much as capitalists abroad feared other brands of communism.

One early success attributed to the organizing power of the Costa Rican Communist Party was a labor stoppage on UFC banana plantations in Limón, often referred to as the Great Banana Strike of 1934. Led by Costa Rican author and labor activist Carlos Luís Fallas, more than 10,000 workers walked off UFC plantations in August of that year. The strike brought banana cultivation to a halt along the Caribbean coast for more than a month and forced company executives to negotiate with workers, who demanded improvements in working conditions and housing. The Costa Rican government eventually called in the military to force an end to the work stoppage, but strikers walked away having won a number of concessions from the UFC. The strike also prompted Fallas, or Calufa as he is referred to in Costa Rica, to write his now classic *Mamita Yunai*, which describes the life of banana workers on the United Fruit Company's Caribbean plantations.

RACE, ENVIRONMENT, AND THE UNITED FRUIT COMPANY

The Great Banana Strike of 1934 took place at a time when the United Fruit Company was renegotiating its contract with the Costa Rican government. A series of contract talks had taken place starting in 1930 as the company sought to expand its operations to the west coast and to work out new terms for its tax obligation. Additionally, government leaders wanted to address the racial composition of the United Fruit Company's workforce. Specifically, some leaders wanted clauses stipulating that the company give Costa Ricans preferential hiring over foreign workers, citing the 1927 census that showed that 55 percent of the population of Limón was of African ancestry. They were particularly concerned that black West Indian workers would migrate to the west coast of the country. A new contract was established in 1930, but two years later government investigators found the UFC not to be in compliance. This finding, combined with the impact of the Great Depression, prompted government leaders to demand yet another renegotiation of the company's contract. New talks began in August of 1934, just as the communist-led banana strike was unfolding in Limón. This time the UFC pushed for an even greater expansion into the Pacific coastal regions as Panama disease spread through UFC lands along the Caribbean coast. Once the disease struck, the only solution was to abandon the land for up to seven years, rendering much of the formerly arable land in eastern Costa Rica useless. By 1938 a new soil affliction had appeared in the Caribbean lowlands. Sigatoka began spreading and prevented banana plants from producing large and healthy bunches of fruit. Like Panama disease, Sigatoka proved resistant to chemical treatments, and the quality of the banana crop in eastern Costa Rica began to decline. The spread of soil diseases combined with the growing labor unrest in Limón prompted the UFC to relocate most of its operations. A final agreement was reached in 1934 that permitted a vast expansion of UFC cultivation into the Pacific region. That agreement was accompanied by legislation that prohibited black workers from migrating to the west coast.

Throughout the late 1930s the United Fruit Company abandoned its banana-cultivating activities in the Caribbean lowlands, although the company continued to produce some other agricultural products in the region. Because the banana industry had come to dominate the coastal economy, the UFC's withdrawal devastated Limón and the surrounding areas. Soil disease and large-scale capitalist agriculture had a disastrous environmental impact on large swaths of land in the area. As its activities dwindled, United Fruit decreased its workforce and eliminated many of the social services it had provided to local workers. A new banana enclave emerged along the Pacific coast, but since the agreement between UFC and the Costa Rican government that allowed the multinational to relocate had specifically limited employment opportunities for people of color, much the Afro-Caribbean population left the country. Costa Rica's recently formed Communist Party attempted to come to the defense of West Indian workers, but geographic distance and cultural differences prevented a cohesive alliance from forming between banana workers and the Central Valley–based communist movement.

THE GREAT DEPRESSION AND RISING SOCIAL EXPECTATIONS

The emergence of Costa Rica's particular brand of communism came about as the culmination of a number of developments. The emphasis on public education put in place by liberal governments of the nineteenth century had produced a population that was generally literate. The government capitalized on expanding literacy by distributing pamphlets and other printed materials to educate the population on the nation's history, advances in medicine and hygiene, and strategies for agriculture production. Peasants and wage laborers read government-generated materials but also sought out other literature as well. Popular novels proliferated, as did the nation's press. By the turn of the century, many Costa Ricans were also reading literature from abroad that challenged the nation's capitalist export economy and class-based society with new socialist and anarchist perspectives.

Furthermore, the nation's relatively stable democratic traditions had resulted in a high degree of political awareness that had taken root not only among the political elite but also within the growing working class. The economic progress created by the export industry paved the way for the introduction of a new "mass culture" including sports, music, the penny press, film, and radio. As the messages disseminated by these media were enthusiastically consumed by the masses, a growing number of Costa Ricans began to challenge the notion of identity and progress that had been imposed from the top by the nation's elite. It was becoming clear in the early decades of the twentieth century that Costa Rica's political and economic leaders would have to make way for even greater political participation in shaping the nation's future. An increasingly socially aware population emerged in the early twentieth century, and while needs and expectations varied across classes, the general belief that the state should be socially responsive was common from the masses to the elite.

While rising levels of social consciousness help to explain the growth of the labor movement and the emergence of the Communist Party in the 1930s, it is also important to note that these events coincided with the onset of the Great Depression. When the capitalist export economy that had provided a foundation for national prosperity in the nineteenth century collapsed, all sorts of assumptions about Costa Rican economic and social institutions were called into question. National leaders responded to the crisis by restructuring and expanding the authority of the state over the economy. The economic liberalism and relative laissez faire policies that had defined the national economy since independence gave way to a new outlook on managing the economy. High levels of state intervention in fiscal and commercial affairs and government oversight of the labor sector characterized that vision.

A more active and regulatory government took action aimed at mitigating the impact of the worldwide economic collapse. Those actions included instituting a minimum wage in 1935 and the passage of bank reform laws the following year. The government took on a much more active role in the economy by regulating the money supply and increasing government spending on public-works projects to provide employment opportunities to the struggling populace. Reforms passed in the 1930s that created a more active role for the state in economic matters set the stage for the implementation of aggressive state-led import substitution industrialization in later decades.

Many Costa Ricans welcomed the expanding role of the state, and throughout the 1930s reforms broadly defined as "social justice" came to the forefront of national politics. This was a common response in many Latin American nations, particularly the South American nations of Chile, Uruguay, Brazil, and Argentina, where an early wave of populism took hold as national governments responded to the Great Depression and the new demands of a rapidly changing population. Leaders in those nations seized the opportunity to consolidate a broad base of support among "the masses"—many of whom had been left out of a political process dominated by elites in earlier decades. South American populists accomplished this task by addressing the needs of a growing pool of urban workers, and the populist platform often included issues such as labor rights, wage protections, price controls, education, and welfare programs. In the heyday of the Great Depression in Costa Rica, labor issues such as employment and wages topped the agenda of populist politicians. It was not until the 1940s that social justice reforms came to include welfare-oriented issues such as health care, social security, and other measures aimed at combating poverty and improving the overall standard of living.

THE RISE OF RAFAEL ANGEL CALDERÓN GUARDIA

The realization of a substantive system of social welfare in Costa Rica came about under the leadership of President Rafael Angel Calderón Guardia (1940–1944). Calderón was the grandson of the nineteenth-century liberal reformer Tomás Guardia and hailed from generations of the *cafetalero* elite. He was handpicked as the presidential candidate for the National Republican Party by his predecessor León Cortes (1936–1940), and Calderón won an overwhelming victory with more than 80 percent of the vote over Communist Party candidate Manuel Mora Valverde. As a physician and staunch adherent to Catholicism, Calderón developed a sincere concern for the plight of the poor. His father, also a physician, became a well-known Catholic reformist layman in the 1920s and had introduced his son to the tenets of Catholic social reform doctrine. The Catholic Church's views on social justice derived first from Pope Leo XIII's 1891 *Rerum Novarum*. That papal encyclical, entitled "Rights and Duties of Capital and Labour," was the Church's response to the social conditions created by rapid worldwide industrialization in the late nineteenth century. It was both an expression of the Church's position against the social and economic trends of nineteenth-century liberalism and an alternative to what Church leaders perceived to be the evils of socialism. Pope Pius XI's 1931 *Quadragesimo Anno*, or *Reconstruction of Social Order*, which was a response to the Great Depression and a reaffirmation of the principles established in the *Rerum Novarum*, also influenced Calderón. But the new encyclical went even further by rebuking the offenses of capitalism and applauding the emergence of a welfare state in many areas of the world. And while Calderón did not promote himself as a populist in the tradition of many of his South American contemporaries, he did make it known—even during his campaign—that he would make protecting the poor one of his highest priorities.

As the 1940 election approached, Calderón secured behind-the-scenes deals that were designed to ensure his election but that also complicated the political realm in later years. First Calderón made an agreement with Victor Manuel Sanabria, the local bishop of Alajuela who shortly thereafter became archbishop of San José. Calderón's relationship with Sanabria was intended to benefit both parties. Sanabria wanted Calderón's support in reversing many of the anticlerical measures that had been introduced as part of liberal reforms of the late nineteenth century. In exchange the church leader pledged his support for Calderón's social reform program that was quietly in the works. A true social progressive, Calderón believed in the merits of a welfare state in its own right. But he also envisioned a social reform program as a way of thwarting the advances made by the Communist Party in the preceding decade. Communism had made substantial inroads in Costa Rica's laboring classes throughout the 1930s by emphasizing social problems such as poverty, unemployment, and living conditions that had been exacerbated by the Great Depression. Calderón and a newly influential Catholic wing of the National Republican Party devised strategies to combat the left by promoting reforms designed to address social problems without resorting to the radical change often demanded by the Communist Party platform. As part of this strategy, Sanabria vowed to support Calderón's program of social welfare as a way to subvert the communists' social reform message.

In another political ploy, Calderón struck a deal with outgoing president León Cortés. Under the agreement, *cortesistas*—as supporters of the incumbent were known—would back Calderón's candidacy and in return Cortés would run for president again in 1944 and enjoy the full support of the *calderonistas*. The assumption in this deal was that, as president, Calderón would work to protect the interests of the *cortesistas*, many of whom were part of the wealthy coffee elite.

Calderón filled his administration with like-minded reformists and set about to expand the welfare state. As a physician he initially targeted medical and hygiene issues by restructuring the Ministry of Public Health and making improvements to rural health programs. He also focused his attention on education and created the University of Costa Rica in 1940. His social reform agenda became more pronounced in 1941 when he formulated a social security program aimed at providing social protections to workers and people in poverty. As he sought to build support for such a program, Calderón forged alliances with the Catholic Church, with labor unions, and eventually even with the Communist Party. In fact the Communist Party changed its name to the Partido Vanguardia Popular (People's Vanguard Party, also known as the Vanguardia or PVP) in 1943 partially in an attempt to mollify any political repercussions Calderón and the Church might face because of their collaboration with the communist group.

The social security system Calderón created included health care coverage and the protection of workers' rights through a series of constitutional amendments known as the Social Guarantees.

DIPLOMACY AND WORLD WAR

Calderón's presidency was also a time when Costa Rica was playing an ever-increasing role in the geopolitical arena. The nation offered a strategic stronghold in issues of hemispheric security, particularly as European hostilities escalated in the late 1930s. After decades of border disputes with Panama, Calderón finalized a new treaty with the southern neighbor in the interest of safeguarding inter-American security. From the earliest days of his presidency, Calderón reached out to the United States as well. He granted the United States access to military bases in Costa Rica as a way to protect the Panama Canal as global tensions rose after the outbreak of World War II. In a strong show of solidarity, he declared war on Germany, Japan, and Italy immediately after the Japanese attack on Pearl Harbor in December 1941. In fact, the Costa Rican declaration of war was finalized several hours before the United States' own declaration.

President Rafael Calderón Guardia and his cabinet ministers sign Costa Rica's declaration of war against the Axis powers, December 8, 1941. (AP Photo)

Calderón continued to act as a strong ally for the United States as the war progressed. Costa Rica produced important raw materials to contribute to the Allied war effort, and the Costa Rican government cooperated by deporting blacklisted Japanese nationals who were considered a security threat. An even more complex policy involved people of German and Italian heritage who were suspected of having fascist sympathies. Even though a large number of German immigrants had married into the influential network of *cafetalero* families, Calderón placed more than 200 individuals of German and Italian descent into internment camps by the war's end.

In exchange for his strong support for the United States in World War II, Calderón received significant foreign assistance earmarked to strengthen Costa Rica's military. The president's reform agenda was evident even in this arena as early negotiations to establish a U.S. military mission in Costa Rica initially stalled due to Calderon's concerns that the nation's own financial obligations to such a venture would detract from his social programs. Only after securing special payment terms from the United States did the Costa Rican leader move forward with the program. Additionally, U.S. leaders helped Costa Rica to secure financial backing from the Export-Import Bank to fund internal improvement projects and to offset the economic difficulties created by the war. One such project was a section of the Pan-American Highway to connect San José with the Panamanian border, which was considered both vital to hemispheric security and a boon to internal economic growth in Costa Rica. The military and economic alliance forged between the two nations during World War II provided the basis for a close relationship in matters of security for the rest of the century.

While Calderon's diplomatic actions during World War II went a long way toward positioning the nation strategically in the world after the war was over, they did little to shore up his political support at home. As the Costa Rican president secured an ever-closer alliance with the United States—and particularly as he capitulated to U.S. demands to intern people of German and Italian descent—Calderón found himself alienating the elite *cafetalero* families that made up such an important part of the national political scene. As his administration seized the property of suspected Axis sympathizers, charges of corruption proliferated. Other charges of graft and profiteering surfaced in connection with the large influx of money entering the country under the guise of wartime cooperation. These incidents, combined with Calderón's ambitious reform agenda, created mounting opposition among the coffee elite and forced the president to rely even more on his tenuous alliance the communist Vanguardia party.

THE CATHOLIC-COMMUNIST ALLIANCE

Calderón's association with communism was somewhat perplexing and certainly a source of consternation from the very beginning. While the president did his best to maintain some distance from the PVP in the early years, Costa Rica's political climate and the nation's labor movement evolved in important ways during the war years. As Calderón lost the support of large segments of the *cafetalero* elite and supporters of Cortés split from the National Republican Party and turned openly against the president in 1941, the PVP and other labor groups were there to fill the void. Two years later, with the backing of the PVP, artisanal unions in the Central Valley joined forces with banana workers along the coast to form the first nationwide union, known as the Confederación de Trabajadores de Costa Rica (Confederation of Costa Rican Workers, or CTCR). Later that year the new union was strengthened when it forged an alliance with the Catholic labor union, the Confederación Costarricense de Trabajadores "Rerum Novarum" (the Costa Rican Confederation of "Rerum Novarum" Workers, or CCTRN). Victor Manuel Sanabria, archbishop of San José and avid proponent of social Catholicism, enthusiastically supported the partnership. This powerful alliance maintained close ties to the Calderón administration, and ensuring the implementation of the president's social reform program became one of its highest priorities.

Even as the Catholic-communist alliance under Calderón gathered political momentum, the opposition condemned the president's affiliation with the left along with the most aggressive measures in his reform program. Costa Rica's increasingly visible role in global politics further complicated this scenario, particularly as the affiliation between the PVP and the Soviet Union was called into question. During the war years, the U.S.S.R. was seen as the lesser of two evils compared to Nazi Germany, and the United States and Western European nations welcomed the Soviets into the anti-Axis alliance. But as the war's end drew near and it became clear that the Soviet Union would become the new enemy, pressure mounted on Calderón in the final years of his administration. He had lost many of the crucial political supporters who had helped to cement his decisive electoral victory in 1940. Furthermore, the archbishop's support of Calderón's platform caused a rift among Catholic leaders, and the president's support among Catholics began to waver. As the 1944 elections approached, accusations of fraud and Calderón's controversial political alliances produced vocal opposition to the governing party.

THE EMERGENCE OF "THE OPPOSITION"

As expected, Cortés ran for president again in 1944. His candidacy caused concern for Calderón, who feared that a Cortés victory would mean an end to his reform program. Since constitutional restrictions prevented Calderón from running for a consecutive term, the outgoing president threw his support behind Teodoro Picado Michalski. Picado was a well-known politician within the National Republican Party. He had held several cabinet positions in the 1930s, including secretary of education and secretary of development, and he served in the Costa Rican Congress in the 1940s. Like Calderón, Picado was an ardent defender of social reform, and he played an instrumental role in securing the passage of the Social Guarantees. With Calderón's support Picado easily won the presidency in 1944 but not without facing charges of being a communist sympathizer. A formal opposition movement formed during the campaign, and that opposition became even more firmly entrenched after the election. Cortés and other members of the opposition charged Picado with electoral fraud, and it became clear that the new president would face significant challenges from a divided population.

As Picado took office, several political groups united to form one cohesive political coalition that became know as "the Opposition." These included El Centro—a think tank created by young politicians and intellectuals in 1940 that was becoming increasingly vocal in the political arena—and the Partido Social Democrático (Social Democratic Party, or PSD), a new political party formed in 1945. The Opposition and the PSD came to be led by José Figueres, or "Don Pepe," the outspoken rival of Calderón who had been forced into exile in 1942. Other leaders of the Opposition included former president Cortés and Otilio Ulate, owner and general editor of *Diario de Costa Rica*, the country's main newspaper. While Cortés and Ulate provided political legitimacy to the Opposition, Figueres gave the group's activities a militant flair.

Figueres's expulsion had marked the first such politically oriented exile since the Tinoco dictatorship, and Calderón's actions only further coalesced the mounting resistance to his administration. While in exile Figueres made contacts with numerous other political refugees from all over Latin America, and his opposition to Calderón became even more firmly entrenched. He became convinced that a forceful overthrow was the only way to challenge the National Republican Party's monopoly control over politics and return Costa Rica to an efficient system of political democracy. He learned about authoritative dictators in neighboring Latin American countries from his contact with other political exiles, and Figueres grew ever more determined to prevent Calderón from becoming Central America's next dictator. Indeed, Figueres convinced other militant exiles that as a less autocratic ruler, Calderón would be an easier target than Nicaragua's Anastasio Somoza or other repressive regimes in the region. The group of Latin American exiles created an informal alliance that journalists and diplomats would later dub the "Caribbean Legion," and Figueres won the group's support in his aims to overthrow the Calderón government. He began recruiting a small band of insurgents to oust the Costa Rican leader, and the Caribbean Legion hoped to use that success as a catalyst for spreading revolutionary insurrection throughout Latin America.

Don Pepe spoke of inciting revolution to bring about the "Second Republic," which he claimed would restore the nation's free institutions. He managed to raise small amounts of money to use for arms and training, and the National Republican Party's victory in the 1944 presidential campaign provided a timely opportunity for Figueres to urge the Opposition to consider his military strategy. The accusations of fraud surrounding Picado's election in 1944 convinced growing numbers of people that an insidious system of corruption was at work within Calderón's National Republican Party. As the Opposition plotted a political strategy to bring down the *calderonistas*, Figueres's militant designs were a constant presence.

Despite a growing organized opposition, Picado pushed through several reform measures during his presidency. As a former minister of education, he advocated policies to safeguard the rights of children and to devote more resources to public education. To pay for higher teachers' salaries and other educational improvements, he pushed through a sweeping tax reform. He also promised to reduce government corruption, and in 1945 he introduced a new electoral code designed to eliminate the accusations of fraud that had surfaced in his own election. Nevertheless, the antigovernment campaign launched by the Opposition only intensified in the coming years. Cortés and the Social Democratic Party continued to denounce Picado's affiliation with the communist PVP. They grew concerned that

José Figueres Ferrer led the War of National Liberation in 1948 and later served three times as Costa Rica's president. (Organization of American States)

Picado's electoral and tax reforms—which were quite popular with the public—would give a boost to the National Republican Party and pave the way for Calderón to be elected once again in 1948.

In 1947 the coalition of parties that made up the Opposition held a convention to select a candidate to run against Calderón the following year. Cortés had died the year before so the anti-Calderón forces needed a new figurehead. Otilio Ulate Blanco, who owned Costa Rica's main newspaper and positioned himself as a staunch ally of the *cafetalero* elite, emerged as the Opposition candidate. A vigorous

campaign ensued with the Opposition painting Calderón as a communist sympathizer and continuing to make accusations of corruption.
Nevertheless, many hoped that the new Electoral Registry and the
ostensibly politically impartial Electoral Tribunal—both of which had
been created under Picado's electoral reform laws—would safeguard
the integrity of the election process.

THE WAR OF NATIONAL LIBERATION

The 1948 presidential election took place on February 8, and the
Electoral Tribunal fielded complaints of various irregularities
throughout the country. Preliminary results showed Ulate as the winner with a margin of roughly 10,000 votes. Both sides charged the
other with fraud while the Electoral Tribunal delayed declaring the
final results and refused to investigate charges of irregularities.
Instead the Tribunal delegated that responsibility to the Congress.
Tensions mounted in the weeks following the election as *calderonistas*
took to the streets in massive demonstrations while Figueres mustered
members of the Opposition at his ranch in southern Costa Rica, where
he had already been training a small militia to form the Army of
National Liberation. Calderón and Ulate initially met to discuss a
compromise, but those talks quickly fell apart, and both sides stood
their ground.

On March 1, the *calderonista*-dominated Congress voted to annul the
election results as part of a strategy to appoint Calderón to the
presidency by Congressional decree. Almost immediately, Figueres
and his Army of National Liberation sprang into action. They seized
the southern town of San Isidro while another contingent took control
of the Pan-American Highway. With the assistance of President Arévalo in Guatemala and the Caribbean Legion, Figueres launched a
bloody civil war that lasted 40 days and resulted in the loss of 2,000
lives. The small and poorly equipped Costa Rican army was unprepared to head off the insurgency, and the Army of National Liberation
expanded its hold to Santa María de Dota and eventually to Cartago in
the Central Valley. Communist leader Manuel Mora rallied union
workers to form ancillary militias, and Mora and Calderón both
resisted Picado's early inclination to negotiate a compromise. Indeed,
there were a number of occasions when Mora's forces seemed to be
operating without the authorization of the central government.

As the Army of National Liberation zeroed in on the Central Valley,
secondary forces targeted Alajuela to the north of San José. Figueres's

forces fortified their positions and prepared to attack the capital while outside forces also rallied to put pressure on Picado, who still nominally held power. Specifically, Nicaraguan forces moved in to occupy strategic positions in the north and U.S. troops mobilized in the Panama Canal Zone, prepared to step in if necessary.

After weeks of fighting it was clear that Figueres and the Army of National Liberation were gaining the upper hand. Figueres inundated the nation, and especially San José, with propaganda aimed at swaying public opinion in his favor. He vowed that his was a prodemocracy movement and not a right-wing campaign. He promised to uphold the election of Ulate and pledged not to nullify Calderón's popular welfare reform legislation. On April 13 Picado and Figueres agreed to a cease-fire, and with U.S. Ambassador Nathaniel Davis acting as mediator, the two sides negotiated an end to the conflict.

The 1948 civil war officially ended when Picado and an emissary from the Army of National Liberation signed the Pact of the Mexican Embassy on April 18. Under the terms of the negotiated peace, Picado turned over power to an interim president, Santos León Herrera, and Figueres promised amnesty to all participants in the conflict. Significantly, the pact also assured that the Social Guarantees and labor rights established under Calderón and Picado would be preserved. At the same time, Ulate and Figueres reached an agreement that became known as the Figueres-Ulate Pact. The pact stipulated that a revolutionary junta would rule during a transitional period of 18 months, during which time the junta would convene an assembly to draft a new constitution. After the transitional period, the junta would recognize Ulate as the first constitutional president of the Second Republic.

Costa Rica's War for National Liberation was over in less than six weeks, and in that time the nation suffered few casualties. Yet the actions of Figueres and his allies reverberated in the region's history for decades. The anticommunist rhetoric employed by Don Pepe against the *calderonistas* was unwarranted, but his denunciations found a receptive audience among many Costa Ricans as the nation found itself caught up in the beginnings of Cold War politics. In the coming years, Costa Rica's foreign policy would continue to be dominated by an ever-present anticommunist mood in the Western Hemisphere. And even though Figueres enjoyed widespread support in his brief civil war, the new government would find it necessary to maintain many of the social justice guarantees that had been so popular under the Calderón government. Further complicating the nation's future, the tenuous alliance between Don Pepe and Ulate was based on the existence of a common enemy—the *calderonistas*—and moving beyond that narrow thread to create a new governing system would prove difficult. It was in the midst of these complexities that Costa Rica's Second Republic was born, and many of the characteristics that define the nation still today took shape.

NOTE

1. Iván Molina Jiménez and Steven Palmer, *The History of Costa Rica: Brief, Up-to-Date and Illustrated*, 1st ed. (San José, Costa Rica: Editorial de la Universidad de Costa Rica, 1998), 99–102.

8

The Cold War and the *Liberación* Era

A CEREMONY AT BELLAVISTA

On December 1, 1948, José Figueres led a civic ceremony outside the walls of the Bellavista military headquarters in the capital city. The site of the ceremony was significant. An imposing structure surrounded by seemingly impenetrable walls and tall gates, the Bellavista headquarters boasted tall towers that loomed over San José. Construction on the installation had begun in 1917, and under the dictatorship of Federico Tinoco it had become widely recognized as a symbol of a strong military presence in Costa Rica. It was precisely its image of fortitude and military supremacy that made the Bellavista such a fitting setting for Figueres's ceremony. With an eloquent and fiery speech, the leader of the National War of Liberation declared an end to Costa Rica's standing army. He then slammed a sledgehammer into the façade of the military barracks, leaving a gaping hole in the once-powerful structure in a move that was as symbolic as it was a real testament to the dismantling of the old ways and the genesis of a new future for the nation.

Figueres enjoyed widespread popular support following the 1948 civil war, and the ruling junta later integrated the abolition of the military into the Constitution of 1949. His actions were indicative of the general tone in Costa Rica following the War of National Liberation. Many citizens had grown weary of the appearance of government corruption and the threat the military had traditionally posed throughout Latin America to civilian reformist movements. Figueres wanted to remove the potential for armed insurrection against his government, and he was confident he could count on the United States to protect Costa Rica against any external threat. Bellavista became a national museum, and much of the military budget was channeled to education and health care programs. For the remainder of the twentieth century, Costa Ricans proudly flaunted the absence of a standing army as a testament to the nation's growing reputation for protecting democratic principles. It also became yet another statement of Costa Rican exceptionalism.

THE FOUNDING JUNTA

On May 8, 1948, José Figueres inaugurated the Founding Junta to lead the Costa Rican Second Republic after the War of National Liberation that successfully overthrew Teodoro Picado and dislodged the dominant National Republican Party led by Rafael Calderón Guardia. As the leader of the civil war, Figueres was the natural choice to head the Founding Junta, and he filled the 11-man group with his closest friends and allies. Each was given the title of minister and served as the leading executive over one of the various cabinet departments. But the authority of the junta extended far beyond the typical powers of government ministers. The constitution was suspended while governing guidelines for the nation derived from the Pact of the Mexican Embassy and the Figueres-Ulate Pact. Despite its extraordinary powers, the Founding Junta was intended to play only a temporary role—to establish a postrevolutionary government that would ensure a democratic process and protect basic freedoms. For his part, Figueres declared that the end of the war and the establishment of the Founding Junta marked the beginning of Costa Rica's Second Republic. He promised a speedy and efficient transition and invited a large degree of public scrutiny from the press and from the general populace to ensure a new governing system was created through an open and honest process.

The junta immediately began issuing decrees aimed at transforming and improving society. It reorganized and streamlined government bureaucracy, but in a process that was presented as a way to make government more efficient, many people lost their jobs. Critics of the junta—including the *calderonistas* and a growing cadre of Ulate supporters—argued that Figueres was resorting to the same strategy of political favoritism that he had denounced in earlier administrations. Those complaints magnified when the junta froze the bank accounts and other assets of *calderonistas*. Figueres and members of the junta increasingly looked at Calderón and Picado supporters as enemies of the Second Republic, and animosity between the two sides mounted. Figueres also faced growing tension in his relationship with Ulate. The one-time allies had significantly different visions for Costa Rica's future, and Ulate was skeptical of Figueres's political aspirations from the very beginning. Despite their agreement that Figueres would hand over power as soon as a sound governing system was restored, Ulate had little faith that Figueres would follow through.

The rivalry between Figueres and Ulate was further strained when the junta began making changes to the tax structure and banking industry. New fiscal reforms were intended to revamp the nation's economic and financial systems after years of mismanagement and graft. In June the junta issued an edict nationalizing banks and creating a 10 percent capital levy tax. Junta leaders stated that the changes were needed to allow the government to control credit and raise the necessary revenue to fund much-needed national improvements. Nevertheless, the changes to the monetary system and increases in taxation had the predictable effect of upsetting those most closely affected by the reform—in this case the wealthy and influential members of the *calderonista* faction.

Those measures also alarmed government leaders in the United States who had been eying potential communist activity in the Western Hemisphere with caution as part of new Cold War foreign policy. Strategies such as major nationalizations and increasing taxes on the wealthy were policies being employed in other countries that were considered communist in the minds of U.S. policy makers. The Costa Rican junta assuaged U.S. fears by stipulating that only public banks were subject to the nationalization decree—effectively removing U.S. institutions from the risk of confiscation. Junta members also specified that the new taxation scheme would not apply to foreign companies that were under an existing contract. That caveat protected the United Fruit Company and other U.S. corporations—a move that allayed many of the concerns U.S. leaders had that the Founding Junta would impose communist-friendly policies. Costa Rican leaders further assuaged those fears by going after the Calderón-friendly

Vanguardia. After multiple reports of PVP plots to incite a coup against the new government, the junta issued a decree in July 1948 outlawing any communist organization in Costa Rica.

The *calderonistas* were vocal in their opposition to the junta, and U.S. leaders were cautiously skeptical, but Figueres's most serious problem was the developing animosity coming from the Ulate camp. Ulate criticized the junta's early fiscal reforms and protested when Figueres supported his allies in the Caribbean Legion in their efforts to depose the Somoza regime in Nicaragua. Ulate reacted by publishing scathing critiques of the junta's foreign policies in his newspaper, and Figueres supporters responded with equally damning criticism of the Ulate camp. The rivalry between the two sides manifested itself most clearly in the political realm, particularly as the junta called for a nationwide election to choose a Constituent Assembly that would be tasked with writing a new constitution. Instead of maintaining the sense of solidarity that had allowed them to overthrow Picado, supporters of Ulate and Figueres split into competing factions. That rift did not allow Calderón's National Republican Party to regain its influence, but it did give Ulate the upper hand in the Constituent Assembly. The election resulted in his supporters in the Partido Unión Nacional (National Union Party, or PUN) gaining a majority of seats, leaving them well positioned to reduce Figueres's influence and to ensure that most of the PUN demands would be addressed.

As the Constituent Assembly election approached, Figueres and the junta made a surprising move by eliminating the standing national army. The governing body issued a proclamation on December 1, 1948 that dissolved the armed forces, stating instead that a strong and efficient national police was a sufficient armed presence to safeguard national security. In the public ceremony detailed in the introduction to this chapter, Figueres handed the keys to the Bellavista Fortress to the minister of public education in a move that made an enormously symbolic statement about the junta's vision for Costa Rica's future. This act was extremely popular among the populace, and the absence of formal armed forces set the country apart from its Central American neighbors, who experienced significant political and military volatility for the rest of the twentieth century.

THE CONSTITUTION OF 1949

The Constituent Assembly met for the first time on January 16, 1949, to consider the nation's political future and draft a new constitution. The growing rift between Figueres and Ulate was immediately evident as deliberations for the new governing document began. As delegates debated political aspects of the postrevolutionary government, Figueres and the junta faced a number of challenges. The relationship between the two leaders was further complicated when the minister of public security, Colonel Edgar Cardona, attempted a coup on April 2; although the insurrection was put down relatively easily, it was an important test of the Figueres-Ulate Pact. Cardona hoped to win Ulate's support, but Ulate remained committed to the Constituent Assembly and was determined to take power only through a legitimate democratic process. Despite their differences, Ulate and Figueres found a way to work together over the coming months to map out Costa Rica's national future.

The new constitution was promulgated on November 9, 1949, and as the document was approved, Figueres handed over power to Ulate in fulfillment of their revolutionary pact. The Constitution of 1949 preserved many of the most democratic aspects that had been established in the Constitution of 1871, but it also went further in protecting individual liberties by integrating Calderón's social guarantees that had been so popular with the masses. It diminished the power of the executive in an attempt to prevent the types of abuses and corruption the revolutionaries had associated with the *calderonista* era. The document also formalized the junta's decree that dissolved the military, and it created new government protections related to property ownership, business, and the distribution of wealth. In the area of electoral reform, the constitution established the Supreme Electoral Tribunal as a fourth branch of government tasked with overseeing elections. Furthermore, it guaranteed suffrage for Costa Ricans of color and granted women the right to vote for the first time in the nation's history.

As Ulate took office, the discord between him and Figueres continued, but the ever-present opposition coming from *calderonistas* forced the two to work together to ensure the nation enjoyed a promising future. Figueres's supporters were concerned that Ulate would dismantle many of the social reforms they held dear, but Ulate did not deviate much from the nationalist and populist spirit that had defined the era under the Founding Junta. Ulate used increased government revenues generated by the junta's 10 percent tax and a renegotiated contract with the United Fruit Company to finance much-needed infrastructure improvements. His government improved roads, funded irrigation projects, built new dams, and constructed an international airport in San José, named after nineteenth-century national hero Juan Santamaría. He also funded programs aimed at expanding the agricultural sector beyond tropical fruit and coffee

exports by providing credit and assistance to farmers wishing to cultivate foodstuffs such as beans, corn, and rice. Ulate increased spending
on education, building hundreds of new primary schools and expanding degree programs at the University of Costa Rica. Additionally, his
government passed health care reforms that provided universal medical care to all Costa Ricans and made major improvements to systems
of public sanitation and preventative medicine.

THE FORMATION OF THE PARTIDO LIBERACIÓN NACIONAL

During the Ulate presidency Figueres did not fade quietly into the
political background. In fact, Ulate often leaned on Figueres to represent Costa Rica at international conferences, and Don Pepe spent
some time traveling internationally, which gave him the opportunity
to place Costa Rican development in the context of all of Latin
America. He became a vocal advocate for Latin American autonomy
and called on the United States to cooperate with Latin American
democratic leaders rather than impose its will unilaterally. Once he
returned to Costa Rica he shifted his focus from the military and emergency strategies he had employed during the armed conflict and
through the era of the Founding Junta to a strictly political and
electoral strategy. Figueres and his supporters within the Social
Democratic Party formalized the growing break with Ulate and began
laying plans to create a new political party that would more closely represent their goals and ideology. Since the PSD had originated as an
alliance between El Centro and the Acción Demócrata—united primarily by the short-term goal of ousting the *calderonistas*—long-term
collaboration between factions whose rivalry was growing was
impractical. In 1951 Figueres and his political allies created the Partido
Liberación Nacional (National Liberation Party, or PLN).

As Figueres began crafting a platform for a formal political movement, he and his advisors carefully considered what kind of ideological foundation they wanted to create. Their decisions were closely tied
to the nation's rich history, and the recent political atmosphere of the
1940s particularly influenced their line of thought. Many of the basic
precepts that had existed at the formation of the PSD carried over into
the formation of the PLN, and those became part of the party's founding ideology, which was articulated specifically in the Fundamental
Charter. Most strongly, the party emerged as an opposition movement
to "Caldero-Communismo" as the cadre of political leaders that had
led the revolution saw Calderón's strong alliance with the Vanguardia

as one of the largest threats to democracy and peace. They did not necessarily oppose most of the social reform policies advocated by the communist-leaning PVP; in fact many of the social policies embraced by the PLN close reflected a pseudosocialist tradition. But the Vanguardia's willingness to use violence and its participation in electoral fraud caused PLN leaders to view communism as one of the greatest enemies to a peaceful and democratic tradition that they saw as the future of the Costa Rican nation.

PLN leaders spoke of themselves as a "generation"—but not one defined by age or even social class, which were groups they considered to be unified primarily by common interests. Rather they united around a set of ideas and a general vision for the nation. Ideologically, PLN founders defined themselves through the concept of "Liberación"—an elusive and specifically Costa Rican concept. They were influenced by a socialist tradition, but modified in a way that they believed would be more suitable for Costa Rica. The staunch Marxist beliefs that drove many leftist political parties in the latter part of the twentieth century were significantly toned down within the circles of the PLN, and a form of liberalism reminiscent of social Christianity emerged as a foundational ideology.

In its initial years in particular, the party focused on the idealistic and moral components of social reform while going to great lengths to avoid the militant, anti-imperialist, and materialist message of traditionally Marxist political movements. Instead party leaders stated that one of the fundamental roles of government was to protect basic freedoms, but they defined basic freedoms as much more than simply political and civil rights. They included equal opportunities for access to education, housing, health, recreation, and a variety of other basic needs. PLN founders believed that a coherent and inclusive platform of social policies must be supported by a deliberate and sound national economy, and they crafted a vision of a "mixed economy" with elements of private ownership combined with degrees of government oversight and control where necessary.

The formation of the PLN coincided with a wave of institutionalized nationalism that swept throughout Latin America in the decades following World War II, and Costa Rica's newest political party certainly followed the nationalist trend. But in other Latin American nations with large and still visible indigenous populations, nationalist movements embraced the concept of *indigenismo*, which celebrated the strengths of pre-Columbian native populations and recognized their contributions in the creation of a national identity. Costa Rica had a much smaller pre-Columbian indigenous population than most of its

Latin American neighbors, and its demographic development followed a different trajectory than that of nations like Mexico, Peru, and Brazil. As a result PLN leaders looked for alternatives to *indigenismo* as a way to celebrate the nation's unique identity and to institutionalize a common sense of nationalism behind the new party.

The institutionalized national character that became the foundation for the PLN was based on idealized notions of Costa Rica's past that depicted an egalitarian, libertarian, and democratic historical trajectory dating back the colonial era. PLN founders emphasized that because Spanish conquistadores found only a small indigenous population in the fifteenth century, a large slave-based economy could not develop. As a result Spanish settlers engaged in manual labor, working their own lands and developing a strong sense of independence and self-sufficiency. Furthermore, PLN founders described the development of an egalitarian system of land ownership in which a flexible class structure took root rather than a system defined by a landed oligarchy exploiting the masses of landless peasants. The PLN's version of national identity also emphasized a strong educational tradition that kept the population politically aware and actively involved in the democratic process. The elimination of the military under the Founding Junta and the decades-long tradition of peaceful democratic government in the first half of the twentieth century reinforced the emerging portrayal of Costa Rican identity.

This carefully crafted national narrative allowed the PLN founders to vilify the *calderonistas* as enemies of the egalitarian and democratic traditions that were uniquely Costa Rican. Furthermore, the Figueres-led civil war in 1948 could be portrayed not as a break from the PLN leaders' inclination for peace but rather as a heroic act to confront the Caldero-communist alliance that had violated Costa Rica's national integrity. The founding principles of the PLN portrayed the War of National Liberation as a necessary interlude to protect Costa Rica's democratic national identity and to restore the important historical traditions that had developed since the colonial period. The "Generation of 48"—those allies of Figueres who participated in the uprising and formed the initial leadership of the PLN—became saviors under this narrative, and they described themselves as "chosen ones" who were following their destiny to redeem the nation.

The notion of Costa Rican exceptionalism created by the PLN in its founding days shaped the way subsequent generations learned the nation's past and formed a collective historical memory. Some recent historians have challenged the historical picture created by the Generation of 48 and have dubbed it Costa Rica's "national myth."

Nevertheless, the creation of a cohesive national identity certainly gave legitimacy to the new political party, and the PLN became the most influential political entity for the rest of the twentieth century.

THE FIGUERES PRESIDENCY

With a solid party foundation behind him, José Figueres announced that he would run for president on March 8, 1952, as Ulate's terms was coming to a close the following year. He used his presidential campaign to publicize the platform of the PLN and emphasized his plans to strengthen the national economy and to promote social justice. He presented himself as a man of the people and spoke at great length about the injustices suffered by the nation's poor and minority classes. The 1953 election marked the first national election since women had been granted the right to vote, and Figueres made a particularly strong effort to win their support as well. He presented himself as defender not just of women's political equality but also their equality in the workplace and in society.

Despite vocal opposition from Ulate's PUN party, Figueres won the presidency with a 65 percent majority on July 26, 1953—coincidentally, the same day that Fidel Castro led his attack on the Moncada Barracks, setting off a series of events that eventually culminated in the Cuban Revolution. With the peaceful transfer of power from Ulate to Figueres in November of that year, the democratic tradition that was such an important foundation of the Liberación ideology was firmly in place. Figueres's PLN dominated the presidency for the rest of the twentieth century, but the new party did not monopolize the political system. Two PUN candidates won the presidency in the coming decades, and candidates from the Partido de Unidad Socialcristiana (Social Christian Unity Party, or PUSC), formed in 1977, have also held the presidency on a number of occasions. In fact, for a time the PUSC coexisted and competed with the PLN in what political experts recognized as a two-party system in the final decades of the twentieth century. With each election, presidential power changed hands smoothly and peacefully, and the Costa Rican political system has been lauded as a model democracy in the region.

THE LIBERACIÓN ECONOMY

Figueres interpreted his presidential victory as a mandate to implement the program outlined under the ideology of Liberación. On domestic issues, he focused much of his attention on economic development. With the mixed economy concept as a backdrop, Figueres strengthened many regulatory agencies that had been created by the Founding Junta. The National Institute of Electricity built a new power plant during his administration in an effort to increase capacity for the nation and to compete with the U.S. company that had traditionally controlled pricing and supply. The government's output of electricity production soon outpaced the competition, and greater access to electrical power allowed for the growth of cities in the coming decades. The advent of the mixed economy meant that the public sector expanded as government agencies oversaw the construction of new schools, highways, and hospitals.

Figueres implemented his plan for the mixed economy concept almost immediately in two sectors that became prototypes for later programs. In 1954 he created the National Fisheries Plan to provide government support to take advantage of the bountiful fish population off Costa Rica's coast and develop a fishing industry. Figueres envisioned a system in which government funding would provide much of the necessary infrastructure—transportation, storage, distribution—through credit and aid programs and the National Council of Production would regulate pricing in the short term. This would allow a local market to grow with the hope of increasing fish consumption at home while freeing up more of the beef supply for the export market where it was more profitable.

In a similar vein, the president also created the National Institute for Housing and Urban Development that same year. Both programs were intended to stimulate the growth of industry in the private sector through government support in the form of credit, seed money, regulation, and other forms of aid. Through the Institute Figueres sought to replace the overrun and unsanitary slums that had grown up in many urban areas with safer, cleaner, and more affordable housing. The Institute helped to plan to urban housing tracts and provided loans and insurance plans to buyers. It sponsored the construction of 2,600 homes during Figueres's administration, and the president heralded both the Institute and the National Fisheries Plan as models of success in his mixed economy model. But greater government involvement in such programs also further expanded the public sector even more, and agencies added jobs and committed government funds to supporting industries.

Funding the expansion of the public sector was delicate business, particularly as the number of state employees grew and the government maintained a consistent policy of ensuring wage increases to match economic growth. The idealistic president was fortunate that the coffee market remained strong throughout the 1940s and into the 1950s and revenue from exports provided some financing for his new programs. Figueres's economic policies took on an increasingly nationalist tone in the early months of his presidency, and one target of that nationalist impulse became foreign companies with large operations in Costa Rica. In particular, Figueres viewed the size and scope of the United Fruit Company's activities as a type of economic occupation. He stated publicly his desire to reform the nation's policies regarding foreign investors with the goal of inducing the UFC and other large-scale foreign companies to reduce their activities on a gradual basis and eventually withdraw from the Costa Rican economy.

Soon Figueres began the process of renegotiating the United Fruit Company's contract. The president saw a number of problems with the nation's traditional relationship with the multinational company, not the least of which included long-standing tax exemptions and the waiving of import duties on heavy machinery. In the past, Costa Rican governments had allowed those concessions—and even looked the other way when abuses occurred—because the United Fruit Company's presence in the banana districts provided employment as well as much-needed services that the government was unable to provide. Those services included roads and housing, schools and health clinics, and other basic-needs services for UFC employees. But as the company expanded and became increasingly powerful, government leaders began looking at UFC's dominance in the national economy as more of a threat. And thus far, Figueres had failed to win full political support from the banana labor sector, which further amplified the urgency for reforming the company's activities.

Figueres envisioned a reform process whereby the government would purchase UFC agricultural land and production responsibilities would be transitioned to domestic operations. He specified at the outset that the government had no intention of carrying out forced expropriations, as was the concern for U.S. investors in other Latin American countries during the Cold War. He intended to leave shipping and distribution operations in United Fruit Company hands. But Figueres outlined his intention to replace UFC social services in the banana districts with state-rendered services. Contract negotiations also included labor provisions, which the president hoped would begin to win him some support among banana workers. But the most sweeping reforms involved taxation. Figueres hoped to establish a 50-50 profit split between the company and the Costa Rican government, and he aimed to introduce tariff obligations for the United Fruit Company's imports of heavy equipment.

While Figueres was negotiating with UFC executives in Costa Rica, the company itself was undergoing significant turmoil in another Central American nation as Guatemalan president Jacobo Arbenz undertook a massive nationalization program and targeted United Fruit Company lands for expropriation. Despite the rising tensions—or perhaps because of them—Figueres managed to win a number of concessions from the company, and he walked away with a new contract that he considered very favorable to the people of Costa Rica. Under the new agreement the Costa Rican government was to take over social services in the banana districts and the company would be subject to import tariffs. Figueres was only able to secure a 30 percent tax on UFC profits, which was higher than in previous contracts but fell short of the 50 percent tax the president had hoped to achieve. He also negotiated a new minimum wage for banana workers, but that concession was attenuated by the president's weak stance on union rights. He particularly avoided supporting banana worker's rights to collective bargaining even though his public statements indicated he hoped one day to see them enjoy that right. Figueres ensured that banana workers' minimum wage rose regularly in accordance with the cost of living, but he distanced himself from collective labor action in an attempt to stifle communism. In fact, when banana workers went on strike in 1955, Figueres initially tried to dissuade striking workers and eventually supported the United Fruit Company in rejecting collective bargaining rights. The president justified his stance on unions as part of Cold War anticommunism, but his actions did little to win him or the PLN support among the labor sector.

LIBERACIÓN FOREIGN POLICY

Figueres's strongly nationalistic position on economic and domestic issues had the potential to cause problems in foreign affairs, and he faced some significant foreign policy challenges during his four-year term. But Figueres navigated his foreign policy stance quite adeptly and managed to maintain a delicate balance between cultivating nationalism at home and negotiating the complexities of Cold War politics abroad. Many of his foreign policy challenges involved maneuvering Costa Rican autonomy and national interest in the face of rising pressures from U.S. leaders to take a strong stance on the Cold War. Oftentimes, the Costa Rican president found those two objectives to be in direct conflict with each other. Figueres watched the United State engage in covert military action in Guatemala in response to nationalist reforms that targeted United Fruit Company lands—policies that were not too dissimilar from the reforms Figueres was attempting to implement in Costa Rica. He became a vocal opponent to the U.S.-friendly dictatorship of Venezuela's Marcos Pérez Jiménez, and in a visible display of protest and independence, he was the lone Latin American leader to boycott the Tenth International Conference of American States held in Caracas in 1954. But Figueres's most serious foreign policy challenge came from neighboring Nicaragua in an episode that threatened the stability of his administration and called into question his earlier decision to abolish the national military.

Animosity between Figueres and Nicaraguan leader Anastasio Somoza dated back to the Costa Rican president's time in exile and his association with the Caribbean Legion. The informal alliance between Figueres and other Latin American political exiles had played a role in inciting the Costa Rican War of National Liberation, and members of the Caribbean Legion had made no secret of their ambition to topple the Somoza regime, along with other Latin American dictatorships. Once he took power Figueres allowed political exiles from Nicaragua and elsewhere to take refuge in Costa Rica, and many of those individuals used San José as a base to organize and train for insurgency missions intended to overthrow dictatorial regimes and even assassinate leaders. Somoza was the prime target of a large group of Nicaraguan exiles, and their presence in Costa Rica only further heightened tensions between Figueres and the Nicaraguan dictator. When members of the Nicaraguan exile group carried out an unsuccessful assassination attempt against Somoza in 1954, their actions provoked vocal protests from the Nicaraguan government and caused an escalation in tensions between Somoza and Figueres.

Somoza exacted his revenge less than one year later. In the late months of 1954 Teodoro Picado, Jr., son of the *calderonista* president ousted in the 1948 War of National Liberation, put together a group of 500 militants to attempt to overthrow Figueres. Aided by the Somoza regime, the group calling itself the Authentic Anti-Communist Revolutionary Army trained in Nicaragua in preparation for an invasion of Costa Rica. That invasion began in January 1955 when Picado's forces crossed the border and occupied the northwestern town of La Cruz. Rather than push his invading force further south, Picado held firm and attempted to incite an uprising similar to the one that had ousted Jacobo Arbenz of Guatemala the year before. He resorted to isolated air raids and broadcast propaganda messages via radio calling for a general uprising among the people. As he fortified his position, Picado continued to receive aid and supplies from Nicaragua, just across the border.

Without a professional military to ensure national defense, Figueres responded by forming a volunteer army. He also invoked emergency executive powers that suspended constitutional liberties. But Figueres's most potent weapon was his diplomatic appeal to the United States and to the Organization of American States (OAS), the regional organization that was chartered in 1948 to maintain peace, stability, and security in the Western Hemisphere. The OAS declared that Costa Rica had been the victim of a major aggression and authorized the United States to supply the Central American nation with four fighter planes for the bargain price of $1 dollar each. For U.S. leaders who viewed Figueres as the last bastion of democracy in a sea of Central American and Caribbean dictators in the 1950s, protecting the Costa Rican president took on particular urgency. With the backing of the United States and the OAS, Figueres thwarted the attempted insurrection rather quickly, but the episode was a clear indication that significant opposition to his administration existed. Nevertheless, Figueres came away from the attempted invasion with a closer tie to the United States and a sense of reassurance that the OAS would support Costa Rican democracy in the interest of protecting regional security.

José Figueres took a sledgehammer to the walls of San José's Bellavista military barracks in 1948, and in one fell swoop he set Costa Rica upon a path that would deviate significantly from that of other Latin American nations in the early years of the Cold War. While neighboring Nicaragua endured the military dictatorship of the Somoza family, Costa Rica abolished its standing army and devoted itself to peace and democracy. As Guatemalan president Jacobo Arbenz was overthrown in response to land reform and other social justice measures that raised communist concerns in the United States, Costa Rican leaders secured social and economic policies that expanded the public sector, introduced a mixed economy, increased funding for education, and raised taxes on powerful multinational corporations such as the United Fruit Company. Costa Rica's carefully crafted position in the early years of the Second Republic allowed its leaders to pursue the ideological platform laid out in the Liberación movement without challenging the delicate Cold War balance in the Western Hemisphere. During that time, José Figueres and his supporters created a new constitution that provided social guarantees, curbed the influence of the United Fruit Company, and withstood a security threat from Nicaragua even in the absence of a standing military. In a short period of time Figueres and the PLN had secured a series of vital successes that allowed *Liberacionistas* to shape the narrative of Costa Rican exceptionalism.

9

State-Led Development and Debt

SOCIAL INDICATORS

By the early 1990s Costa Rica stood as a quintessential success story for advocates of social justice reform, particularly in comparison with many of its Latin American neighbors. Even though Costa Rica ranked eighth among Latin American nations in terms of income—measured as GDP per capita—the nation held either the number one or number two position in the region in 10 other indicators of social well-being. Those measures included such things as life expectancy, infant mortality, daily calorie supply, access to clean water and sanitation, and access to social security. Almost all Costa Ricans had access to reliable health care, and nearly 90 percent of the nation's children were immunized against communicable diseases. Furthermore, Costa Rica's unemployment rates were the lowest of any nation in Latin America, and it had the lowest poverty rates in the region. Nearly 100 percent of Costa Rican children were enrolled in primary school, and adult literacy rates stood at roughly 95 percent.[1]

By these measures, Costa Rica's social justice initiatives had been enormously successful, and the nation's social indicators placed it on a par with developed, industrial nations in the rest of the world. Yet these statistics belie the fact that Costa Rica spent the preceding 10 years in the midst of a devastating economic crisis and a dramatic overhaul of trade and investment policies. Indeed, Costa Rica's experiences in the 1980s mirrored those of most Latin American nations where economic development and social spending policies put in place in the 1960s and 1970s proved unsustainable and gave way to enormous foreign debt. As one Latin American country after another defaulted on foreign loans, the region suffered debt crises, high inflation, exchange rate problems, and imposed austerity measures. The economic crisis in the region became so serious that most nations saw their economies stagnate or even decline, and the 1980s became known throughout Latin America as the "lost decade." Given the severity of the crisis, it is no surprise that many Latin American nations saw indicators of social well-being deteriorate over the course of the decade. What is surprising is that the small and unassuming Central American nation that had fought a violent civil war just a few decades earlier weathered the crisis with considerable aplomb. And even though Costa Rica's economy did not emerge from the lost decade unscathed, social and political institutions managed to endure a number of potential challenges as the economy faltered.

IMPORT SUBSTITUTION INDUSTRIALIZATION

The 1948 War of National Liberation and its immediate aftermath brought dramatic changes to Costa Rica through constitutional reform, new citizenship and suffrage rights, the abolition of the military, and the institutionalization of the Social Guarantees and other basic individual freedoms. Those developments endured the war and the political consolidation that took place after the war was over; they became permanent fixtures in Costa Rican society throughout the remainder of the twentieth century and are generally held up as markers of the strength of the Costa Rican system. Other changes were equally dramatic, if not also similarly long lasting, but eventually failed to reinforce the notion of Costa Rican exceptionalism. In particular, the economic model put in place by Figueres brought short-term gains to the nation, but the long-term consequences of some economic decisions were ultimately devastating.

Figueres's mixed economic model aimed to expand economic output, diversify the nation's productive capacity, and generally modernize the nation's economy through a combination of government initiatives and private-sector involvement. Figueres and other presidents who followed him were concerned that the nation's economy relied so heavily on bananas and coffee—two commodity agricultural products that were subject to immense volatility in the global market. Any number of factors could affect the price of and demand for Costa Rica's two main exports, not the least of which included climate conditions at home, economic downturn abroad, and any of the variety of global security concerns that were so common during the Cold War. Furthermore, the banana industry in particular had developed as a foreign economic sector with the United Fruit Company wielding enormous influence over Costa Rican affairs. The dominant position of the UFC—or any other foreign enterprise—did not conform to the nationalist tone among Costa Rica's post–World War II leaders. Generations of leaders had talked about changing the structure of the nation's economy; Figueres and his successors in the 1950s and 1960s took very real steps to do just that.

The PLN's mixed economic system generally conformed to the model of import substitution industrialization (ISI) that was common throughout Latin America in the several decades following World War II. ISI policies had their roots in the nationalist and protectionist response in Latin America to the economic crisis following the Great Depression. But the United Nations' Economic Commission for Latin America and the Caribbean (ECLAC), formed in 1948, formalized the model as a policy recommendation for Latin American nations throughout much of the last half of the twentieth century. ECLAC economists pressed developing nations such as Costa Rica to transform the national economic base by developing a more diversified manufacturing sector and prioritizing industrialization. They envisioned the development of industries devoted to the manufacture of small consumer goods such as textiles, processed foods, and some small appliances. ECLAC leaders looked to the massive industrialization process that had taken place in the United States and Western Europe in the nineteenth century as a model. But in the global economy of the twentieth century, newly industrializing economies were at a disadvantage, particularly when trying to compete with long-standing and well-developed industries abroad. An emerging school of economic thought known as dependency theory influenced many proponents of ISI and helped to shape their economic recommendations. This theory posited not only that developing nations were at a disadvantage but also that, as they pursued their own industrial expansion, developed and industrialized nations had actually prevented economic progress from taking root in areas such as Latin America.

To mitigate the many challenges faced by developing economies and to give them a competitive edge, ISI advocates recommended a significant degree of government involvement through state investment in industry and tax incentives. Protectionist trade policies such as tariffs and quotas were also used as a way to make imports from competing countries more expensive and encourage the consumption of nationally produced goods. ECLAC leaders envisioned ISI as a system that would help small, developing nations weather the difficult early stages of industrialization with the hope of creating a strong foundation that would give those nations more self-sufficiency and economic stability.

While many of ECLAC's leaders initially envisioned ISI policies primarily as a solution for the economic woes of larger Latin American nations—such as Mexico, Argentina, and Brazil—many leaders in smaller nations adopted similar economic models as a solution to underdevelopment and economic stagnation based on centuries of relying on commodity agricultural exports. Costa Rican leaders were no exception. The nation's long-running volatility caused by having an economy dominated by commodity exports led many political leaders to begin seeking alternative models for Costa Rica's economic future. The nationalist impulse generated by José Figueres was firmly entrenched by the end of his presidency so that even when Mario Echandi, the opposition PUN candidate, defeated the Liberación candidate in 1958 to succeed Figueres, nationalist economic policies and Costa Rica's own version of ISI remained.

THE COLD WAR AND THE ALLIANCE FOR PROGRESS

Costa Rica's turn toward ISI economic policies came at an inauspicious time in U.S.-Latin American relations. Concern among U.S. leaders over the possible expansion of communism dictated foreign policy decisions, especially in Latin America. Those decisions were increasingly defined by an expansion of militarism and strong denunciations of any policies that included even the slightest hints of nationalism. Nationalist rhetoric combined with economic reform and the expropriation of United Fruit Company properties in Guatemala had generated a strong anticommunist backlash in Washington, DC. U.S. concerns eventually translated into a covert intervention in 1954 that drove democratically elected president Jacobo Arbenz from power.

Costa Rican economic nationalism was not as pronounced as the policies in Guatemala, but the expansion of state enterprises, the creation of trade barriers, and the preference for nationally owned industries over foreign investment were not welcome developments among U.S. policy makers. U.S. president Dwight Eisenhower and his vice president Richard Nixon generally regarded Costa Rica's democratic tradition as a positive feature, and U.S. diplomatic leaders publicly promoted the expansion of democracy in the Western Hemisphere. Nevertheless, in the Cold War climate a paradoxical preference for right-wing dictators began to emerge in policy decisions.

U.S. military aid to Latin America increased significantly during the 1950s, and by 1957 the United States had developed close military links with all Central American nations except Costa Rica and El Salvador. U.S. leaders also strongly encouraged all Latin American nations to embrace policies that would facilitate direct investments by U.S. businesses in the local economies. Costa Rican leaders remained leery of such economic policies, particularly as the national economy declined due to a steep drop in coffee prices in the late 1950s. The expansion of Cold War military programs also concerned national leaders, and in 1957 Costa Rican diplomats submitted a proposal to the Organization of American States calling for a reduction in the arms buildup throughout Latin America. The proposal was quickly rejected by other OAS nations, an increasing number of which were under military regimes and enjoying large military aid packages from the United States.

U.S. strategies in Latin America shifted—at least temporarily—following the success of the 1959 Cuban Revolution. As Fidel Castro and his supporters adopted progressively more and more socialist-oriented policies, the concern among U.S. leaders over the spread of communism in the Western Hemisphere became particularly acute. The new administration of John F. Kennedy adopted a new approach to fighting communism in Latin America by introducing the Alliance for Progress in the early 1960s. The new plan included aid programs to fight poverty in the region while continuing to devote resources to preventing revolutions. Alliance programs included funding for health and education as well as economic aid to help Latin American nations recover from trade deficits that had become problematic in the 1950s. Under Kennedy, U.S. aid to Costa Rica increased, and much of that aid was devoted to social programs under PLN president Francisco José Orlich Bolmarcich. The Alliance for Progress magnified U.S. influence in the Costa Rican economy while allowing the Costa Rican government to expand its emphasis on ISI policies.

THE CENTRAL AMERICAN COMMON MARKET

While leaders in Costa Rica and other smaller Latin American nations accepted the validity of the ISI model for twentieth-century economic development, they also understood that the theory's goal of economic and productive self-sufficiency was not a realistic scenario in smaller economies with fewer national resources. To overcome that challenge, ISI advocates in Central America began considering how they could cooperate with each other by integrating their economies to expand the market as well as the productive capacity in the region. ECLAC economists proposed economic integration—or the creation of a "common market"—for nations like Costa Rica, in which trade treaties would link regional economies and those networks would be protected by common external tariffs. Such a strategy—in theory—would restrain competition from industrialized nations and allow new industries within the common market to develop.

In the 1950s leaders from Guatemala, Costa Rica, El Salvador, Nicaragua, and Honduras began experimenting by forming bilateral treaties with neighboring nations that established common market trade regulations on specific products. The formation of the Organization of American States coincided with these new economic agreements, and even though the OAS was primarily an organization devoted to hemispheric security, it did foster a greater sense of cooperation among Central American nations and gave new efforts to foster economic collaboration a greater sense of legitimacy. By 1956 each Central American country had signed at least one bilateral trade agreement with one of its neighbors, and the activities of the ECLAC ensured that multilateral collaboration would soon follow.

ECLAC leaders, following the example being set by founding nations of the European Economic Community—which was the early institution that eventually became the European Union—formed a Committee of Economic Cooperation, and government officials from the five Central American nations began considering the establishment of a common market. By 1959 the efforts of the Committee resulted in formal integration agreements, which collectively established a free trade zone around signatory nations for specified products. U.S. leaders eventually became involved in the trade negotiations as well, and support for regional integration in Central America became part of the Kennedy administration's platform under the Alliance for Progress. A U.S. plan known as the General Treaty of Central American Economic Integration created a regional trade block in Central America known as the Central American Common Market (CACM); it was signed in 1960 by leaders from Guatemala, El Salvador, Nicaragua, and Honduras. Costa Rica did not sign on to the agreement immediately, but by 1962 Costa Rica had joined the other Central American nations in an experiment in economic integration. Signatory countries phased in a system in which they eliminated most tariffs on goods traded among each other and adhered to common external tariffs on goods traded outside of the trading block.

Initially the regional integration scheme produced positive results. Manufacturing output rose significantly in Costa Rica throughout the 1960s, and the value of industrial exports increased by a factor of 25. Furthermore, total trade within the Central America trading block expanded from $32 million in 1960 to $136 million in 1969.[2] With the strategy's emphasis on consumer goods, the manufacture of processed foods and textiles naturally saw the most notable expansion while imports of those products from outside the CACM declined considerably. To facilitate the expansion of local industry and regional trade, Central American governments committed to vital infrastructure projects that were intended to develop more efficient transportation and communications networks. Regional development organizations, financed by the U.S. Agency for International Development (USAID) and the Alliance for Progress, facilitated many of those projects. Others were undertaken by individual national governments. While the initial expansion in regional manufacturing and trade was impressive, it

U.S. president John F. Kennedy with Central American leaders at a Central American Common Market meeting in San José, March 1963. (AP Photo)

was not necessarily a sign of success. Indeed, by 1965 the first signs of structural problems with the CACM integration model started to become apparent. The creation of a regional trading bloc in Central America had yielded a larger market for member nations' manufactured goods, but the majority of the population was poor—many of the people lived in extreme poverty—and could not afford to purchase the goods being produced in the new manufacturing sectors. As a result the size of the market among CACM nations was necessarily limited. Furthermore, wealth and resource inequality persisted among member nations, and the more developed industrial sectors in Guatemala and El Salvador thrived while industries in Costa Rica, Nicaragua, and Honduras were less developed and required larger outlays of cash. But perhaps the most significant obstacle to the CACM's success was the long-standing animosities that festered among several Central American nations. Border tensions between Honduras and El Salvador culminated in 1969 in the "Soccer War," which was so named because skirmishes that broke out among fans after a soccer match between the two national teams eventually provoked military hostilities between the two nations. Trade between the two countries came to a virtual halt, and Honduras eventually withdrew from the CACM in 1971. The organization became defunct, and policies aimed at regional integration in Central America ceased over the coming decades.

STATE-LED DEVELOPMENT PROGRAMS

Costa Rican leaders believed that they could fundamentally alter the trajectory of the nation's economy by expanding the role of the government in the economic sector through state-led development programs. Protectionist trade barriers, government subsidies for industry, and the promotion of regional commercial integration were all measures the government put in place to promote import substitution industrialization. Formal development programs were seen as the next step in diversifying the nation's economy and transforming Costa Rica into a viable force in the global marketplace. In 1968 the Orlich administration created the Center for the Promotion of Exports and Investments (CENPRO), which was dedicated to promoting nontraditional exports to markets outside of Central America. Throughout the 1970s, CENPRO provided advice and technical assistance to businesses in Costa Rica in an attempt to diversify exports and generate foreign revenue.

In 1970 José Figueres Ferrer was elected to the presidency once again, and his PLN won a majority of seats in the Congress. Figueres devoted his third and final presidential term to continuing the nationalist and populist policies he had implemented in the 1950s. The CACM had not produced the level of economic independence that he had envisioned, but Figueres and his supporters remained committed to the theory behind import substitution industrialization. Regional integration in Central America continued and even expanded throughout the 1970s despite the dissolution of the CACM, and the Figueres administration ramped up the government's participation in the economy as a way of guiding and regulating development activities.

In 1972 the government created the Costa Rican Development Corporation (CODESA), which was a government agency that operated as a majority partner and entered into joint ventures with private companies. Government leaders envisioned CODESA as a way to provide investment support to national businesses interested in expanding their activities into industries that were deemed essential for national growth. The creation of CODESA marked a distinct turn to state-led development programs, compelling many observers to refer to Costa Rica as an "entrepreneur state." Figueres and other PLN leaders believed that moving toward an entrepreneur state was necessary because the promises of ISI remained unfulfilled. Specifically, ISI had failed to benefit the nation fully because the structure of Costa Rica's economy still allowed significant participation by foreign corporations. Those foreign entities invested much-needed capital into Costa Rican industries, but profits generally did not make their way back into the national economy. Figueres hoped that the government-operated CODESA would replace large multinational corporations in providing investment support to national businesses. CODESA was to act as a holding company until the businesses could operate without government support, at which time they would be completely privatized, ideally with ownership transferring to the Costa Rican private sector.

Although it was created in 1972 under President Figueres, CODESA did not begin operating fully until four years later under Figueres's successor and fellow PLN leader, Daniel Oduber Quiros; after that time its activities expanded significantly. The agency backed new ventures in heavy industry such as railroads, cement, and aluminum production, and it also made new agricultural investments in cotton, sugar, and fertilizers. CODESA acquired large subsidiaries, but instead of providing basic support, the government holding company often provided nearly 100 percent of investment funds. Furthermore, most subsidiaries of CODESA never became profitable, and the government investment backing that was supposed to be temporary remained in place, effectively propping up inefficient and unprofitable industries.

The PLN's political adversaries pounced on CODESA from the beginning, pointing out many of these structural problems and accusing agency leaders of corruption. Indeed, there was rampant and blatant misspending associated with CODESA as employees of the agency enjoyed lavish perks and funded projects that more often reflected political calculation rather than strategic investment in promising industries with a high profit potential. Many of the subsidiaries remained fully owned by the CODESA holding company and never became profitable in their own right. As a result government spending increased substantially in the 1970s as CODESA continued to provide a seemingly endless supply of credit to companies that were not viable and that were not contributing to the overall growth of the economy.

The Costa Rican government's decision to create CODESA and adhere to expansive fiscal policies unfortunately coincided with a series of major upheavals in the global economy. In 1973 the Organization of Petroleum Exporting Countries (OPEC) manipulated the production and supply of oil as part of a strategy to raise the price of oil substantially in the global marketplace. The OPEC-led price increase affected Costa Rica in two important ways. First, since Costa Rica is not a petroleum-producing country, it must import oil from abroad to provide fuel and raw materials for its industrial sector and to support its transportation networks. The rise in oil prices in 1973 meant that the nation had to pay substantially more for oil imports. The 1973 oil shock occurred as the prices of many of Costa Rica's agricultural exports were dropping, making it even more difficult for the small nation to absorb higher oil prices.

Second, as oil importers were forced to pay higher prices, OPEC nations found themselves flush with cash as the higher oil revenues also yielded much larger profits. Members of OPEC deposited large sums of money into major banks around the world, and those banks in turn looked to convert that money into loans that would yield high interest rates. Costa Rica and other nations in the developing world found themselves in urgent need of borrowing large sums of money just as world banks were intent on making large loans. Rising oil prices combined with the government spending required through CODESA and other such developmental programs created a new sense of urgency for the Costa Rican government to take out substantial foreign loans.

Government spending and a heavy reliance on foreign borrowing created enormous fiscal problems for Costa Rica by the end of the decade. Populist leaders, particularly among the PLN, had made deficit spending and the accumulation of public debt a part of their political strategies since the creation of the Second Republic. Increased public spending was necessary to support the social programs that became the foundation of populist leaders' political platforms. Politicians found themselves unable to raise sufficient tax revenue to fund such programs since taxing the wealthy would result in losing significant political support. Instead the Costa Rican system of revenue generation relied on sales taxes and some tariffs on foreign goods, which did not come close to covering government expenditures. To make up the difference national leaders turned to foreign loans to pay for populist programs.

Between 1950 and 1970 Costa Rica's public debt increased from $29 million to $164 million while the national deficit increased from less than ₡1 million (colones, Costa Rica's national currency) to more than ₡90 million colones. The creation of CODESA and the proclaimed dedication of the Figueres and Oduber administration to expanding the government's role in the economy required even more public spending—expenditures that were also not covered by tax income. Foreign debt increased substantially throughout the 1970s, going from $164 million to more than $1 billion by 1978.[3]

DEBT CRISIS

The structural problems with CODESA combined with the extensive reliance on foreign loans proved to be unsustainable for the Costa Rican government. A second sharp rise in oil prices in 1979 coincided with a dramatic decrease in the global price for coffee and bananas—two of Costa Rica's primary export commodities. As the nation's expenditures for oil and other imports increased, the outlay of government resources for CODESA and other development programs did not decline to offset the new budgetary pressures. Rather, government spending on social programs continued to rise throughout the 1970s, and as the national government took out more and more foreign loans to fund such spending, the national debt ballooned.

By 1980 international investors had become jittery about the level of debt being carried by nations in the developing world. Of particular concern was the proportion of national income that many nations needed to devote to interest payments alone. Costa Rica was no different, and as international lenders began to lose confidence in the Costa

Rican economy, their concerns were reflected in increasingly unfavorable conditions on new loans. In 1981 interest rates on foreign loans rose substantially, and that proved to be the death knell for Costa Rican borrowing and by extension the entrepreneur state's development strategies.

In July 1981 Costa Rica suspended interest payments on its foreign debt and became one of the first Latin American nations to default on its loans. The rest of the region soon followed as the international banking community lost confidence in developing economies and, one after another, Latin American nations defaulted on debt payments throughout 1982. The region entered a period of economic decline and fiscal crisis that became known as the "lost decade." In Costa Rica the colón lost more than half its value to the dollar, and by 1982 inflation had skyrocketed to 90 percent. This combination made all goods— but particularly imports—considerably more expensive. Costa Rica was already suffering from a severe economic decline that had started in 1979 when oil prices rose. The additional financial pressures brought on by the debt crisis strained the nation nearly to the breaking point, and many Costa Ricans vented their frustration towards Rodrigo Carazo Odio, the Partido Renovación Democrática (Democratic Renovation Party, or PRD) president who was elected in 1978.

Costa Rica and other nations that suffered through the debt crisis of the 1980s had to appeal to the International Monetary Fund (IMF) and the World Bank for assistance in an attempt to put their economies back on track. As organizations dedicated to stabilizing the global economic system, the IMF and the World Bank offered structured "bailout" packages and loans that provided an immediate infusion of emergency cash along with long-term aid and debt restructuring. In return, the organizations required struggling nations to adopt more disciplined economic and fiscal policies. The United States has always exerted disproportionate influence in both organizations so countries relying on economic aid found themselves beholden to U.S. policy priorities. Further complicating this scenario, the U.S. government often granted unilateral aid to certain developing nations in the wake of the 1980s debt crisis, and those decisions were nearly always tied to foreign policy priorities. In the volatile economic and diplomatic environment of the 1980s, Costa Rican leaders played a careful balancing act of cultivating a closer relationship with the United States while still maintaining a degree of national sovereignty. While President Carazo had developed an antagonistic relationship with the IMF, his successor Luis Alberto Monge of the PLN committed to cooperating with the international agency despite the painful reform measures stipulated in the IMF bailout package.

In 1982 Costa Rica accepted nearly $100 million in IMF aid. At the same time, the United States Agency for International Development sent advisors to Costa Rica, and U.S. unilateral economic assistance also began to flow into the Central American nation. In fact, after 1982 Costa Rica received more direct aid from the United States than it did from the IMF, the World Bank, and other international organizations combined. Between 1982 and 1989 the United States provided more than $1 billion in financial assistance to the small Central American nation.[4] The IMF, the World Bank, and the Inter-American Development Bank also granted substantial aid packages to Costa Rica. Since those organizations were heavily influenced by U.S. policy priorities, Costa Rica found itself increasingly bound by U.S. economic and foreign policy demands.

AUSTERITY AND THE ECONOMIC REFORM

In exchange for large IMF and USAID assistance packages, the Monge administration implemented aggressive reforms designed to limit government spending and boost revenue by encouraging exports. Those reform policies became known as austerity measures because they required governments to rein in spending to its most basic levels. Costa Rican social programs—such as education, welfare, and subsidies—that had required high levels of government funding in the preceding decades were significantly diminished or eliminated completely. Slashing public spending also meant that the large government expenditures in CODESA and other development programs that formed the backbone of the ISI model were also reduced or eliminated. President Monge and his successor Oscar Arias Sánchez—also of the PLN—became strong proponents of the new economic model that defined IMF reform initiatives. Know as neoliberalism, the economic approach preferred by many world leaders in the 1980s prescribed opening trade and reducing government spending as a way for developing economies like Costa Rica's to recover from the debt crisis and build a solid financial foundation for the future.

One important target of austerity measures in Costa Rica was the government holding company, CODESA. Since its creation in 1972, the PLN-favored agency had come under intense scrutiny by political opposition within Costa Rica, and the debt crisis of the 1980s brought CODESA under fire by the IMF and USAID as well. The state-run financier had become a symbol of the cronyism, inefficiency, and bloated bureaucracies that critics of the ISI model often attributed to state-led development programs. By the late 1970s private-sector entrepreneurs in Costa Rica had already been calling for the dissolution of the agency, and USAID advisors were brought into the debate after the nation defaulted on its foreign debt. In 1984 a coalition of USAID representatives and Costa Rican private-sector business leaders began privatizing CODESA. This became a complicated scenario as it became clear that many CODESA firms were not active, and only seven companies accounted for 90 percent of the holding company's investments.[5] The privatization process that was supposed to last two years was not fully completed until 1997 when the last—and one of the most profitable—of CODESA's firms was finally sold off.

One strategy for promoting economic recovery and opening trade was the establishment of the Coalición Costarricense de Iniciativas de Desarrollo (the Costa Rican Coalition of Development Initiatives, or CINDE), which was created in 1982 by 76 national business leaders. CINDE was formed as a private-sector, nonpartisan export and investment promotion organization, but it received funding from USAID and was empowered by the Costa Rican government to facilitate major economic policy changes. The objectives of the new organization included safeguarding measures to ensure social justice and general national well-being, but CINDE leaders focused their efforts on expanding the nation's export market and attracting direct foreign investments, which are investments in permanent assets, such as land and factories. Many of CINDE's programs duplicated the mandate of CENPRO, the Costa Rican government's export promotion agency, but supporters argued that a private-sector initiative was better suited to overhaul the nation's economic sector.

Backed by increasing amounts of USAID funding between 1983 and 1989, CINDE sponsored training seminars to guide government and business leaders toward an export economy. The group worked to attract foreign investors to Costa Rica's export sector, and it successfully lobbied for the passage of numerous laws providing tax breaks and other incentives to new investors in the export market. By some estimates, CINDE was responsible for attracting more than $330 million in direct foreign investments by 1990. Largely because of those direct investments, new factories producing plastics, textiles, chemicals, and small machine parts opened throughout Costa Rica. USAID statistics indicate that Costa Rica's manufacturing exports increased by more than 60 percent per year by 1991. Many of those manufacturers operated in newly established free trade zones, whose creation was promoted by CINDE and which provided tax-free promotions and other incentives to new export industries. CINDE leaders also focused their efforts on encouraging the cultivation of nontraditional exports in the agricultural sector, including strawberries, flowers, melons, and diverse foodstuffs.

As CINDE's strategies were evolving in the 1980s, other private initiatives backed by USAID funding silently emerged in the Costa Rican economy as well. In 1988 investigative journalists and other observers uncovered an extensive network of schools, private banks, and development agencies (like CINDE) that had been operating in Costa Rica to promote export-oriented development strategies and to encourage privatization of banking, education, and other Costa Rican institutions. Critics of this "secret" U.S.-backed network referred to it as a "parallel state," and a scandal erupted as leaders within USAID were charged with cronyism, legal irregularities, and threatening Costa Rican sovereignty.

Regardless of the scandal surrounding USAID's "parallel state," austerity measures and economic reform did bring notable economic recovery. Inflation decreased to manageable levels, and the nation's economy grew by a respectable 4.4 percent between 1983 and 1994. The Costa Rican economy that emerged during that 10-year period was hardly recognizable as the one that had existed in the 1960s and 1970s. Free trade zones and export-oriented manufacturing dominated the economic sector. Many of the social justice initiatives that had been put in place under the Figueres and the Liberación movement had either been privatized or eliminated completely. ISI development strategies became a distant memory by the end of the century, and a wider array of free-trade initiatives replaced the failed attempt to establish a regional trading block through CACM.

Significantly, the economic turmoil Costa Rica experienced throughout this period did not undermine the democratic traditions that came to define the "national myth" put in place by Figueres and the PLN. The PUN, which had played such a dominant role in national politics, gradually lost ground and dissolved by the end of the 1970s. But as the PUN disbanded, the PUSC emerged to challenge the dominance of the PLN, and by the 1990s other opposition parties had emerged as well. Many of the social justice measures implemented after the War of National Liberation remained, elections occurred peacefully, and political power changed hands relatively smoothly even in the midst of economic turmoil. Even though the mixed economic model put in place by Liberación leaders proved unsustainable, other measures that were fundamental to their reform agenda stood the test of time.

NOTES

1. Carmelo Mesa-Lago, "Social Development with Limited Resources," in Steven Palmer and Iván Molina Jiménez, *The Costa Rica Reader: History, Culture, Politics* (Duke University Press, 2004), 323–33.

2. Walter LaFeber, *Inevitable Revolutions: The United States in Central America*, 1st ed. (New York: Norton, 1983), 191.

3. Iván Molina Jiménez and Steven Palmer, *The History of Costa Rica: Brief, Up-to-Date and Illustrated*, 1st ed. (San José, Costa Rica: Editorial de la Universidad de Costa Rica, 1998), 142–43.

4. Mary A. Clark, *Gradual Economic Reform in Latin America: The Costa Rican Experience* (Albany: State University of New York Press, 2001), 48.

5. Ibid., 53.

10

Contemporary Costa Rica

"THE HAPPIEST PEOPLE"

On January 6, 2010, Nicholas Kristof published an op-ed column in the *New York Times* entitled "The Happiest People." In the piece, Kristof reported that according to the World Database of Happiness, the scholarly "happy life years" measure, and the Happy Planet Index, Costa Rica was the happiest country in the world. The three indices all use different measures to gauge happiness, but whether assessing contentment through polling, life expectancy, or environmental impact, Costa Rica topped the list every time. Kristof surmised that the reason for such high levels of happiness in Costa Rica was tied directly to the nation's decision to abolish the military in 1948 and devote more resources to education. This, in turn, promoted stability and economic growth for the people of Costa Rica. Kristof also argued that recent environmental conservation efforts had produced an appreciation for the nation's spectacular ecological setting. Beautiful beaches, impressive rainforests, and sophisticated urban areas all bred contentment, according to the op-ed piece.

The *New York Times* column is indicative of the reputation for peace, stability, and happiness that Costa Rica has garnered over the course of its history. But it should be noted that the nation faced a number of challenges throughout the last half of the twentieth century that made the long-term success of the Costa Rican system far from certain. The economic instability that afflicted the region in the 1980s was further exacerbated by Cold War security concerns and guerrilla insurgencies in neighboring countries. U.S. leaders complicated the situation even more by supplying weapons and aid to anticommunist forces and by tying debt relief aid to antileftist cooperation in Central America. While Costa Rica managed to escape the appalling bloodshed that revolutionary violence brought to Guatemala, Nicaragua, and El Salvador in the 1970s and 1980s, the spillover effects of insurrections in other Central American nations and the posturing of the United States caused enormous concern for the Costa Rican people and threatened to destabilize the nation.

It was against this backdrop that Costa Rican leaders pledged to defend Central American peace and democracy in the 1980s and to find a regional solution to the violence that plagued neighboring nations. Facing what many deemed to be insurmountable odds, Costa Rica's Oscar Arias brought Cold War foes throughout Central American together to bring an end to the civil wars that had torn the region apart. Costa Rica—the nation that had appeared on the verge of collapse at the beginning of the 1980s—ended the decade with a Nobel Peace Prize and an economic recovery plan that was already beginning to create prosperity. Furthermore, Costa Rica's reputation as a staunch defender of democracy, peace, and human rights was reinforced through those experiences, and recent developments in contemporary Costa Rica continue to reflect that reputation. There have been bumps along the road, to be sure, particularly when charges of corruption surfaced that were tied to high-ranking politicians in the 1990s. But Costa Rica seems to have weathered the storm, electing its first female president in 2010 and recommitting itself to democracy, environmental protection, and peace. And while Nicholas Kristof's classification of Costa Ricans as "the happiest people" may seem a bit cliché, the fact remains that the nation's recent history amplified the notion of Costa Rican exceptionalism. The tendency of tourists, the media, and others around the world to portray Costa Rica as the happiest nation on earth serves to sustain that idea.

THE ARIAS PEACE PLAN

Even though Costa Rica faced considerable economic volatility by the 1980s, it remained a bastion of peace and democratic stability.

The same could not be said for its Central American neighbors. Unequal income distribution, dire poverty, and corrupt dictatorial regimes had engendered a decades-long civil war in Guatemala. Similar political and socioeconomic currents in Nicaragua led to the 1979 Sandinista Revolution that finally ousted the dictator Anastasio Somoza Debayle, son of the famed 1950s dictator who had supported the opposition to the Figueres administration. In both countries, internal insurrection took shape under the auspices of militant leftist guerrilla movements, and the right-wing governments became increasingly repressive in an attempt to stamp out the rebellions. In the context of the Cold War, the guerrillas' leftist leanings sparked fears of communism in the region and among diplomatic leaders in Washington, DC. U.S. military aid poured in to the region while an estimated 200,000 Guatemalans either were killed or disappeared at the hands of the military regime.

Leftist violence and right-wing military repression escalated in Central America throughout the 1970s just as economic pressures intensified in the region. Costa Rica, already struggling with its own skyrocketing debt and subsequent default on foreign loans, viewed the turbulence in neighboring countries with concern while striving to prevent the bloodshed from spilling over into its own borders. Costa Rican leaders faced mounting pressure from U.S. president Ronald Reagan, who was newly inaugurated in 1981 and whose administration attempted to tie debt relief to support for U.S. antileftist policies in Central America.

The Reagan administration aggressively sought to bring the perceived leftist threat in Central America under control. Administration officials began a covert policy of supporting anticommunist *contras*—right-wing paramilitary rebels who organized to destabilize the Sandinista regime in Nicaragua. Some *contra* groups were based in northern Costa Rica, where they operated training facilities funded by U.S. military aid. The Reagan administration put enormous pressure on President Monge to allow *contra* activity on Costa Rican soil and also to begin building up a national military presence with the help of U.S. aid. In 1985 Costa Rica received $11 million in military aid from the United States and the Civil Guard was receiving specialized training from U.S. special forces.[1]

The Costa Rican public remained committed to antimilitarism, and Monge publicly proclaimed his resolve to keep the nation neutral in the face of escalating conflict in Central America. Costa Ricans also continued to espouse nationalist and populist attitudes toward economic and social policies, but those nationalist leanings were increasingly difficult for political leaders to accommodate. The government found itself virtually held hostage by U.S. leaders who offered much-needed debt relief aid, but it was assistance that came with strings attached. Just as the IMF and the World Bank demanded structural economic reform in exchange for financial assistance, so too did the United States. And since USAID provided more relief to Costa Rica than the IMF and World Bank combined, U.S. leaders were able to influence Costa Rican economic reforms in significant ways.

Furthermore, the Reagan administration was urging Costa Rica to militarize and fully support the United States in its anti-Sandinista efforts in Nicaragua. Indeed, much of the economic assistance being offered by the United States in the 1980s came with unwritten, yet very real, anticommunist expectations. In 1983 the Reagan administration created the Caribbean Basin Initiative (CBI), which offered economic aid to Central American and Caribbean nations in an effort to prevent the spread of revolutions by stabilizing governments through economic growth. The program established trade relationships through a system of duty-free imports of certain Latin American goods into the United States. It also directed USAID and other support agencies to promote programs that facilitated U.S. investment in Central America and the Caribbean. Costa Rica's strong democratic tradition made it an archetypal recipient of U.S. aid, and by 1983 the nation had received $70 million of CBI-allocated aid.[2] But U.S. debt relief was not limited to CBI initiatives, and the Reagan administration regularly allotted "extraordinary concessionary aid" to Costa Rica. Between 1982 and 1989 the amount of U.S.-sponsored assistance received by Costa Rica amounted to 3.6 percent of its entire GDP, and CBI trade initiatives allowed the United States to absorb more than 11 percent of Costa Rican exports.[3] It was clear to Costa Rican leaders that the nation's precarious economic situation left it under the thumb of the United States on other foreign policy issues. As the U.S.-led anticommunist crusade escalated in Nicaragua and other regions of Central America, Costa Rica felt itself pulled ever closer to the conflict.

The Monge administration disliked U.S. policies in Central America, but despite growing public demands for Costa Rican neutrality, it did little to challenge those policies. Monge's successor, though, made no secret of his disdain for the tactics being used by U.S. leaders to combat communism. Oscar Arias publicly opposed the *contras*, and his bold statements against U.S. strategies coincided with the decision by the Reagan administration to withhold aid in 1986. U.S. leaders justified this move by accusing Costa Rica of violating some of the clauses in the economic aid agreements, but many observers in Costa Rica found the timing to be more than coincidental and some even accused the United States of holding the Central American nation's aid packages hostage over Arias's refusal to support the *contra* policy.

Despite Costa Rica's reliance on debt relief aid from the United States in the 1980s, Oscar Arias refused to bow to U.S. pressure to militarize the nation and to commit to supporting *contra* activity. He considered the civil wars and extreme violence that plagued his Central American neighbors to be a grave problem for the region as a whole as well as for Costa Rica specifically. Costa Rica had taken in roughly 200,000 refugees who had fled the fighting in Nicaragua and El Salvador, and that sudden large influx of people strained the resources of the already-struggling nation. Furthermore, political instability and a lack of security in the region had disrupted trade networks within Central America and dissuaded many nations from establishing long-term economic ties with any Central American nation—Costa Rica included. These security issues combined with near constant pressure from Washington, DC, to militarize Costa Rica and draw the nation more fully into the conflict compelled Arias to act. But he denounced the assumptions put forth by U.S. leaders that only a military solution would bring effective peace to the region. Instead, Arias—an admirer of John F. Kennedy and a self-proclaimed idealist—insisted that Central Americans could find viable solutions to their own problems without the interference of the United States.

Arias's stance on Central American peace followed other Latin American initiatives to bring an end to the violence in Nicaragua, Guatemala, and El Salvador. Between 1983 and 1985 the Contadora Group attempted to mediate a resolution to Central American civil wars. Made up of leaders from Panama, Mexico, Venezuela, and Colombia, the Contadora Group put forth a 21-point Document of Objectives that aimed to subdue military violence, put in place a process of democratization, and ensure the protection of human rights in the war-ravaged countries. The United Nations and Central American leaders eventually supported the plan, and some observers believed an end to the bloodshed was near. Nevertheless, U.S. leaders opposed the Contadora initiative, arguing that the complete destruction of the Sandinistas and other leftist groups must be part of any peace strategy.

Costa Rica's Arias learned from the failures of the Contadora Group, and even before his 1986 inauguration he began promoting a peace initiative that would largely sidestep the United States in laying out a way forward for Central America. Arias was personable and persuasive, but he was also the fortunate beneficiary of good timing. The Contadora Group fell apart shortly before the extent of illegal covert aid given by the United States to anti-Sandinista rebels was being made public. The resulting *contra* scandal captured the attention of the U.S. public as government investigations and Congressional hearings paraded a host of military and administration leaders in front of news cameras. As a result support in the United States for anticommunist activities in Central America began to wane.

In May 1986, months before the *contra* scandal broke in Washington, Arias had already convened a meeting with the other Central American heads of states. At the summit that became known as Esquipulas I Arias mediated while the presidents of Guatemala, Honduras, El Salvador, and Nicaragua worked through a long list of grievances. Right-wing military leaders in Guatemala, Honduras, and El Salvador had welcomed U.S. military aid and had allowed *contras* to operate in their territory—often just across the border from Nicaragua. The tendency of those leaders to allow U.S. interference in the region's affairs became a main source of the animosity among the Central American leaders. Also troubling was the socialist orientation of the Sandinista government under Daniel Ortega in Nicaragua. The Sandinistas had invited advisers from Cuba, the Soviet Union, and other communist nations after taking power in 1979 and instituted controversial policies such as censoring the press, canceling elections, and expropriating private property. For its part, Nicaragua had received vital aid from the Soviets, further exacerbating the tension with its Central American neighbors.

Arias viewed the large sums of foreign military aid pouring into Central America as one of the gravest challenges to the region's quest for peace. The United States and its Central American allies found the Sandinistas' relationship with communist nations to be unacceptable, and they were quick to criticize the Sandinista government for violating the basic rights of the Nicaraguan people. But the populations of other Central American nations faired no better. U.S.-funded *contras* and right-wing military regimes became renowned for cruel and repressive tactics. They targeted anyone suspected of having leftist ties, and death squads in El Salvador and Guatemala slaughtered many innocent civilians throughout the 1970s and 1980s. Those atrocities contributed significantly to the refugee crisis that threatened economic and political stability in Costa Rica and in other areas.

Few expected the leaders of the Central American nations to agree to talk, and even fewer believed they could come to an agreement on how to proceed toward achieving peace. But the Esquipulas I talks yielded promising results, and Arias convened a series of follow-up meetings throughout 1987 as he presented his fellow Central American leaders with a peace proposal. The Esquipulas II Peace Accord that emerged from this series of negotiations called for an immediate cease-fire throughout the region and compelled each nation to hold free elections at the next scheduled election cycle. Furthermore, the agreement required that all foreign military aid would cease and that human rights would be guaranteed. This included a stipulation that called for amnesty for all political prisoners and a Sandinista pledge to grant amnesty for the *contras*. To the surprise of U.S. leaders and many other outside observers, Arias walked away from the final peace summit in August 1987 with the signatures of all other Central American heads of state on his peace agreement. The Costa Rican president, it seemed, had managed to find common ground and secure for the region a peace that for decades had seemed so elusive.

Central Americans were cautiously optimistic about Arias's peace accord, but officials in the Reagan administration reacted quite differently. U.S. leaders were incredulous and rather disgruntled that the Costa Rican president had bypassed the United States and had secured a peace agreement without the support of the Western Hemisphere's superpower. U.S. officials publicly questioned the peace agreement's chances for success, arguing that the only way to end violence in Central America and to ensure the emergence of democracy in Nicaragua and elsewhere was to maintain a strong military presence. To punctuate that assertion, the Reagan administration submitted a request to Congress for nearly $300 million more in military aid to be earmarked for the Central American anticommunist campaign.

While Washington officials remained skeptical of and even irritated by the Arias peace plan, leaders in the rest of the international community did not share those opinions. Support and admiration for Arias's efforts quickly emerged among leaders in Western Europe and the rest of Latin America. In October 1987, the Norwegian Nobel Committee announced that the Nobel Peace Prize that year would be awarded to Oscar Arias for his efforts in bring peace to Central America. Costa Ricans and other Central Americans predictably reacted with pride to the news while some U.S. leaders publicly rebuked the Nobel Prize Committee for its decision, arguing that such an honor was premature since the peace process was far from assured in Central America. Despite Washington's aloof response, Arias accepted the honor as a testament to the peaceful and democratic traditions of the Costa Rican people. The Nobel Prize Committee also weighed in to justify its decision, maintaining that the incompleteness of the Central American peace process did not detract from its importance. Committee members insisted that they hoped the prize itself would have a positive impact on the ongoing efforts still unfolding among Central American leaders.

It is difficult to ascertain what impact, if any, Arias's Nobel Peace Prize had on the success of the Central American peace process, but some important developments can be tied directly to the Nobel Prize Committee's decision. Shortly after the October 1987 announcement, Nicaragua's Daniel Ortega began easing his restrictions on the nation's press, and by the early months of 1988 Ortega was engaged in direct negotiations with the *contras*. Eventually neighboring Honduras agreed to shut down rebel base camps in its territory, and Arias personally mediated a dispute between leftist rebels and the El Salvadoran government. But perhaps the most significant ramification of Arias's Nobel Peace Prize was the change in posture it forced onto U.S. policy makers. The U.S. Senate passed a resolution publicly sanctioning Arias's peace plan and congratulating the Costa Rican leader for his admirable efforts. At the same time Reagan's request for additional *contra* funding died in the Congress. It simply was not

Oscar Arias accepts the Nobel Peace Prize in Oslo, Norway, December 19, 1987. (AP Photo/Pool/Norsk Telegrambyraa, Inge Gjellesvik)

politically expedient to stand against peace, and an endorsement by the United States went a long way toward solidifying the commitment to peace in Central America.

Oscar Arias's Nobel Peace Prize had far-reaching effects on the small Latin American nation. Central America, which had become known for the horrific atrocities carried out during bloody civil wars in recent decades, now became part of a global conversation about peace and democracy. And Costa Rica, which many people around the world would have struggled to find on a map prior to 1987, now found itself in an intense media spotlight. Oscar Arias's ability to stand so steadfastly for peace and to challenge the status quo being championed by the United States gave the country a sense of respectability and legitimacy around the world.

TOURISM AND THE ENVIRONMENT

Even as Costa Ricans struggled through economic crisis and neoliberal reform in the 1980s, a strong foundation in environmental conservation had already been established. Policies put in place in the 1970s were safeguarded even in the face of economic decline, and through those policies national leaders developed a robust system of national parks and other legally protected lands. Today Costa Rica is viewed as a leader in environmental programs, and a new focus has emerged around ecotourism in recent decades. Late-twentieth-century policies were intended to correct the environmental problems that had developed over several centuries in Costa Rica. National leaders also hoped that laws to protect the country's natural resources would become an instrumental part of building a more prosperous future.

Environmental devastation and gradual deforestation became particularly problematic during the colonial period as Europeans introduced new crops, animals, and agricultural techniques to Costa Rica. After the development of the coffee industry in the early nineteenth century the rate of deforestation increased considerably. Large landowners took advantage of government incentives, such as tax breaks, and converted large tracts of forestland into coffee estates. Small farmers also participated in the coffee economy and contributed to the transformation of forestland. Nevertheless, the overall environmental impact of these activities was relatively mild for a number of reasons, not the least of which was Costa Rica's small population and relative isolation throughout the colonial period and for much of the nineteenth century. Furthermore, landowners and government leaders demonstrated an early awareness of the need for environmental preservation. As early as the late eighteenth century local leaders passed laws aimed at regulating soil usage and curbing the rate of deforestation. Other decrees attempted to govern hunting practices and to protect important watershed areas.

Costa Ricans witnessed a significant environmental impact in the late nineteenth century as Minor Keith introduced mass-scale banana cultivation to Costa Rica. The immediate effects of banana production were a result of the need to clear lowland rainforests to make room for large-scale plantations. The emergence of Panama disease and other soil afflictions led the United Fruit Company and other growers to abandon mature cultivation areas in favor of virgin lands. In the early decades of the twentieth century the Caribbean coast was dotted with depleted fields made barren by overcultivation and a lack of ecological foresight. But in addition to the direct consequences of banana cultivation, ancillary activities also wrought their share of environmental devastation. Clearing land for railroad construction and the rapid growth of cities put additional pressures on Costa Rica's ecological landscape.

The relatively new focus on ecotourism in the late twentieth century seems fitting for a country with a long history of attracting natural scientists and other researchers, many of whom began venturing to Costa Rica in the middle of the nineteenth century. At that time, the expanding coffee export sector and international interest in the construction of a trans-isthmian canal through Central America drew foreign scientists' attention to Costa Rica. They quickly discovered the extent of the region's biodiversity. Over time, the efforts of researchers received some support from the government as national leaders invited foreign scientists to contribute to the emerging system of higher education. In the early decades of the twentieth century the Costa Rican government created a National Agricultural Society, a National Observatory, and a National Geographic Institute. Those agencies collected and studied data on agriculture, climate, topography, and the nation's biodiversity, and their activities positioned Costa Rica as a leader in Latin America in initiatives to facilitate scientific and biological research.

Despite those initial first steps, scientific research and initiatives to study the nation's biodiversity declined throughout the first half of the twentieth century. But in the 1950s biologists at the University of Costa Rica began playing an increasingly important role not only in promoting research into the nation's natural environment but also in protecting the richness of vulnerable natural resources. By that time Costa Rica's ballooning population was putting immense strains on the nation's resources, and rural areas were inundated with squatters seeking new farmlands. New laws were passed calling for conservation procedures in some forestlands—such as those alongside the recently built Pan-American Highway—and the Wildlife Conservation Law of 1956 specified that wildlife was part of the nation's natural resources.

It did not take long for some national leaders to realize that protecting Costa Rica's diverse natural landscape could also attract tourists to the small nation. The Instituto Costarricense de Turismo (Institute of Costa Rican Tourism, or ICT) was formed in 1955, and the government began taking initial steps to develop a cohesive plan to attract foreign travelers. Two years later the Juan Santamaría International Airport opened in San José to facilitate foreign travel to the capital city. From the beginning, Costa Rican leaders seemed to identify a connection between an incipient tourism industry and conserving the nation's national resources. The ICT was charged with designating national park lands around the country's multitude of volcano craters, partially as environmental policy and partially as a way to showcase the nation's natural habitat to travelers. Nevertheless the notion of conservation—particularly of forestlands—did not meet a receptive audience in most of the country. And a lack of enforcement and monitoring meant that these initial policies did little to create a coordinated and effective system of conservation.

It was not until the 1970s that meaningful environmental policies took root in Costa Rica. In 1969 the national congress passed the Forestry Law, which established basic protections for forests and natural resources, and that law proved to be just the first of many important conservation developments in the coming years. In 1974 government leaders ratified the Convention on International Trade in Endangered Species, followed in 1976 by the Convention for the Protection of Flora, Fauna, and Places of Natural Scenic Beauty in the Countries of the Americas. These laws coincided with deliberate attempts by the government to cultivate the nation's tourism industry, and developing a cohesive system of national parks and biological reserves became an important part of that strategy. The creation of the National Parks Service in 1977 gave merit to the interests of those concerned about conservation. The activities of the new agency allowed government officials to promote responsible biotourism as a part of national conservation efforts.

In the coming years, government leaders began to envision tourism as a new area of economic development that could bolster the nation's income, particularly in the wake of the economic problems caused by the debt crisis. In 1985 the Tourism Investment Incentives Law was passed, which granted tax exemptions and other incentives to tourism-related businesses in an effort to encourage investment into the services and infrastructure necessary to expand the tourism industry.

Perhaps the biggest boon to Costa Rican tourism came when President Arias won the Nobel Peace Prize in 1987. The country became more internationally visible and also secured its reputation as a nation of peace. Security concerns no longer dissuaded international travelers from venturing to the Central American nation; in fact many tourists were curious to visit the small, unassuming country whose leader had made such an impact in the quest for Central American peace. Other initiatives in the coming years aimed at promoting mass tourism, such the construction of a second international airport and allowing international investors to develop large-scale resorts along the coast.

Government leaders were concerned that a rapid expansion in tourism could have a negative affect on the nation's natural resources. By the end of the 1990s a number of initiatives were in place to promote sustainable practices in the tourism industry. The Institute of Costa Rican Tourism began monitoring the environmental practices of hotels, beaches, and other tourist attractions and rating those establishments on their level of environmental sustainability. These efforts, combined with the diversity and richness of Costa Rica's natural environment, have made the country a favorite destination for ecotourists—those travelers who combine vacation with ecological experience. By 2009 Costa Rica was the top-ranking Central American nation for tourism and ranked 42nd overall in the world. The income generated from the tourism industry has helped to sustain and expand the Costa Rican economy, and the attention tourism has brought to Costa Rica has bolstered the nation's reputation as a peaceful and stable country.

NEOLIBERALISM

The Costa Rican economy has been transformed substantially since the debt crisis of the 1980s. The rise of the tourism industry accounted for many of those changes, but the nation has also diversified its productive capacity in other ways. Neoliberal economic reforms that prioritized trade liberalization in the 1980s—coupled with Costa Rica's reputation for peace and stability—allowed the nation to attract new investments from multinational corporations in high-technology enterprises. A drastic reduction in tariffs combined with lucrative tax exemptions put in place in the late 1980s resulted in an increase in direct foreign investment of more than 200 percent between 1990 and 1997.[4] Attracting new sources of direct foreign investment was one of the most important goals of the neoliberal economic reforms put into place by Costa Rican leaders following the economic crisis of the 1980s. But neoliberal economists in Costa Rica sought foreign investment opportunities that would go far beyond the exploitation and economic dependency that had marked the nation's relationship with the United Fruit Company throughout much of the twentieth century. Instead, they pursued investors in new, high-value industries in a move away from foreign investment in agricultural commodity products.

As early as 1981, the Costa Rican government passed the Export Processing Zone and Industrial Parks Law, which established free trade zones in specific areas of the country. The first free trade zones were located along important port cities and within the Central Valley, and foreign manufacturers operating within those zones could take advantage of 100 percent tax exemptions on the import of raw materials, partially manufactured components, machinery and replacement parts, work vehicles, and other items necessary for the manufacturing of goods destined for the export market. Other tax exemptions applied to capital, assets, real estate, and profits; companies within free trade zones were generally exempt from local taxes as well. As the economic crisis and security concerns of the 1980s subsided, Costa Rica successfully attracted foreign investment in a variety of industries. Technology manufacturers in particular found an enticing investment climate in Costa Rica, and in 1997 Intel Corporation opened a microchip manufacturing plant there. That company's activities alone helped Costa Rica's economy to grow by 8 percent in 1998 and 1999.[5] Other information technology companies soon followed, and the nation gained a reputation as an ideal economy for the IT industry.

By 2004 Costa Rica had become home to more than $500 million of annual foreign direct investment, with more than 60 percent of that money supporting companies in free trade zones.[6] Electronics and technological products make up a significant portion of that economic activity, with textiles, medical equipment, pharmaceuticals, processed food, and plastic goods making up the rest. Costa Rican leaders publicly tout what they perceive as the successes of trade liberalization and the nation's push to expand the production of nontraditional exports in recent decades. Laws passed as recently as 2011 are aimed at continuing that trend.

While Costa Rica's economic transformation has been dramatic, it has also brought some questionable consequences to the small nation. Neoliberal reform called for a decrease in government spending and a massive push to privatize much of the economy. As a result public sector employment fell by more than 30 percent between 1980 and 2003. Privatization also spread to health care and public safety as government spending in those areas diminished and private companies stepped in to fill the void. Furthermore, a rush of private schools opened in the last decades of the twentieth century, and even as austerity measures required decreased government spending on social programs, Costa Rica maintained its reputation for producing a highly educated population.

Neoliberal reforms induced a series of changes in the nation's labor sector. The number of Costa Ricans employed in the agricultural sector diminished by nearly 44 percent while the number of people employed in service sectors rose to include roughly two-thirds of the population between 1984 and 2004. The shift in employment demographics that took place in the 1980s and 1990s has transformed the nature of Costa Rica's middle class and has put pressure on the traditional political power of labor unions. In fact the number of labor unions operating in Costa Rica fell by approximately 15 percent between 1984 and 2004, and an alternate form of labor organizing known as *solidarismo* rose instead.[7] Under this system workers and management belong to a Solidarista Association, which is funded by worker dues and employer matching contributions. Funds are used to pay for schools, medical care, and other services to benefit employees, but the downside of the system is that it limits workers' rights of collective bargaining. Many Costa Ricans praise the system as a viable alternative to the often contentious relationship between management and traditional unions. But others, including the International Labor Organization and other prolabor groups, consider *solidarismo* to be a violation of general labor rights.

DRUG TRADE

Costa Rica has managed to maintain its reputation as a peaceful and stable nation in recent decades, and indeed it has set itself apart from other problematic regions of Latin America. The nation is known for having a solid respect for human rights, a strong democratic tradition, and an economic climate favorable to foreign investors. But Costa Rica has not escaped all of the problems that have afflicted its neighbors, and despite its distinction as arbiter of Central American peace, the scourge of organized crime and the drug trade that has stricken other nations of the hemisphere began to permeate Costa Rica as well.

Drug trafficking in Costa Rica was initially tied to the activities of the *contras* in the northern regions of the country. Nicaraguan rebels often resorted to smuggling drugs from Colombia to the United States as a way to finance arms purchases and to carry out militant activities against the Sandinista government. In later years, Colombian cartels continued to funnel drug shipments designated for the United States through Central America, and many of those shipments are still transported by land through Costa Rica or by boat close to the nation's shore. A deeply rooted system of corruption in Costa Rican political and business circles allowed drug shipments and money laundering activities in Costa Rica to expand substantially in the 1990s as the country became part of an intricate Central American drug network. By 2008 authorities were confiscating more cocaine in Central American every year than in Mexico and the Caribbean combined.

RECENT DEVELOPMENTS

The insecurities created by the expansion of corruption and the drug trade also produced a sense of disillusionment among the Costa Rican people. Voter participation fell, and in 2002 Costa Rica was forced to hold a run-off presidential election as neither candidate captured the necessary 40 percent of the electorate. Abel Pacheco of the PUSC was eventually declared the winner, and his administration negotiated the Central American Free Trade Agreement (CAFTA-DR) with the United States, the Dominican Republic, and the other Central American nations in 2004. The agreement's provisions for privatizing state-run monopolies in utilities, telecommunications, and insurance prompted protests among many of the working classes in Costa Rica, and the president delayed sending the legislation to the Legislative Assembly for approval because of intense opposition among some sectors of the population. The free trade deal became a controversial issue in the next presidential election when, following a change in the nation's constitutional provisions for reelection, Oscar Arias was allowed to run for president again. Arias won the 2006 election, and one year later the CAFTA agreement narrowly passed a national referendum with 52 percent of the vote.

While Arias had enjoyed enormous popularity following his Nobel Peace Prize in the 1980s, he faced a drastically different political climate during his second presidential administration. In the years leading up to his election, corruption and bribery scandals had come to light surrounding a number of prominent politicians. In 2004, former president Miguel Angel Rodríguez resigned his post as secretary-general of the Organization of American States after allegations surfaced that he had taken illegal kickbacks from a foreign telecommunications company. At the same time, other allegations circulated that the PUSC had accepted large political donations from foreign companies, and former president Rafael Angel Calderón was accused of money laundering through a Finnish pharmaceutical company. Costa Ricans grew increasingly disillusioned as news of suspected corruption circulated, and they vented their frustrations by abstaining from voting and by shifting their political support to up-and-coming opposition parties. Indeed, after 2002 Costa Rica's two-party political system began to unravel as opposition parties began to gain strength. Most political analysts agree that the nation's political environment has effectively become a multiparty system.

Arias's ambitions to run for president again further complicated the political climate. He had long cultivated his reputation as an upright and honest politician, but in seeking a second term the former president led an initiative to amend the constitution, which, since 1969, had previously barred reelection to the nation's highest office. The process of securing a constitutional amendment was itself enormously controversial and caused a rift within Arias's own PLN. His support for the CAFTA-DR generated significant opposition at home as many Costa Ricans accused Arias of selling out to neoliberal forces abroad. A number of political foes lambasted his environmental policies, charging that Arias was abandoning Costa Rica's long history of ecological protection in the interest of attracting investment from multinationals. Security concerns created by the growing drug trade through Central America caused Costa Ricans to question the competence of the Arias administration even more. To punctuate the extent to which Arias—and indeed Costa Rica's reputation in general—had been tainted through rising political discontent, most Western Hemisphere leaders took little heed of the Nobel Peace Prize winner's attempts to mediate after a coup d'état deposed Honduran president Manuel Zelaya in 2009. Arias served out his term, but the groundswell of national unity and political support that had surrounded his presidency in the 1980s never materialized during his second term.

Despite Arias's flagging support, the 2010 PLN candidate—and Arias's vice president—ran a strong campaign promising to make security concerns and social inequality two of her highest priorities. As Costa Rica's first female president, Laura Chinchilla had campaigned on restoring the prestige of Costa Rica's educational system and strengthening the nation's reputation as an environmental haven.

Even though some portrayed her as a lackey of Arias and the old guard of the PLN, many Costa Ricans supported her candidacy in the hope that Chinchilla would renew the notion of Costa Rican exceptionalism. At 50 years old when she took office, for many Chinchilla represented shifting attitudes toward gender in the political system. But she also stands as the embodiment of the hope that a new generation will restore the values that many believe still define their nation.

As Costa Ricans welcomed their first female president, the effects of globalization and neoliberal economic policy were evident. The nation's close diplomatic and trade relationship with the United States has resulted in an overwhelming presence of U.S. cultural markers in Costa Rican society. Hollywood films and music and U.S. fashion trends are notably present throughout the country, as are consumer products manufactured by U.S. companies. English is widely spoken among the Costa Rican population, and there are many private schools and specialized language centers that offer English language instruction. All of these factors continue to make Costa Rica an appealing destination for a wide variety of U.S. tourists, including those looking for an ecological adventure and those seeking a luxury beach resort. Costa Rica has also become a favorite spot for language students looking for study-abroad opportunities to learn Spanish. And its low cost of living and safe, laid-back reputation is quickly making the nation a preferred retirement spot for U.S. expatriates interested in living abroad.

As Ticos continued to greet each other with the expression *pura vida* in recent years, there were many who began to question the notion of Costa Rican exceptionalism that had become so fundamentally ingrained in national identity. The reputation that the nation had so carefully cultivated as a stalwart defender of peace and democracy was increasingly called into question as Costa Rica suffered economic crises in the 1980s, a scaling back of social justice measures, political corruption scandals, and the growing presence of drug trafficking. But despite those challenges, many Costa Ricans have remained optimistic that the nation has not lost its greatness. Costa Rica continues to be a favorite tourist destination, and a resurgence of economic stability has created a diverse commercial sector that is intricately linked to the global market. A new generation of politicians, epitomized by the election of the nation's first female president, has renewed the hopes of a population that has historically demonstrated an upbeat and confident outlook. Furthermore, the country maintains a high standard of living and continues to boast impressive socioeconomic indicators, measures that compelled Nicholas Kristof to label Costa

Ricans "the happiest people" in 2010. Even through the turmoil of recent decades, *pura vida* has not lost its luster.

NOTES

1. Walter LaFeber, *Inevitable Revolutions: The United States in Central America*, 1st ed. (New York: Norton, 1983), 320.

2. Mary A. Clark, *Gradual Economic Reform in Latin America: The Costa Rican Experience* (Albany: State University of New York Press, 2001), 47.

3. Ibid.

4. Ricardo Monge-Gonzalez, Julio Rosales-Tijerino, and Gilberto Arce-Alpizar, "Cost-Benefit Analysis of the Free Trade Zone System: The Impact of Foreign Direct Investment in Costa Rica," OAS Trade, Growth and Competitiveness Studies (Washington, DC: Organization of American States, 2005), 10.

5. Felipe Larrain Bascuñan, Luis F. Lopez-Calva, and Andres Rodriguez-Clare, "Intel: A Case Study of Foreign Direct Investment in Central America," CID Working Paper No. 58 (Center for International Development at Harvard University, 2000), 14.

6. Gonzalez et al., 11.

7. All employment and labor data from Iván Molina Jiménez and Steven Palmer, *The History of Costa Rica: Brief, Up-to-Date and Illustrated*, 1st ed. (San José, Costa Rica: Editorial de la Universidad de Costa Rica, 1998), 162–64.

Notable People in the History of Costa Rica

Arce, Manuel José (1787–1847). El Salvadoran general who served as the first president of the United Provinces of Central America (1825–1829). He participated in the independence movement and opposed the annexation of Central America by the Mexican empire in 1821. When the empire dissolved and the United Provinces was formed, Arce was chosen as its first president in a contested selection process. During his administration he faced numerous conflicts among liberal and conservative factions, eventually resulting in a civil war from 1826 to 1829. His time in office is an example of the problems faced by the short-lived United Provinces. Arce spent most of the 1830s in exile. He tried unsuccessfully to return to political life before he died in 1847.

Arias Sánchez, Oscar (1940–). Two-time president of Costa Rica (1986–1990, 2006–2010) and winner of the 1987 Nobel Peace Prize for his efforts to mediate a peaceful resolution to violent civil wars throughout Central America. Arias is a career politician and long-time member of the National Liberation Party (PLN). He was elected president for the first time in 1986 when Central America was embroiled in bloody civil wars, complicated by U.S. military aid flowing to Nicaraguan anticommunist *contras* and other right-wing movements. Arias sponsored the Esquipulas talks, bringing the leaders of Central American nations together and working for a regional solution to a regional problem. He brokered a peace deal that was not initially backed by the United States, but after winning the Nobel Peace Prize Arias won U.S. support and garnered worldwide attention for Costa Rica. He supported neoliberal economic policies in an effort to pull Costa Rica out of the debt crisis of the 1980s, which required him to curtail many of the social programs that had become the hallmark of his political party. Arias won a second presidential term in 2006. He was succeeded in 2010 by his own vice president, Laura Chinchilla, who is Costa Rica's first female president.

Calderón Guardia, Rafael Angel (1900–1970). President of Costa Rica (1940–1944) and creator of the nation's system of Social Guarantees, which outline individual rights and social justice measures. Calderón Guardia was trained as a physician and rose to power with the support of Costa Rica's *cafetalero* elite. Once in office, he promoted policies that aimed to protect the nation's poor, creating a system of national health care and a social security program. He allied Costa Rica closely to the United States during World War II and cracked down harshly on people of German descent living in Costa Rica. Calderón backed the growing labor movement, and he eventually established close ties with the Communist Party. José Figueres Ferrer denounced his administration for its communist affiliation and for suspicions of corruption in 1942, and Calderón Guardia responded by having Figueres expelled from the country. After sitting out one term, Calderón Guardia ran for president again in 1948 in a much-disputed election and claimed victory over opposition leader Otilio Ulate. That move prompted Ulate and Figueres to join forces and lead the War of National Liberation to overthrow the government. After 44 days, Calderón Guardia was forced to flee Costa Rica, and Figueres seized power, ushering in the era of the Second Republic. In later years Calderón Guardia attempted unsuccessfully to overthrow Figueres. Eventually he returned to Costa Rica and was elected as a congressman. He died in San José in 1970. His son, Rafael Angel Calderón Fournier, served as Costa Rica's president in the 1990s.

Carrillo, Braulio (1800–1845). President of Costa Rica on two occasions (1835–1837 and 1838–1842). He served as a judge on the Supreme Court and represented Costa Rica in the Congress of the United Provinces of Central America. He implemented early liberal reforms and withdrew Costa Rica from the United Provinces in 1838. He became increasingly autocratic and passed laws giving the executive considerable authority and making himself president for life. Carrillo was overthrown by Francisco Morazán and Vicente Villaseñor in 1842. He was killed in El Salvador in 1845.

Chinchilla, Laura (1959–). Costa Rica's first female president (2010–). Chinchilla has been a career politician and was one of the vice presidents under Oscar Arias Sánchez (2006–2010). She resigned her vice presidential position in 2008 to launch her campaign for the 2010 presidential election. She won the presidency during a time when many had begun to question the political system in Costa Rica as allegations of corruption surfaced against former presidents and other major political figures. She promised to restore the nation's reputation for education and environmental protections. At 50 years old when she took office, many in Costa Rica viewed her as the leader of a new generation and a fresh start for Costa Rican politics.

Cortés Castro, León (1882–1946). President of Costa Rica (1936–1940). Cortés was a lawyer and educator from Alajuela. During his presidency, he supported the *cafetalero* elite and supported policies favorable to multinational banana interests like the United Fruit Company. As his presidential term expired, Cortés handpicked Rafael Angel Calderón Guardia to be his successor in a backroom deal of questionable integrity. Calderón Guardia and his supporters agreed to support Cortés in the subsequent presidential election, and in exchange Cortés gave Calderón Guardia his support in the 1940 election. But Calderón Guardia reneged on the deal and instead backed Teodor Picado Michalski over Cortés in the 1944 election. Cortés eventually joined the emerging anti-Calderón opposition movement led by Otilio Ulate and José Figueres. He died in March of 1946.

Fallas, Carlos Luis (1909–1966). Labor activist and literary figure who became famous for his affiliation with the Communist Party and his literary works denouncing the United Fruit Company. Fallas, also known as Calufa, was born into poverty and was raised in Limón province on the Caribbean coast. At a young age, he was already working in the coastal banana industry, and there he was exposed to the exploitative working conditions on UFC plantations. He was influenced by early labor movements and eventually helped to lead several major strikes in the 1930s—the most famous of these being the Great Banana Strike of 1934 that involved more than 10,000 disgruntled workers. His most famous literary work was the novel *Mamita Yunai*, which was published in 1941 and described the deplorable working conditions on UFC banana plantations. He also wrote *Marcos Ramírez*, a work that won him a major literary prize from the William Faulkner Foundation. Carlos Luis Fallas died in San José in 1966.

Fernández Oreamuno, Próspero (1834–1885). President of Costa Rica (1882–1885) and one of the liberal leaders who made up "the Olympians." Fernández was elected president after the death of Tomás Guardia in 1882. He continued many of the liberal development programs initiated by Guardia, including installing electric street lights in San José, secularizing education, and allowing civil marriage and divorce. Under his administration Costa Rica entered into the Soto-Keith Contract, which granted U.S. entrepreneur Minor Keith exclusive rights to finish and run Costa Rica's first railroad and awarded the U.S. businessman a 99-year lease on nearly 7 percent of Costa Rica's national territory. He died in office in March of 1885.

Figueres Ferrer, José (1906–1990). President of Costa Rica (1948–1949, 1953–1958, 1970–1974) and leader of the War of National Liberation in 1948. Known as Don Pepe, Figueres was born into a coffee-growing family and developed a social consciousness at an early age. In 1942 he gave a radio address in which he denounced President Rafael Angel Calderón Guardia for corruption and for communist sympathies. He was arrested and sent into exile in Mexico, where he met with other Central American dissidents; the group, which became known as the Caribbean Legion, began plotting to overthrow dictatorial regimes throughout the region. In 1948 Figueres launched a rebellion against the Costa Rican government, accusing Calderón of electoral fraud as the former president sought a second term and claimed victory over Otilio Ulate. Outgoing president Teodoro Picado attempted to quell the insurrection, but Figueres's uprising quickly spread into a full-scale civil war. The War of National Liberation lasted 44 days and ended with the ousting of Picado and with Figueres taking power. In his first administration, he abolished the military, oversaw the writing of the Constitution of 1949, and guaranteed the continuation of social justice measures. Figueres and his supporters founded the National Liberation Party (PLN) and initiated a series of economic reforms that introduced Costa Rica to import substitution industrialization policies. He served two additional terms as president and died on June 8, 1990.

Guardia Gutierrez, Tomás (1831–1882). President of Costa Rica (1870–1876, 1877–1882) and one of "the Olympians," known for his liberal vision and for bringing stability and progress to the nation. Guardia was a military man who rose through the ranks after serving in the National Campaign of 1856 against William Walker. He overthrew the presidency of Jesús Jiménez Zamora in 1870 and ruled in an authoritarian manner in an attempt to bring order to the country. He dissolved Congress and imposed reforms in the military, which allowed him to end the cycle of barracks coups that had plagued the nation throughout much of the nineteenth century. Guardia oversaw the drafting of the Constitution of 1871, a liberal document that remained in place until 1948. His administration expanded the nation's education system, abolished the death penalty, and founded the national archives. He worked to expand Costa Rica's economic base by pursuing the construction of a railroad and by actively courting foreign investors. It was during the Guardia administration that Minor Keith began experimenting with banana exports, eventually developing a major industry and creating the United Fruit Company. Guardia died in office on July 6, 1882.

Jiménez Zamora, Jesús (1823–1897). President of Costa Rica (1863–1866, 1868–1870) who instituted numerous liberal reforms. Jiménez was trained in medicine but entered politics at an early age. He was elected president in 1863 and took office in a peaceful transfer of power from José María Montealegre. He is known for dissolving Congress just a few short months into his presidency and calling for new elections. He also offered asylum to ousted El Salvadoran president Gerardo Barrios, which caused a major diplomatic rift between his administration and other leaders in Central America. He served out his three-year term and handed over power to his successor, José María Castro Madriz, who had won the presidency for a second time. But just two years into the Castro Madriz presidency, Jiménez launched a coup d'état and took power once again. During his second administration, Jiménez declared free and obligatory public education and created a normal school for teacher training. Despite implementing some popular liberal reforms, he faced intense opposition and was overthrown by Tomás Guardia Gutiérrez in 1870. He died in 1897, and his son later served as president on three separate occasions.

Keith, Minor Cooper (1848–1929). U.S. businessman who entered into a contract with the Costa Rican government to complete a railroad connecting the Central Valley to the Caribbean coast. Keith first became involved in the project that was initiated by his uncle, Henry Meiggs. Keith worked on the railroad project and eventually took over after his uncle's death. He also began growing and exporting bananas along Costa Rica's Caribbean coast. After the Costa Rican government defaulted on the foreign loans that were intended to finance the railroad project, Bernardo Soto negotiated with Keith on behalf of the administration of President Próspero Fernández. The result of those negotiations was the 1883 Soto-Keith Contract, in which Minor Keith took over financial responsibility for the railroad and was granted the right to run the railroad after its completion. He also negotiated a lease on 800,000 acres of land, which amounted to roughly 7 percent of Costa Rica's national territory. Keith eventually married the daughter of one of Costa Rica's most powerful political families, giving him significant influence in several presidential administrations. With control of the railroad—which was completed in 1890—and vast landholdings to expand his banana cultivation, Keith became one of the wealthiest and most influential individuals in Costa Rica in the late nineteenth century. Keith eventually combined his banana enterprise with the Boston Fruit Company to form the United Fruit Company. The UFC expanded its activities to other regions of Central America and into northern South America as well. Keith eventually controlled most railroad activities throughout Central America, and the reach of the United Fruit Company continued to expand throughout the twentieth century. Keith died in New York in 1929.

Montealgre Fernández, José María (1815–1887). Costa Rican president (1859–1863), known for his liberal and progressive reform agenda. Like most of Costa Rica's nineteenth-century presidents, Montealgre was born into an elite *cafetalero* family. He studied medicine in Europe but dedicated himself to the coffee export business. He came to power in 1859 as a result of the coup d'état that overthrew Juan Rafael Mora. Montealgre then oversaw the drafting of a new constitution, and he was elected outright to the presidency in 1860 under the electoral system outlined in the new governing document. During his administration he established a Department of Public Works to oversee liberal development programs. He also passed a series of laws to encourage European immigration and the establishment of coffee colonies. Montealgre served out his three-year term, but due to growing hostilities from the Tomás Guardia administration in the 1870s, he moved to the United States. He died there in 1887.

Mora, Juan Rafael (1814–1860). President of Costa Rica (1849–1859) and leader of the National Campaign against U.S. filibuster William Walker. He ruled during the expansion of coffee cultivation, and his administration oversaw a number of expansion and development projects, including major improvements to the highway connecting Cartago and the port of Puntarenas. Mora is best known for leading the army that prevented William Walker from invading Costa Rica in 1856 and for continuing to pursue the U.S. filibuster to drive him from Central America. Mora was deposed in 1859 after attempting to establish a national bank that would have weakened the power of the *cafetalero* elite. One year later he attempted to retake power, but he was captured and executed by firing squad.

Mora Fernández, Juan (1784–1854). First president of Costa Rica under the United Provinces of Central America (1825–1833) and notable liberal leader of the nineteenth century. Trained as a schoolteacher, Mora Fernández became involved in politics during the independence era. He was elected president of the province of Costa Rica in 1825 and served two terms. During his administration, Mora Fernández supported the establishment of Costa Rica's first newspaper, and he supported other important entities such as the first mint and the first printing press. He was declared a national hero in 1848 and died in San José in 1854.

Morazán, Francisco (1792–1842). Honduran general who served as president of the United Provinces of Central America and later as president of Costa Rica. He was committed to the idea of a unified Central American federation and spent his military and political career trying to keep the region politically unified. The United Provinces dissolved in 1838, and Morazán fled to exile in South America in 1840. But he returned in 1842 and launched an attempt to overthrown Costa Rican dictator Braulio Carrillo. On April 11 he signed the Jocote Pact with General Vicente Villaseñor, who had been sent by Carrillo to stop Morazán, but instead the two formed an alliance to depose the dictator. Morazán took power and for several months he pursued plans to restore the United Provinces. Costa Ricans rebelled and overthrew Morazán. He was executed by firing squad on September 15.

Picado Michalski, Teodoro (1900–1960). President of Costa Rica (1944–1948) and leader of the government that was ousted by the War of National Liberation in 1948. Teodoro Picado was a career

politician and became a political ally of President Rafael Angel
Calderón Guardia (1940–1944). He helped to gain passage of Calderón
Guardia's signature Social Guarantees that enacted sweeping social
reforms. In return Calderón Guardia supported Picado's bid for
president in 1944, at times using questionable means to ensure Picado's election. Accusations of corruption and fraud led to the formation
of an opposition movement led by José Figueres Ferrer—a movement
that was aimed more at Calderón Guardia than at Picado. In the disputed 1948 election, Calderón Guardia claimed victory over the
opposition candidate, Otilio Ulate. Picado's support for Calderón
Guardia prompted an insurrection against the government that escalated into the War of National Liberation. After 44 days of civil war
Picado and Calderón Guardia were forced to flee Costa Rica, and José
Figueres took over as interim president. In 1955 Picado and his son led
a group of dissidents from Nicaragua in a failed attempt to overthrow
the Figueres administration. He died in Managua in 1960.

Presbere, Pablo (??–1710). Talamancan native who led a major
uprising against Spanish colonial officials in 1709. The insurrection
was in response to attempts by Spanish religious and political leaders
to bring the southern regions of Costa Rica more fully under control,
and it united many disparate indigenous groups against colonial
authorities. Ten Spanish soldiers and one woman were killed in the
uprising, and dozens of chapels and military outposts were destroyed.
Presbere was later captured along with 500 other natives, and the
group was forced to march to Cartago in a journey that lasted two
weeks and resulted in the deaths of 200 natives. After a brief trial,
Pablo Presbere was executed by Spanish authorities on July 4, 1710.

Santamaría, Juan (??–1856). Peasant soldier who is credited with
sacrificing himself to help the Costa Rican army claim victory over
the invading forces of U.S. filibuster William Walker in the National
Campaign. Very little is known about Santamaría's early life. He
joined the militia put together by Juan Rafael Mora to defend the
nation against the expansionist aims of William Walker, who had
already occupied neighboring Nicaragua. At the Battle of Rivas,
Santamaría charged into a hail of gunfire to set fire to the structure
where Walker's forces were installed. He was fatally wounded in the
process, but not before succeeding in his mission and turning the tide
of the battle in favor of the Costa Rican forces. Decades later, national
leaders appropriated the memory of Juan Santamaría by building statues and memorials to create a sense of unity around the national hero.

Today there are statues to Juan Santamaría throughout the country, and the San José airport is named for him.

Soto Alfaro, Bernardo (1854–1931). President of Costa Rica (1885–1889) and member of "the Olympians." Alfaro Soto served in the cabinet of his predecessor, Próspero Fernández, and he was responsible for negotiating the Soto-Keith contract in 1883, which granted U.S. entrepreneur Minor Keith exclusive rights to finish and run Costa Rica's first railroad and awarded the U.S. businessman a 99-year lease on nearly 7 percent of Costa Rica's national territory. That contract allowed Keith to create the United Fruit Company and to dominate the emerging tropical fruit export industry. Soto assumed the presidency upon the death of Fernández and was later elected to the office in his own right. He continued the liberal reform agenda that had characterized the era of the Olympians. He strengthened education reform laws and continued to promote national development policies by favoring the activities of Minor Keith and sponsoring additional infrastructure projects. His presidency came to an end with the election of 1889, when new electoral freedoms granted by the Olympians allowed the conservative opposition to gain momentum and challenge the liberals. Bernardo Soto died in 1931.

Tinoco Granados, Federico (1868–1931). Dictator who seized power by force (1917–1919) and ousted President Alfredo González Flores. Tinoco had served as the minister of war under the González administration, but he took advantage of growing opposition to the president and carried out his coup on January 27, 1917. Even though he seized power by force, Tinoco was well received at first by Costa Ricans. Nevertheless, he faced considerable challenges from the United States as the administration of Woodrow Wilson refused to recognize the Tinoco regime and exerted intense diplomatic pressure on the country. Despite his initial popularity within Costa Rica, Tinoco ruled as a military dictator, jailing the opposition and limiting personal freedoms. Discontent with his rule began to mount, and Tinoco was eventually forced out by grassroots opposition movements within Costa Rica in 1919. He fled into exile in France, where he died in 1931.

Ulate, Otilio (1891–1973). President of Costa Rica (1949–1953) following the War of National Liberation. Ulate was a journalist by trade and the owner of Costa Rica's main newspaper, *Diario de Costa Rica*. He helped to lead the opposition movement against Rafael Angel Calderón Guardia and ran as the opposition candidate against the former president in the 1948 election. When Calderón Guardia claimed victory in a process that Ulate disputed, the opposition movement rose in revolt against the government. Ulate, along with José Figueres Ferrer, led the War of National Liberation and forced Calderón Guardia and outgoing president Teodoro Picado into exile. In accordance with the Figueres-Ulate Pact, Figueres took over as interim president and called for a constituent assembly to write a new constitution. After 18 months, Ulate finally became president and served a four-year term. He continued the platform of social reform that had been prioritized under Figueres, and Costa Rican women won the right to vote under his administration. He died in San José in 1973.

Vásquez de Coronado, Juan (1523–1565). Spanish explorer and conquistador who became governor of Costa Rica during the age of conquest. He arrived in Costa Rica in 1562 with the charge of bringing local indigenous communities under Spanish control. Vásquez de Coronado became known for his fairness and humane treatment of the native population, and he led successful early efforts to settle areas of the Central Valley. He founded the city of Cartago and transferred the main Spanish settlement there. In 1565 he was granted the title of governor and *adelantado* of Costa Rica, but he died in a shipwreck during his voyage to Spain to receive his title.

Walker, William (1824–1860). U.S. filibuster who led an invasion of Costa Rica in 1856. Walker began his filibustering adventures by attempting to establish an independent republic in northern Mexico in 1853. He was eventually arrested, tried, and acquitted in a U.S. court. In 1855 he set his sights on Nicaragua, launching an invasion and setting up his own government. From there he moved southward toward Costa Rica where President Juan Rafael Mora was putting together an armed force to defend against Walker in a war that became known as the National Campaign. Walker was defeated and retreated back into Nicaragua, where he passed a number of laws, including reestablishing the institution of slavery. Mora continued to pursue Walker and led a Central American coalition against the filibuster, and Walker was captured and sent back to the United States in 1857. He was captured and killed in Honduras in 1860 after leading one last failed filibustering attempt.

Glossary

ALLIANCE FOR PROGRESS—U.S. aid program for Latin America created by President John F. Kennedy that aimed to fight poverty and prevent revolutions. Costa Rica received substantial aid under this program, which allowed national leaders to continue to pursue import substitution industrialization policies.

AUDIENCIA **OF GUATEMALA**—A judicial administrative unit in colonial Latin America that encompassed present-day Guatemala, El Salvador, Belize, Honduras, Nicaragua, Costa Rica, and a small part of Mexico. In 1609 the area was also made a captaincy general, which was a military and political administrative unit under the Spanish system.

AUTHENTIC ANTI-COMMUNIST REVOLUTIONARY ARMY—Group headed by Teodoro Picado, Jr., son of the *calderonista* president ousted in the 1948 War of National Liberation. Aided by the Somoza regime in Nicaragua, the Authentic Anti-Communist Revolutionary Army launched an invasion of Costa Rica in 1954. It was put down with the help of the United States and the Organization of American States.

BATTLE OF RIVAS—1856 battle that pitted a hastily assembled Costa Rican army against the forces of U.S. filibuster William Walker.

Humble foot soldier Juan Santamaría sacrificed himself in an act of bravery that turned the battle in favor of the Costa Rican military and made Santamaría into a national hero.

BELLAVISTA—The military headquarters in San José, built under the dictatorship of Federico Tinoco. Bellavista was the site of José Figueres's public ceremony in which he abolished the nation's standing military. He slammed a sledgehammer into the side of Bellavista as a symbolic gesture.

BOURBON REFORMS—A series of administrative, economic, military, and social reforms dealing with the Latin American colonies and implemented by the Bourbon monarchs in Spain in the eighteenth century. The reforms were intended to make the colonies more efficient, but they also produced a growing sense of resentment toward the Spanish Crown.

CABILDO—A town council in colonial Latin America.

CACAO—Bean from which cocoa products are extracted. Cacao cultivation became an important part of the Costa Rican economy in the last half of the seventeenth century.

CACICAZGO—An indigenous chieftainship in pre-Columbian Costa Rica. Ruled by a *cacique*.

CACIQUE—An Indian chief in pre-Columbian Costa Rica. Ruled over a *cacicazgo*.

CACM (CENTRAL AMERICAN COMMON MARKET)—A regional trade block among Central American nations formed in 1960.

CAFETALEROS—Costa Rica's coffee elite who dominated political and economic development through most of the nineteenth century.

CAFTA-DR (CENTRAL AMERICAN FREE TRADE AGREEMENT)—Free trade agreement between the United States, the Dominican Republic, and the nations of Central America passed in 2004.

CALDERONISTAS—Supporters of Rafael Angel Calderón Guardia in the 1940s.

CAÑAS-JEREZ TREATY—Treaty reached between Costa Rica and Nicaragua in 1858 to settle border disputes between the two countries.

CARIBBEAN LEGION—A group of Central American and Caribbean political activists formed in the 1940s and dedicated to overthrowing dictators in the region. José Figueres was a member of the Caribbean Legion, and other members provided vital assistance to him in the War of National Liberation.

CBI (CARIBBEAN BASIN INITIATIVE)—A program created by U.S. president Ronald Reagan in 1983 that offered economic aid to Central American and Caribbean nations in the hope of stabilizing governments through economic growth and preventing the spread of revolutions.

CENPRO (CENTER FOR THE PROMOTION OF EXPORTS AND INVESTMENTS)—The export promotion agency of the Costa Rican government, initially formed in 1968 to promote nontraditional exports to markets outside of Central America.

CENTRO PARA EL ESTUDIO DE LOS PROBLEMAS NACIO-NALES (CENTER FOR THE STUDY OF NATIONAL PROBLEMS, ALSO KNOWN AS EL CENTRO OR CEPN)—A staunchly anticommunist think tank of young political activists and intellectuals in the 1940s. It became part of a formal opposition movement to the government of Rafael Angel Calderón Guardia and members of El Centro launched the War of National Liberation in 1948.

CHACRAS—Small farms in colonial Costa Rica, often public lands surrounding cities that were rented out to farmers.

CINDE (COSTA RICAN COALITION OF DEVELOPMENT INI-TIATIVES)—A private-sector, nonpartisan export and investment promotion organization created in 1982 by 76 national business leaders. It received funding from USAID and was empowered by the Costa Rican government to promote measures that would expand the export market and attract direct foreign investment.

CLAYTON-BULWER TREATY—Treaty negotiated in 1850 between the United States and the British, under which both sides agreed not to pursue exclusive rights over a trans-isthmian canal in Central America.

CODESA (COSTA RICAN DEVELOPMENT CORPORATION)—Government agency created in 1972 to operate as a majority partner and enter into joint ventures with private companies. CODESA was part of the Costa Rican government's strategy to encourage national involvement in industry by providing investment assistance. It became an inefficient and bloated government bureaucracy.

COFRADÍAS—Associations of Catholic laymen.

CONSTITUTION OF 1871—Governing document put in place by President Tomás Guardia. It called for three branches of government and open suffrage, but it also created a powerful executive with considerable authority. This constitution was in effect until it was replaced by the Constitution of 1949.

CONSTITUTION OF 1949—Costa Rica's current governing document. It was written by the Founding Junta during the period of transitional government following the War of National Liberation.

CONSTITUTION OF CÁDIZ—Spain's first constitution, written in 1812. It was a liberal document that inspired many independence leaders in Latin America. Liberal constitutions throughout Latin America in the nineteenth century were modeled after the Constitution of Cádiz.

CONSTITUTIONAL DEMOCRATIC PARTY (PARTIDO CONSTITUCIONAL DEMOCRÁTICO)—One of Costa Rica's first formal political parties, formed in the late nineteenth century by elite conservative interests.

CONTADORA GROUP—A group made up of leaders from Panama, Mexico, Venezuela, and Colombia that attempted to mediate a resolution to Central American violence between 1983 and 1985.

CONTRAS—Right-wing paramilitary rebels who organized to destabilize the Sandinista regime in Nicaragua.

CORTESISTAS—Supporters of León Cortés in the 1940s.

CTCR (CONFEDERACIÓN DE TRABAJADORES DE COSTA RICA, OR CONFEDERATION OF COSTA RICAN WORKERS)—Costa Rica's first nationwide labor union, formed in 1943.

DEPENDENCY THEORY—An economic theory promoted by ECLAC economists that suggested that industrialized nations were preventing economic progress from taking root in Latin America. Advocates of dependency theory advocated import substitution industrialization as a strategy through which Latin American nations could pursue their own industrial expansion.

ECLAC (ECONOMIC COMMISSION FOR LATIN AMERICA AND THE CARIBBEAN)—Commission of the United Nations formed in 1948 to address the economic needs of Latin American nations. ECLAC economists urged Latin American leaders to adopt economic policies based on import substitution industrialization in the 1950s.

EL CENTRO—*See* Centro para el Estudio de los Problemas Nacionales.

ELECTORAL TRIBUNAL—A politically impartial body that is charged with overseeing Costa Rican elections. It is considered a fourth branch of government in the Constitution of 1949.

ENCOMIENDA—A Crown grant to Spanish conquistadores in the Americas giving them jurisdiction over a group of natives. Spanish *encomenderos* could make labor demands and exact tribute payments from natives, and in exchange Spaniards were to provide security and religious conversion.

ENTREPRENEUR STATE—A term referring to state-led development programs and high levels of government involvement in the promotion of industry under import substitution industrialization programs.

ESQUIPULAS (I & II)—Peace agreements brokered by Costa Rican president Oscar Arias Sánchez that brought an end to the violence that plagued Central America in the 1980s and eventually won Arias a Nobel Peace Prize.

EXPORT PROCESSING ZONE AND INDUSTRIAL PARKS LAW—Law passed in 1981 that established free trade zones in ports and major cities in Costa Rica.

FIGUERES-ULATE PACT—Agreement between José Figueres and Otilio Ulate at the conclusion of the War of National Liberation in 1948. The pact stipulated a revolutionary junta would rule during a transitional period of 18 months, during which time the junta would convene an assembly to draft a new constitution. After the transitional period, the junta would recognize Ulate as the first constitutional president of the Second Republic.

FILIBUSTERS—U.S. soldiers of fortune who launched their own private expeditions into Latin America in the nineteenth century in an attempt to claim new lands for the United States. One of the most famous filibusters was William Walker, who occupied Nicaragua and attempted to extend his reach into Costa Rica in 1856.

FORESTRY LAW—Law passed in 1969 that established basic protections for forests and natural resources in Costa Rica.

FOUNDING JUNTA—Ruling body, led by José Figueres, that served for 18 months following the War of National Liberation in 1948 and that wrote the Constitution of 1949.

GENERATION OF 48—Term referring to José Figueres and his allies who participated in the War of National Liberation and formed the initial leadership of the Partido Liberación Nacional.

GREAT BANANA STRIKE—Major work stoppage on a United Fruit Company plantation in 1934 involving more than 10,000 disgruntled workers.

GUANACASTE—An administrative province in northwestern Costa Rica. The Gaunacaste region was home to the largest of Costa Rica's native civilizations in the pre-Columbian era, and its contested border with Nicaragua made it the site of a number of boundary disputes in the nineteenth century.

HACENDADO—Owner of a large landed estate.

HACIENDA—Large landed estate.

ICT (INSTITUTO COSTARRICENSE DE TURISMO, OR INSTI-TUTE OF COSTA RICAN TOURISM)—Government agency formed in 1955 to attract foreign travelers.

ISI (IMPORT SUBSTITUTION INDUSTRIALIZATION)—Economic program popular in Latin America in the last half of the twentieth century. It called for protectionist trade measures to allow local manufacturers to develop durable consumer goods industries. ISI policies relied on significant government involvement in the economic sector and generally produced inefficient industries and inferior products.

ISTHMUS OF RIVAS—Narrow stretch of land in northern Costa Rica along the Nicaraguan border. It connects Lake Nicaragua with the Pacific Ocean, and its strategic location and potential as a site of a trans-isthmian canal made it the subject of border disputes between the two countries in the nineteenth century.

JOCOTE PACT—An agreement in 1842 between Francisco Morazán, who had launched an invasion of Costa Rica, and Vicente Villaseñor, who had been sent by President Braulio Carrillo to repel the invading force. Under the agreement, the two generals joined forces and overthrew Carrillo.

JUNTA—A governing council.

LA NEGRITA—The Black Madonna, patron saint of Costa Rica, named for a small black figurine of the Virgin Mary discovered by a peasant woman in 1635. Also known as the Virgen de los Angeles.

LA PASADA—Annual procession to celebrate the feast day of the Virgen de los Angeles, Costa Rica's patron saint. The statue of *La Negrita* is moved from the Basilica to the main cathedral in Cartago.

LATIFUNDIO—A system of land tenure characterized by very large estates held by relatively few elites. The system had its roots in colonial Latin American systems of landholding and became particularly prevalent throughout the nineteenth century. Costa Rican coffee and banana estates have historically exhibited many characteristics of *latifundio*.

LAW ON INDIVIDUAL RIGHTS—Law passed in 1877 by President Tomás Guardia. It established personal liberties such as freedom of religion, freedom of expression, rights to privacy, and freedom of movement.

LEY DE LA AMBULANCIA—A cumbersome administrative system, created in 1834 by Rafael Gallegos, whereby the seat of the executive in Costa Rica rotated among the four principal cities of Cartago, Heredia, Alajuela, and San José. The law was abolished one year later by President Braulio Carrillo in an act that provoked the War of the League.

LEY GENERAL DE EDUCACIÓN COMÚN—Law passed in 1885 by Bernardo Soto that created a public school system. Specifically it mandated primary schooling for both boys and girls, established a national curriculum for primary education, called for age-specific instruction, and diminished the influence of the Catholic Church over school curriculum.

LIBERACIÓN—The political philosophy articulated by José Figueres and his supporters in the years following the 1948 War for National Liberation. *Liberación* focused on social reform, a mixed economy, and institutionalized nationalism.

LIBERALISM—A nineteenth-century political philosophy, common throughout Latin America, that privileged secularism, modernization, private property, individualism, laissez faire economic policies, and the development of commodity export markets. Most Costa Rican political leaders of the nineteenth century were influenced by liberalism.

LIBERAL PROGRESSIVE PARTY—One of Costa Rica's first formal political parties, formed in the late nineteenth century by elite liberal interests.

LIGA FEMINISTA **(COSTA RICAN FEMINIST LEAGUE OR CRFL)**—Women's activist group formed in 1923. The CRFL demanded greater equality for women in the workplace and in the political arena. The group tried unsuccessfully to push through women's suffrage in 1925.

LIMÓN WORKERS' FEDERATION—Labor movement formed by West Indian banana workers in Limón in the early twentieth century.

LOST DECADE—Term referring to the economic stagnation experienced throughout Latin America in the 1980s as a result of severe austerity measures imposed by the International Monetary Fund after nations defaulted on foreign loans.

MAMITA YUNAI—Novel by Costa Rican literary figure and labor activist Carlos Luis Fallas in 1941. The novel describes the labor exploitation and other injustices of a United Fruit Company banana plantation in the province of Limón.

MANIFEST DESTINY—A commonly held notion in the United States in the nineteenth century, which stated that the United States had a God-given mission to expand its territory across the continent and spread U.S. political, economic, and religious institutions. Some political leaders and filibusters used the notion of Manifest Destiny to justify U.S. expansion into Latin America.

MIXED ECONOMY—Economic program implemented by José Figueres and his supporters in the Partido Liberación Nacional from the 1950s to the 1970s. It called for private ownership combined with degrees of government oversight and control. The mixed economy concept gave rise to import substitution industrialization in Costa Rica, and government involvement in the economy expanded significantly.

NATIONAL CAMPAIGN—Military campaign launched by Costa Rican president Rafael Mora in 1856 to drive the forces of U.S. filibuster William Walker from Central America.

NEOLIBERALISM—Economic policies implemented by most Latin American nations in the 1980s in an attempt to recover from the debt crisis. Neoliberal reforms included trade liberalization, attracting foreign investments, privatizing government-owned industry, and cutting social spending.

NICOYA PENINSULA—Large peninsula on Costa Rica's northwest coast.

NUEVO CARTAGO Y COSTA RICA—Administrative province created by the Spanish Crown in 1540. It encompassed present-day Nicaragua, Costa Rica, and Panama, and it was reorganized in 1565 with the creation of Costa Rica Province.

OAS (ORGANIZATION OF AMERICAN STATES)—Regional organization chartered in 1948 to maintain peace, stability, and security in the Western Hemisphere.

OLYMPIANS—Term self-ascribed by Presidents Tomás Guardia, Próspero Fernández, and Bernardo Soto in the 1870s and 1880s to describe and promote their staunch political liberalism.

PACT OF THE MEXICAN EMBASSY—Treaty signed on April 18, 1948 that ended the War of National Liberation.

PANAMA DISEASE—A soil disease that inflicts banana plantation lands. Panama disease struck United Fruit Company lands in eastern

Costa Rica and compelled the company to relocate much of its cultivation to the Pacific coast in the 1930s.

PARALLEL STATE—Refers to a secret network of U.S.-backed schools, private banks, and development agencies whose operations in Costa Rica were uncovered in 1988.

PATRONATO REAL—Royal patronage. Describes the relationship between the Spanish Crown and the Catholic Church in Latin America during the colonial period. Under this system, the Spanish Crown could supervise church appointments, revenue, and other activities.

PLN (PARTIDO LIBERACIÓN NACIONAL, OR NATIONAL LIBERATION PARTY)—Political party formed by José Figueres in 1951 to articulate the *liberación* agenda.

POSITIVISM—A philosophy popular in Latin America in the late nineteenth century that privileged the role of science in the pursuit of knowledge. Positivists promoted modernization and empirical thinking, and they became influential in many Latin American governments.

PUSC (PARTIDO DE UNIDAD SOCIALCRISTIANA, OR SOCIAL CHRISTIAN UNITY PARTY)—Opposition party to the Partido Liberación Nacional, formed in 1977.

PVP (PARTIDO VANGUARDIA POPULAR, OR PEOPLE'S VANGUARD PARTY)—Created in 1943 by the former Communist Party of Costa Rica.

REFORMIST PARTY—Short-lived political party formed by Catholic priest, scholar, and politician Jorge Volio Jiménez in 1924. The party became an influential presence in the administration of Ricardo Jiménez and pushed through reforms such as the institution of a secret ballot and an expansion of social welfare programs.

SANDINISTAS—Socialist-oriented leaders in Nicaragua in the 1980s.

SAN JUAN RIVER—Costa Rica's largest river. It runs more than 100 miles along the Costa Rica–Nicaragua border and connects Lake Nicaragua to the Caribbean Sea. In the nineteenth century it was a favored location for the construction of a trans-isthmian canal. Navigation rights along the river and boundary disputes in the region were a long-standing source of conflict between Costa Rica and Nicaragua.

SAN PABLO **INCIDENT**—The sinking of United Fruit Company cargo ship the *San Pablo* by Nazi submarines in 1942. The episode eventually led to protests and riots against the national government in San José.

SECOND REPUBLIC—José Figueres's vision for Costa Rica's future after the War of National Liberation in 1948. He convened the Founding Junta to write a new constitution and oversee new democratic elections.

SIGATOKA—A disease that inflicts banana plants. It appeared on United Fruit Company plantations in Costa Rica in the 1930s.

SOCIAL DEMOCRATIC PARTY—Political party formed in 1945 in opposition to Rafael Angel Calderón Guardia.

SOCIAL GUARANTEES—A series of constitutional amendments passed by Rafael Angel Calderón Guardia in 1943 that established a social security system, including health care coverage and the protection of workers' rights.

SOLIDARISMO—A system for labor organizing introduced in the 1990s that guarantees access to social services but limits workers' rights of collective bargaining.

SOTO-KEITH CONTRACT—Contract reached between Bernardo Soto and U.S. entrepreneur Minor Keith in 1883 under which Keith renegotiated Costa Rica's external railroad debt with London investors. Keith absorbed much of the financial risk to complete the railroad project in exchange for direct control over the administration of the rail lines. He also received a 99-year lease on 800,000 acres of property in the Caribbean lowlands—a grant that amounted to roughly 7 percent of Costa Rica's national territory.

TICO-COMMUNISM—A moderate version of communism that emerged in Costa Rica in the 1930s. Tico-Communist leaders advocated some social justice reform primarily aimed at improving workers' lives.

TIERRAS BALDÍOS—Large swaths of public land in unoccupied or frontier regions in colonial and early nineteenth century Costa Rica. Also known as *tierras públicas.*

TIERRAS DE LEGUA—Costa Rican land tenure system of the colonial period and early nineteenth century under which municipal governments rented large tracts of communal land to users.

TIERRAS PÚBLICAS—*See* tierras baldíos.

TOURISM INVESTMENT INCENTIVES LAW—Law passed in 1985 that granted tax exemptions and other incentives to tourism-related businesses in an effort to expand the tourism industry.

TRIBUTE—Payment obligations required by the Spanish Crown of native inhabitants of Costa Rica and elsewhere in Latin America. Tribute payments could be made in specie, but they were most often made in kind.

UFC (UNITED FRUIT COMPANY)—Banana and tropical fruit company formed by U.S. entrepreneur Minor Keith. The UFC became enormously powerful in Costa Rica and in other areas of Latin America, exerting influence over political and economic decisions throughout the twentieth century.

UNITED PROVINCES OF CENTRAL AMERICA—A federation established after achieving independence from Spain in 1823 by present-day Guatemala, El Salvador, Honduras, Nicaragua, and Costa Rica. Beset from the start by regional rivalries, political infighting, and inefficient bureaucracy, the United Provinces disbanded in 1838.

USAID (UNITED STATES AGENCY FOR INTERNATIONAL DEVELOPMENT)—A U.S. government–backed development agency created in 1961 that provided aid packages to Latin America, particularly in the aftermath of the debt crisis in the 1980s.

VICEROYALTY OF NEW SPAIN—A large administrative unit of the Spanish colonies in the Americas. Initially created in 1521, the viceroyalty of New Spain eventually encompassed all of colonial Mexico, all of the Spanish Caribbean, the Philippines and other Pacific colonial possessions, and all of Central America as far south as Costa Rica.

VIRGEN DE LOS ANGELES—The patron saint of Costa Rica, named for a small black figurine of the Virgin Mary discovered by a peasant woman in 1635. Also known as *La Negrita*.

WAR OF NATIONAL LIBERATION—A 44-day civil war carried out in 1948 by the opposition forces of José Figueres against the supporters of Rafael Angel Calderón Guardia.

WAR OF THE LEAGUE—A short-lived civil war in 1835 that erupted when Costa Rican president Braulio Carrillo abolished the *Ley de la ambulancia*, which had created a power-sharing system among Costa Rica's four main cities. Cartago, Heredia, and Alajuela rose in revolt against San José, but the insurrection was quickly put down, and San José became the nation's sole administrative center.

WILDLIFE CONSERVATION LAW—Law passed in 1956 that specified that wildlife was part of Costa Rica's natural resources.

ZAMBOS MOSQUITOS—Interracial descendants of escaped African slaves and the indigenous population, who occupied the eastern portion of Costa Rica and Nicaragua in the seventeenth and eighteenth centuries.

Bibliographic Essay

For an excellent general history of Costa Rica, see Iván Molina Jiménez and Palmer Steven, *The History of Costa Rica: Brief, Up-to-Date and Illustrated* (San José, Costa Rica: Editorial de la Universidad de Costa Rica, 1998). Two excellent historical readers that include scholarly essays as well as an array of primary sources are Steven Paul Palmer and Iván Molina Jiménez, *The Costa Rica Reader: History, Culture, Politics* (Durham, NC: Duke University Press, 2004), and Marc Edelman and Joanne Kenen, *The Costa Rica Reader* (New York: Grove Weidenfeld, 1989). For basic overviews organized thematically, see Mavis Hiltunen Biesanz, Richard Biesanz, and Karen Zubris Biesanz, *The Ticos: Culture and Social Change in Costa Rica* (Boulder, CO: Lynne Rienner, 1999), and Meg Tyler Mitchell and Scott Pentzer, *Costa Rica: A Global Studies Handbook* (Santa Barbara, CA: ABC-CLIO, 2008). Other general works that provide an overview of Costa Rican history in the context of Central America include Leslie Bethell, *Central America since Independence* (New York: Cambridge University Press, 1991), and Edelberto Torres-Rivas, *History and Society in Central America* (Austin: University of Texas Press, 1993).

Most studies of the pre-Columbian era in Costa Rica come from the field of archaeology and focus on artifacts. Some excellent sources specifically on Costa Rica include Doris Stone, *Pre-Columbian Man in Costa Rica* (Cambridge, MA: Peabody Museum Press, 1977), and Mark Miller Graham and Julie Jones, *Jade in Ancient Costa Rica* (New York: Metropolitan Museum of Art, 1998). Other studies examine ancient cultures of the Central American region: Frederick W. Lange and Doris Stone, *The Archaeology of Lower Central America* (Albuquerque: University of New Mexico Press, 1984); Jeffrey Quilter and John W. Hoopes, *Gold and Power in Ancient Costa Rica, Panama, and Colombia: A Symposium at Dumbarton Oaks, 9 and 10 October 1999* (Washington, DC: Dumbarton Oaks Research Library and Collections, 2003); Mark Miller Graham, *Reinterpreting Prehistory of Central America* (Niwot: University Press of Colorado, 1993); and Frederick W. Lange, *Precolumbian Jade: New Geological and Cultural Interpretations* (Salt Lake City: University of Utah Press, 1993).

There are few comprehensive histories in English of the colonial period in Costa Rica. But a number of specialized studies on narrow topics do exist. For the conquest era, see Ricardo Fernández Guardia, *History of the Discovery and Conquest of Costa Rica* (New York: Gordon Press, 1978). For studies of the Costa Rican economy, see Elizabeth F. Keithan, "Cacao in Costa Rica," *Economic Geography* 16, no. 1 (1940): 79–86, and Lowell Gudmundson, *Costa Rica before Coffee: Society and Economy on the Eve of the Export Boom* (Baton Rouge: Louisiana State University Press, 1986). An excellent examination of race in colonial Costa Rica is Michael D. Olien, "Black and Part-Black Populations in Colonial Costa Rica: Ethnohistorical Resources and Problems," *Ethnohistory* 27, no. 1 (1980): 13–29. For the history and legacy of Costa Rica's patron saint, the Virgen de Los Angeles, see Russell Leigh Sharman, "Re/Making La Negrita: Culture as an Aesthetic System in Costa Rica," *American Anthropologist* 108, no. 4 (2006): 842–53.

Many studies of the nineteenth century examine Costa Rica in the context of the rest of Central America. One example that begins in the colonial era and continues through the decades following independence is Miles L. Wortman, *Government and Society in Central America, 1680–1840* (New York: Columbia University Press, 1982). An excellent study of the rise of liberalism in all of Central America is James Mahoney, *The Legacies of Liberalism: Path Dependence and Political Regimes in Central America* (Baltimore: Johns Hopkins University Press, 2001). On early nineteenth-century Costa Rican society, see Lowell Gudmundson, "The Expropriation of Pious and Corporate Properties in Costa Rica, 1805–1860: Patterns in the Consolidation of a National Elite," *The Americas* 39, no. 3 (1983): 281–303. For trade and infrastructure development, see Richard J. Houk, "The Development of Foreign

Trade and Communication in Costa Rica to the Construction of the First Railway," *The Americas* 10, no. 2 (1953): 197–209. Two fascinating studies on the emergence of nationalism in the nineteenth century are Steven Palmer, "Getting to Know the Unknown Soldier: Official Nationalism in Liberal Costa Rica, 1880–1900," *Journal of Latin American Studies* 25, no. 1 (1993): 45–72, and Marshall C. Eakin, "The Origins of Modern Science in Costa Rica: The Instituto Físico-Geográfico Nacional, 1887–1904," *Latin American Research Review* 34, no. 1 (1999): 123–50. For sources on Costa Rica's diplomatic history as part of larger trends in Central America, see Thomas D. Schoonover, *The French in Central America: Culture and Commerce, 1820–1930* (Wilmington, DE: SR Press, 2000), and Thomas David Schoonover, *The United States in Central America, 1860–1911: Episodes of Social Imperialism and Imperial Rivalry in the World System* (Durham, NC: Duke University Press, 1991). An excellent history of early education programs and the mobilization of women is Steven Palmer and Gladys Rojas Chaves, "Educating Señorita: Teacher Training, Social Mobility, and the Birth of Costa Rican Feminism, 1885–1925," *Hispanic American Historical Review* 1, no. 1 (1998): 45–82.

The United Fruit Company (UFC) historically played a fundamental role in Costa Rican economic and social development. Much scholarship has been generated examining the company and its impact on Costa Rica and other Latin American nations. General histories of the UFC include Peter Chapman, *Bananas: How the United Fruit Company Shaped the World* (Canongate: New York, 2007); Steve Striffler and Mark Moberg, *Banana Wars: Power, Production, and History in the Americas* (Durham, NC: Duke University Press, 2003); Stacy May and Galo Plaza, *The United Fruit Company in Latin America* (New York: Arno Press, 1976); Thomas P. McCann and Henry Scammell, *An American Company: The Tragedy of United Fruit* (New York: Crown Publishers, 1976); and Lester D. Langley and Thomas David Schoonover, *The Banana Men: American Mercenaries and Entrepreneurs in Central America, 1880–1930* (Lexington: University Press of Kentucky, 1995). For a dated but informative study of the banana industry in Costa Rica, see Clarence F. Jones and Paul C. Morrison, "Evolution of the Banana Industry of Costa Rica," *Economic Geography* 28, no. 1 (1952): 1–19.

Many other specialized studies examine race and labor issues on UFC plantations: Aviva Chomsky, *West Indian Workers and the United Fruit Company in Costa Rica, 1870–1940* (Baton Rouge: Louisiana State University Press, 1996); Elisavinda Echeverri-Gent, "Forgotten Workers: British West Indians and the Early Days of the Banana Industry in Costa Rica and Honduras," *Journal of Latin American Studies* 24, no. 2 (1992): 275–308; Philippe I. Bourgois, *Ethnicity at Work: Divided Labor on a Central American Banana Plantation* (Baltimore, MD: Johns Hopkins University Press, 1989); Avi Chomsky, "Afro-Jamaican Traditions and Labor Organizing on United Fruit Company Plantations in Costa Rica, 1910," *Journal of Social History* 28, no. 4 (1995): 837–55; Ronald N. Harpelle, "Racism and Nationalism in the Creation of Costa Rica's Pacific Coast Banana Enclave," *The Americas* 56, no. 3 (2000): 29–51; Trevor W. Purcell, *Banana Fallout: Class, Color, and Culture among West Indians in Costa Rica* (Los Angeles: University of California, 1993); Ronald N. Harpelle, "The Social and Political Integration of West Indians in Costa Rica: 1930–50," *Journal of Latin American Studies* 25, no. 1 (1993): 103–120; Charles W. Koch, "Jamaican Blacks and Their Descendants in Costa Rica," *Social and Economic Studies* 26, no. 3 (1977): 339–61; and Lowell Gudmundson and Justin Wolfe, *Blacks and Blackness in Central America: Between Race and Place* (Durham, NC: Duke University Press, 2010). For an examination of labor and gender, see Lara Putnam, *The Company They Kept: Migrants and the Politics of Gender in Caribbean Costa Rica, 1870–1960* (Durham: University of North Carolina Press, 2002).

Specialized topics on twentieth-century Costa Rica include works on the Tinoco era: Richard V. Salisbury, "Domestic Politics and Foreign Policy: Costa Rica's Stand on Recognition, 1923–1934," *Hispanic American Historical Review* 54, no. 3 (1974): 453–78; George W. Baker, Jr., "Woodrow Wilson's Use of the Non-Recognition Policy in Costa Rica," *The Americas* 22, no. 1 (1965): 3–21; and Richard Salisbury, "Costa Rica and the 1920–1921 Union Movement: A Reassessment," *Journal of Interamerican Studies and World Affairs* 19, no. 3 (1977): 393–418. For a general overview of diplomacy in Central America, including excellent sections on Costa Rica, see Walter LaFeber, *Inevitable Revolutions: The United States in Central America* (New York: Norton, 1993). For studies of women and gender, see Ilse Abshagen Leitinger, *The Costa Rican Women's Movement: A Reader* (Pittsburgh, PA: University of Pittsburgh Press, 1997), and Nicola Foote, "Rethinking Race, Gender and Citizenship: Black West Indian Women in Costa Rica, c. 1920–1940," *Bulletin of Latin American Research* 23, no. 2 (2004): 198–212. On literacy, see Iván Molina and Steven Palmer, "Popular Literacy in a Tropical Democracy: Costa Rica 1850–1950," *Past & Present*, no. 184 (2004): 169–207.

Costa Rica's War of National Liberation has attracted the attention of scholars, and a number of studies examine the events leading up to and following the 1948 civil war. On the Calderón era, see Mark B. Rosenberg, "Social Reform in Costa Rica: Social Security and the

Presidency of Rafael Angel Calderón," *Hispanic American Historical Review* 61, no. 2 (1981): 278–96, and Eugene D. Miller, "Labour and the War-Time Alliance in Costa Rica 1943–1948," *Journal of Latin American Studies* 25, no. 3 (1993): 515–41. On the 1948 civil war, see John Patrick Bell, *Crisis in Costa Rica: The 1948 Revolution* (Austin: University of Texas Press, 1971); Fabrice Edouard Lehoucq, "Class Conflict, Political Crisis and the Breakdown of Democratic Practices in Costa Rica: Reassessing the Origins of the 1948 Civil War," *Journal of Latin American Studies* 23, no. 1 (1991): 37–60; Kyle Longley, "Peaceful Costa Rica, the First Battleground: The United States and the Costa Rican Revolution of 1948," *The Americas* 50, no. 2 (1993): 149–75; and Marcia Olander, "Costa Rica in 1948: Cold War or Local War?" *The Americas* 52, no. 4 (1996): 465–93. Two excellent studies of José Figueres are Charles D. Ameringer, *Don Pepe: A Political Biography of José Figueres of Costa Rica* (Albuquerque: University of New Mexico Press, 1978), and Kyle Longley, *The Sparrow and the Hawk: Costa Rica and the United States during the Rise of José Figueres* (Tuscaloosa: University of Alabama Press, 1997), which focuses on Costa Rican-U.S. diplomacy. For a detailed examination of the emergence of the Partido Liberación Nacional, see Susanne Bodenheimer, "The Social Democratic Ideology in Latin America: The Case of Costa Rica's Partido Liberación Nacional," *Caribbean Studies* 10, no. 3 (1970): 49–96.

Costa Rica's experiences with import substitution industrialization from the 1950s to the 1970s and the economic reform efforts that followed in the 1980s have been the subject of much scholarship in recent years. An older study of the initial attempts at economic integration in Central America is James D. Cochrane, "Costa Rica, Panama and Central American Economic Integration," *Journal of Inter-American Studies* 7, no. 3 (1965): 331–44. The events leading up the 1980s debt crisis are covered in Mitchell A. Seligson and Edward N. Muller, "Democratic Stability and Economic Crisis: Costa Rica, 1978–1983," *International Studies Quarterly* 31, no. 3 (1987): 301–326. Other studies consider the attempts at economic reform in the 1980s. General studies of Costa Rican and Central American economic reform include Mary A. Clark, *Gradual Economic Reform in Latin America: The Costa Rican Experience* (Albany: State University of New York Press, 2001); Eduardo Lizano Fait, *Economic Policy Making: Lessons from Costa Rica* (San Francisco: ICS Press, 1991); and Jolyne Melmed-Sanjak, Carlos Santiago, and Enrique Magid Alvin, *Recovery or Relapse in the Global Economy: Comparative Perspectives on Restructuring in Central America* (Westport, CT: Praeger, 1993). Two works that specifically examine the trend to replace import substitution industrialization policies with export-led growth policies are Mary A. Clark, "Nontraditional Export Promotion in Costa Rica: Sustaining Export-Led Growth," *Journal of Interamerican Studies and World Affairs* 37, no. 2 (1995): 181–223, and Mary A. Clark, "Transnational Alliances and Development Policy in Latin America: Nontraditional Export Promotion in Costa Rica," *Latin American Research Review* 32, no. 2 (1997): 71–97. A study of the impact of neoliberal reform on public employees can be found in Diego Sánchez Ancochea, "Domestic Capital, Civil Servants and the State: Costa Rica and the Dominican Republic under Globalisation," *Journal of Latin American Studies* 37, no. 4 (2005): 693–726.

Many studies exist that examine Central American violence in the 1980s and Costa Rica's role in the peace process. For a general overview of Central American conflict with a particular view of the role of the United States, see William M. LeoGrande, *Our Own Backyard: The United States in Central America, 1977–1992* (Chapel Hill: University of North Carolina Press, 1998), and Thomas W. Walker and Ariel C. Armony, *Repression, Resistance, and Democratic Transition in Central America* (Wilmington, DE: Scholarly Resources, 2000). Many studies were published in the mid-1980s that provide a contemporaneous analysis of the unrest. See Kenneth M. Coleman and George C. Herring, *The Central American Crisis: Sources of Conflict and the Failure of U.S. Policy* (Wilmington, DE: Scholarly Resources, 1985); Martin Diskin, *Trouble in Our Backyard: Central America and the United States in the Eighties* (New York: Pantheon Books, 1983); Robert S. Leiken, *Central America: Anatomy of Conflict* (New York: Pergamon Press, 1984); and Steve C. Ropp and James A. Morris, *Central America: Crisis and Adaptation* (Albuquerque: University of New Mexico Press, 1984). For an accessible biography of Oscar Arias Sánchez and an account of his role in the peace process, see Vicki Cox, *Oscar Arias Sánchez: Bringing Peace to Central America* (New York: Chelsea House, 2007).

Costa Rica's reputation for environmental protection has generated considerable scholarship. Two excellent overviews of the country's environmental history are Sterling Evans, *The Green Republic: A Conservation History of Costa Rica* (Austin: University of Texas Press, 1999), and Luis Antonio Vivanco, *Green Encounters: Shaping and Contesting Environmentalism in Rural Costa Rica* (New York: Berghahn Books, 2006). Other more specialized studies include Stuart McCook, " 'Giving Plants a Civil Status': Scientific Representations of Nature and Nation in Costa Rica and Venezuela, 1885–1935," *The Americas* 58, no. 4 (2002): 513–36; Charles D. Brockett and Robert R. Gottfried, "State Policies and the Preservation of Forest Cover: Lessons from Contrasting Public-Policy Regimes in Costa Rica," *Latin American*

Research Review 37, no. 1 (2002): 7–40; Eduardo Silva, "The Politics of Sustainable Development: Native Forest Policy in Chile, Venezuela, Costa Rica and Mexico," *Journal of Latin American Studies* 29, no. 2 (1997): 457–93; Anja Nygren, "Deforestation in Costa Rica: An Examination of Social and Historical Factors," *Forest & Conservation History* 39, no. 1 (1995): 27–35; and Lori Ann Thrupp, "Pesticides and Policies: Approaches to Pest-Control Dilemmas in Nicaragua and Costa Rica," *Latin American Perspectives* 15, no. 4 (1988): 37–70.

For studies on the history of tourism in Costa Rica, see David Matarrita-Cascante, "Tourism Development in Costa Rica: History and Trends," *e-Review of Tourism Research (eRTR)* 8, no. 6 (2010): 136–56, and Brian Coffey, "Investment Incentives as a Means of Encouraging Tourism Development: The Case of Costa Rica," *Bulletin of Latin American Research* 12, no. 1 (1993): 83–90.

Index

Note: "p" indicates a photo

Accessory Transit Company, 59–60
Acción Demócrata, 118
Acosta García, Julio, 91
Agriculture, 3, 7–8, 48, 63, 99,
  156; colonial period, 21,
  23–24, 27–30, 32; commodity
  exports, 42–47, 73–74, 76,
  80, 93, 97, 129, 136;
  diversification, 117, 130, 135,
  141; environmental impact,
  99, 150–52; pre-Columbian,
  16, 18. *See also* Bananas
Aguilar, Manuel, 41
Alajuela, 10, 29, 102;
  independence, 38–39; War of
  National Liberation, 109–10;
  War of the League, 41
Alfaro Zamora, José María, 53

Alliance for Progress, 130–31;
  CACM, 132–33
Angel Rodríguez, Miguel, 158
Anti-imperialism, 87–89. *See also*
  UFC
Arbenz, Jacobo, 124, 125, 130–31
Arce, Manuel José, 42
Arévalo, Juan José, 109
Arias Sánchez, Oscar: Central
  American peace plan, 144–51,
  150p; and neoliberalism, 159;
  Nobel Peace Prize, 10, 144,
  149–51, 150p; second
  presidency, 157–58; and
  tourism, 154
Army of National Liberation,
  109–10. *See also* War of
  National Liberation

Artisan's and Labourer's
    Union, 86
Audiencia of Guatemala, 23, 30;
    independence, 36, 38
Austerity, 128, 139–41
Authentic Anti-Communist
    Revolutionary Army, 125

Banana Massacre, Colombia,
    79–80
Bananas, 3, 7, 8, 79–80, 83p,
    93–94, 129, 137; and creation
    of UFC, 80–84; development
    of, 75–76; and environmental
    devastation, 98–99, 152; and
    labor issues, 84–87, 97–98,
    105; and taxation, 89,
    123–24
Barrios, Gerardo, exile in Costa
    Rica, 62
Bellavista, 113–14, 116, 126
Blanco, Máximo, 66
Border disputes: Honduras and
    El Salvador, 134; Nicaragua,
    55, 60; Panama, 103
Boston Fruit Company, 82
Bourbon Reforms, 36
Brazilwood, 44

CACM (Central American
    Common Market), 132–34,
    133p, 135, 141
Cafetaleros, 47, 52, 54, 73; and
    Calderón Guardia, 101, 104,
    105, 108; diminishing
    influence, 84; politics, 60–61,
    63, 67. *See also* Coffee
CAFTA-DR (Central American
    Free Trade Agreement),
    157–58
Calderón Fournier, Rafael
    Angel, 158

Calderón Guardia, Rafael Angel,
    103p; Catholic Communist
    alliance, 105–6; expulsion of
    Figueres, 96, 106; the
    Opposition, 106–9; rise of,
    101–12; social reform, 102;
    War of National Liberation,
    109–10; World War II, 103–5.
    See also Calderonistas
Calderonistas: 1948 election, 109;
    agreement with Cortés, 102;
    attempted coup against
    Figueres, 125; *Liberación* era,
    115–16, 117, 120; opposition
    to, 107
Calufa. *See* Fallas, Carlos Luis
Canal, interest in, 54–56, 58, 66,
    153. *See also* Cañas-Jerez
    Treaty; Clayton-Bulwer
    Treaty; Panama Canal
Cañas-Jerez Treaty, 60
Carazo Odio, Rodrigo, 138
Cardona, Edgar, 117
Caribbean Legion, 107, 109,
    116, 125
Carranza, Bruno, 67
Carrillo, Braulio: dissolution of
    United Provinces, 41–43;
    overthrow of, 35–36, 43–44;
    reforms, 40–41, 45
Cartago: administrative
    province, 10; colonial capital,
    21–22, 23, 32; earthquake, 5;
    execution of Pablo Presbere,
    15–16; independence, 39;
    transportation, 54, 63; and
    Virgen de los Angeles, 26;
    War of National Liberation,
    109; War of the League,
    40–41
Castro Madriz, José María, 53,
    62–63

Castro, Fidel, 121, 131
Catholic Church, 11, 38, 39; in colonial era, 22, 25–26, 31; and nineteenth-century liberal reform, 41, 42, 52, 68–69, 70–73, 77; and twentieth-century politics, 92, 101–2, 105–6
CBI (Caribbean Basin Initiative), 146
Cecilio del Valle, José, 39
CENPRO (Center for the Promotion of Exports and Investments), 134, 140
Central America, 9; Arias peace plan in, 10, 144–50; and canal issues, 54–56, 152; and Caribbean Legion, 107; conservatives in, 42; diplomacy and, 62, 134; drug trade in, 156–57; filibusters in, 51–52, 56–60; geography, 2, 4, 35–36, 38; independence of, 37–38; pre-Columbian people, 17–18; UFC in, 8, 80–82, 124. *See also* CACM; CAFTA-DR; United Provinces of Central America
Central Valley: agriculture in, 27, 44–47, 84; in colonial period, 15–16, 21, 23–24, 32–33; geography of, 3, 4, 5; and labor, 99, 105; population of, 6, 7, 85; and pre-Columbian people, 17; and trade, 8, 155; transportation in, 48, 74–75, 80; and War of National Liberation, 109
Centro para el Estudio de los Problemas Nacionales, 96, 106, 118
Chinchilla, Laura, 10, 158–59

Cholera, 59–60
CINDE (Coalición Costarricense de Iniciativas de Desarrollo), 140–41
Cinema, 93
Civil Codes, 72–73
Clayton-Bulwer Treaty, 55–56
Climate, 3–4, 8, 20, 81
CODESA (Costa Rican Development Corporation), 135–37, 139, 140
Coffee, 6, 8, 12, 44–48, 97; and the environment, 151; and politics, 52–54, 60–63, 66, 69, 84, 90, 102, 105; and the railroad, 73–74, 81; volatility, 129, 131, 137. *See also* *Cafetaleros*
Colegio Superior de Señoritas, 71
Colombia, 79–80, 82, 88, 147, 157
Colombian Land Company, 82
Communism, 92, 105–6; and Cold War fears, 115–16, 126, 130–31; outlawed, 116. *See also* *Contras*
Communist Party, 92, 96, 99–100, 101, 102. *See also* PVP
Confederación Costarricense de Trabajadores, "Rerum Novarum," 105
Confederación de Trabajadores de Costa Rica, 105
Conservation, 143, 151, 153
Constitutional Democratic Party, 76–77
Constitution of 1871, 70
Constitution of 1949, 9, 11, 114, 116–17
Constitution of Cádiz, 37, 39
Contadora Group, 147–48
Contra scandal, 148
Contras, 145–48, 149, 150, 157

Convention for the Protection of Flora, Fauna, and Places of Natural Scenic Beauty in the Countries of the Americas, 153

Convention on International Trade in Endangered Species, 153

Corruption, 40, 61, 67, 77, 104, 107, 114, 136, 144, 157–58

Cortés, León, 101–2, 105, 106, 107–8

Coups d'état, 41, 48, 53, 61, 63, 66–67; New Republic, 116, 117. *See also* Tinoco Granados, Federico

Cuba, 88, 121, 131, 148

Cuban Revolution, 121, 131

Davis, Nathaniel, 110

Debt crisis, 8, 137–39, 154

Debt, foreign, 40, 61, 128, 144–46; and railroad construction, 74–75, 81. *See also* Debt crisis

Deforestation, 151–52

Democracy, 9, 62, 77, 89–90, 107, 121, 126, 131, 144

Dependency theory, 129

Diario de Costa Rica, 106

Drug trafficking, 93, 156–57

Duranista Party, 90

Earthquakes, 4, 5–6, 25, 54

Echandi, Mario, 130

ECLA (Economic Commission for Latin America and the Caribbean), 129–30, 132

Ecotourism, 4, 151–52. *See also* Tourism

Education, 7, 10–11, 102, 118–19, 158; under Alliance for Progress, 131; and liberalism, 40, 47, 53, 62, 65–66, 68–69, 70–72; military budget devoted to, 114, 116; for women, 63, 70–71

Eisenhower, Dwight, 131

El Centro. *See* Centro para el Estudio de los Problemas Nacionales

Electoral Tribunal, 9, 109, 117

El Salvador, 10, 18, 62; and Arias peace plan, 144, 147–48, 150; and CACM, 132–34; and United Provinces, 39, 42–43

Enlightenment, 37, 53

Entrepreneur state, 135, 138

Environment, 12, 79, 87, 151–54; and UFC, 98–99

Esquipulas (I & II), 148–49. *See also* Arias Sánchez, Oscar

Esquivel, Ascención, 77

European Union, 132

Export-Import Bank, 104

Export Processing Zone and Industrial Parks Law, 155

Exports, 8, 28; commodity, 42, 44–46, 69, 73–76; decline in Great Depression, 97–98, 99–100; diversification of, 117–18, 122, 130, 133–34, 140–41, 155. *See also* Bananas; Coffee; UFC

Fallas, Carlos Luis, 80, 97–98

Feminism, 71, 91–92

Ferdinand VII, 37

Fernández, Cristina María, 82

Fernández, Pacífica, 53

Fernández, Próspero, 66, 68, 75, 82

Figueres Ferrer, José, 108p; abolition of military, 113–14; Caribbean Legion, 107; Constitution of, 1949, 116–18;

creation of PLN, 118–21; economic policies, 121–24, 128–30, 135–37; exiled by Calderón Guardia, 96, 106; Founding Junta, 114–16; opposition to Calderón Guardia, 106–9; presidency, 121–26, 128–30, 134–37; War of National Liberation, 109–111
Figueres-Ulate Pact, 110, 117
Filibusters, 9, 11, 51, 54, 56, 58, 59–60, 88. *See also* Walker, William
Foreign investment, 8, 76, 131; direct, 140, 154–55
Forestry Law, 153
Founding Junta, 114–16
Free trade zones, 8, 132–33, 140–41, 155

García Marquez, Gabriel, 79–80
General Treaty of Central American Economic Integration, 132–33. *See also* CACM
General Workers' Confederation, 87
Generation of 48, 120
González Flores, Alfredo, 90
Great Banana Strike, 80, 97–98
Great Depression, 84, 96–98, 99–101, 102, 139
Guardia Gutiérrez, Tomás, 65–66; liberal reform, 69–72; railroad, 74–76; rise of, 67–68. *See also* Olympians
Guatemala, 7, 10, 17, 62; and Arias peace plan, 146–48; and CACM, 132–34; and Caribbean Legion, 109; UFC in, 82, 124–26, 130–31; and

United Provinces, 38–39, 41–42. *See also Audiencia* of Guatemala

Hacienda Santa Rosa, 59
Happiest country, 143–44
Health care, 7, 101, 103, 114, 118, 127, 156
Heredia, 10; independence, 38–39; War of the League, 41
Honduras, 10, 18, 28, 62; and Arias peace plan, 148, 150; and CACM, 132–34; UFC in, 82; and United Provinces, 38–39, 41–43; William Walker in, 60

ICT (Instituto Costarricense de Turismo), 153
Independence, 9, 36–38
Indigenismo, 119–20
Indigenous people, 6–7, 68, 119–20; during conquest, 20, 22, 24–25; population decline of, 23; pre-Columbian, 16–19. *See also Zambos mosquitos*
Industry, 8, 122, 130, 134–35; IT, 155. *See also* CACM; ISI
Infant mortality, 7, 127
Inflation, 128, 138, 141
Intel Corporation, 155
Inter-American Development Bank, 139
International Monetary Fund, 8, 138–39, 146
International Railways of Central America, 82
ISI (import substitution industrialization), 8, 128–30, 131, 135, 139–40; and CACM, 132–34. *See also* CODESA

Isthmus of Rivas, 55
Iturbide, Agustín, 38

Jiménez Oreamuno, Ricardo, 89, 92
Jiménez Zamora, Jesús, 62
Jocote Pact, 35–36, 43
Juan Santamaría International Airport, 117, 153

Keith, Minor Cooper, 8, 75–76, 80–82, 84–85, 88, 90, 93. *See also* UFC
Kennedy, John F., 131–32, 133p, 147

Lake Nicaragua, 55
Land tenure, 8; and coffee elite, 44–47, 63; colonial era, 23–24, 27–28, 30–32; reforms of, 40, 42, 45–46, 54, 72. *See also* UFC
La Negrita. *See* Virgen de los Angeles
Law of Foundations and Guarantees, 40
Law on Individual Rights, 73, 76
León Herrera, Santos, 110
Ley de la Ambulancia, 41
Ley general de educación común, 71
Liberación, 119–21, 141; economy, 121–24; foreign policy, 124–26. *See also* PLN
Liberalism, 11, 40, 42–46, 52–54, 61–63, 66, 67–73, 76–77; in Nicaragua, 58
Liberal Progressive Party, 76–77
Life expectancy, 7, 143
Liga Feminista, 92–93
Limón Workers' Federation, 85–86, 87
Literacy, 7, 11, 53, 76, 99, 127. *See also* Education

Literature, 12, 99. *See also Mamita Yunai*
Lost decade, 128, 138. *See also* Debt crisis

Mamita Yunai, 12, 80, 98
Manifest Destiny, 56–57
Meiggs Keith, Henry, 74–75
Meiggs, Henry, 74
Mexico, 17–18, 56–57, 147, 157; empire of, 37–39, 40; Figueres in exile in, 96
Military, 41, 43–44, 62, 66–67; abolition of, 10, 113–14, 117, 120, 125–26; and labor unrest, 86, 97; in National Campaign, 51–52, 58–60; and World War II, 103–4. *See also* Coups d'état
Mixed economy, 119, 122, 126
Monge, Luis Alberto, 138–39, 145–46
Montealegre Fernández, José María, 61–62, 66
Mora Fernández, Juan, 39–40
Mora Valverde, Manuel, 97
Mora, Juan Rafael, 53–54, 56; National Campaign, 58–61
Morazán, Francisco: execution, 36, 44; invasion of Costa Rica, 43; Jocote Pact, 35, 43; president of Costa Rica, 43–44; president of United Provinces of Central America, 42
Mt. Arenal, 4–5, 5p

Napoleon Bonaparte, 36–37
National Agricultural Society, 152
National Campaign, 59–60, 61, 63, 88
National Fisheries Plan, 122

National Geographic Institute, 152
National Institute for Housing and Urban Development, 122
National Observatory, 152
National parks, 4, 151, 153
National Parks Service, 153
National Physical-Geographic Institute, 66
National Republican Party, 90, 101, 105–7, 108, 114, 116. *See also* Calderón Guardia, Rafael Angel; War of National Liberation
Neoliberalism, 8, 139, 151, 154–56, 158
New Grenada, 37
New Spain, 23, 28, 38
Nicaragua, 2, 3, 4, 17, 18, 20–21, 28, 62; and Arias peace plan, 146–48, 149, 150; attempted invasion from, 125–26; border dispute with, 54–55; and CACM, 132–34; and Caribbean Legion, 107, 116; and drug trafficking, 157; filibusters in, 58–60; and United Provinces, 37–39, 43; U.S. military in, 88, 91
Nicoya Peninsula, 2, 3, 4; colonial period, 24; pre-Columbian, 18, 20
Nixon, Richard, 131
Nonrecognition, 91

OAS (Organization of American States), 126, 131–32
Oduber Quiros, Daniel, 135, 136
Oil shock, 136, 137–38. *See also* OPEC
Olympians, 66, 68–69, 70, 72, 73, 76–77

One Hundred Years of Solitude, 79–80
OPEC (Organization of Petroleum Exporting Countries), 136
Opposition, the, 106–9, 116
Orlich Bolmarcich, Francisco José, 131, 134
Ortega, Daniel, 148, 150

Pacheco, Abel, 157
Pact of the Mexican Embassy, 110, 114
Panama, 2, 4, 10, 19, 60, 88; and Arias peace plan, 146–48; border dispute with, 103; UFC in, 82. *See also* Panama Canal
Panama Canal, 56, 88, 103
Panama disease, 83, 98, 152
Pan-American Highway, 104, 109, 153
Parallel state, 141
Partido Renovación Democrática, 138
Partido Republicano Nacional, 90
Partido Social Democrático, 106
Pearl Harbor, 103
Pérez Jiménez, Marco, 125
Picado Michalski, Teodoro: presidency of, 106–9; War of National Liberation, 109–110
Picado, Jr., Teodoro, 125
Pinto, Antonio, 44
Pittier, Henri François, 65–66, 72
PLN (Partido Liberación Nacional), 124, 126, 131, 134, 138, 158–59; economic policies, 129, 135–37; formation, 118–21; neoliberalism, 139, 141.

See also Figueres Ferrer, José; Liberación
Political parties, Nicaragua, 58
Populism, 92, 94, 100–101, 117, 135, 137, 145
Positivism, 69, 71–72, 93
Postal service, 61
Poverty, 92, 101, 102, 127, 131, 134, 145
Prisons, 72, 92
Prostitution, 72, 93
Public works, 47, 61, 69, 100; Department of, 166
Puerto Limón, 3, 5–6, 7, 19, 63, 74, 75, 81; labor unrest in, 85–87, 97; and *San Pablo* incident, 95–96; withdrawal of UFC from, 98–99
Puerto Rico, 88
PUN (Partido Unión Nacional), 116, 121, 130, 141
Puntarenas, 2, 10, 48, 54, 74
Pura Vida, 1–2, 10, 13, 159–60
PUSC (Partido de Unidad Socialcristiana), 121, 141, 157–58
PVP (Partido Vanguardia Popular), 102, 105, 107, 116, 118–19

Quadragesimo Anno, 101

Racial conflict, 7, 56–57, 85–87, 98
Radio, 93, 99; address by José Figueres Ferrer, 96
Railroads, 3, 7, 8, 48, 135; and banana industry, 80–82, 84–85, 87–88, 93; construction of, 73–78; and the environment, 152
Rainforests, 3–4, 143, 152

Reagan, Ronald, 145–46, 150
Reformist Party, 92
Refugees, Central American, 147–48
Rerum Novarum, 101
Rivas, Battle of, 51–52, 59
Rivas, Isthmus of, 55
Rodríguez Zeledón, José Joaquín, 77
Roosevelt, Theodore, 88

Salazar, Lorenzo, 66
Sanabria, Victor Manuel, 102, 105
Sandinistas: and Arias peace process, 147–49; and drug trafficking, 157; and Reagan administration, 145–46
San José, 5, 6, 29, 44; administrative province, 10; development in, 47, 54, 63; education in, 65–66, 72; independence, 38–39, 40, 41; land reform in, 45–46; as national capital, 21, 40; protests in, 77, 96; transportation, 74, 104; War of National Liberation, 109–10; War of the League, 40–41
San Juan River, 2; border disputes, 55, 58, 60
San Pablo, 95–96
Santamaría, Juan, 11, 51–52, 59–60, 72, 88, 117
Santos Zelaya, José, 88
Second Republic, 107, 110–11, 114–15, 126, 137
Sigatoka, 98
Slavery, 7, 24, 29–30, 39; in conquest, 19–20; and William Walker, 58–59
Snyder Banana Company, 82
Soccer War, 134

Social Guarantees, 103, 106, 110, 117, 126, 128
Social security, 7, 101, 102–3, 127
Solidarismo, 156
Somoza Debayle, Anastasio, 145
Somoza, Anastasio, 107, 116, 125–26
Soto-Keith Contract, 75–76
Soto, Bernardo, 65, 82; and liberal reform, 66, 71–72; and the railroad, 75–76
Soviet Union, 105, 148
Spanish-American War, 88
Strikes, 86–87, 97–98, 124; in literature, 79–80. *See also* Great Banana Strike
Suffrage, 39, 70, 128; and people of color, 117; secret ballot, 92; and women, 93, 117
Supreme Electoral Tribunal, 9, 117

Taft, William Howard, 88
Taxes, 36, 43, 69, 90, 97, 107–8, 115, 117, 130, 137, 140; and neoliberal reform, 154–55; and tourism, 151, 154; and UFC, 87, 89, 98, 123–24, 126
Teatro Mora, 47
Telegraph, 63
Terrenos baldíos, 45–46
Theater, 12–13, 47, 77, 78p
Tico-Communism, 97–98
Ticos, 6
Tierra de legua, 45
Tierras públicas. See Terrenos baldíos
Tinoco Granados, Federico, 89–91, 92, 94, 113
Tobacco, 24, 36, 40, 62
Tourism Investment Incentives Law, 154

Tourism, 2, 4–6, 9, 12, 144, 151–54, 159. *See also* Ecotourism; Tourism Investment Incentives Law
Transportation, 7, 47, 48, 64, 68, 69, 73, 122, 133, 136. *See also* Canal, interest in; Railroads
Tropical Trading & Transport Company, 81, 82

UFC (United Fruit Company), 8, 95, 129; anti-imperialism against, 87–89; contract renegotiations, 98–99; 123–24; formation of, 82–84; in Guatemala, 124; and labor issues, 84–87, 97–98; in literature, 79–80, 98
Ulate Blanco, Otilio, 106, 109–10; and Founding Junta, 114–18. *See also* PUN; War of National Liberation
Unions, 86, 102, 105, 109, 124, 156
United Committee of Anti-Totalitarian Associations, 96
United Provinces of Central America: and border issues, 55; creation of, 38–39; dissolution of, 41–44
United States: and Arias peace plan, 147–49, 151; and canal interest, 54–56; cultural influences from, 13; economic aid from, 8, 138, 139, 146–47; economic involvement, 73, 81; interventions, 51–52, 56–60; military aid from, 114, 126, 131, 145; as WWII ally, 96, 103–4, 105. *See also* Anti-imperialism; Keith, Minor Cooper; Nonrecognition; UFC

Universidad de Santo Tomás, 53, 71
University of Costa Rica, 102,
    118, 152
USAID (U.S. Agency for
    International Development),
    133, 139–41, 146
U.S.-Mexican War, 57

Vanderbilt, Cornelius, 59–60
Venezuela, 30, 37, 125, 147
Villaseñor, Vicente, 35, 43–44
Virgen de los Angeles, 25–26,
    27p, 31, 72
Volcanoes, 4–5, 153
Volio Jiménez, Jorge, 92

Walker, William, 11, 51, 56–60,
    57p. *See also* Filibusters;
    National Campaign

War of National Liberation, 96,
    109–10, 114, 125
War of the League, 41, 43
Welfare state, 101–2
Wildlife Conservation
    Law, 153
Wilson, Woodrow, 91, 94
Women, 72, 91, 92–93; and
    education, 63, 71; and
    suffrage, 117, 121
World Bank, 138, 139, 146
World War I, 91
World War II, 95–96, 103–4,
    119, 129

Yglesias Castro, Rafael, 77

Zambos mosquitos, 30
Zelaya, Manuel, 158

About the Author

MONICA A. RANKIN, PhD, a pioneer in the study of Mexican diplomacy, gender, fashion, and identity in the 1940s, is assistant professor of history at the University of Texas–Dallas. Rankin specializes in the history of Mexico, Latin America, and U.S.–Latin American relations. Her published works include *Á México, la patria! Propaganda and Production during World War II* and *Encyclopedia of Latin American History and Culture: The Search for National Identity, 1820s–1900*. She has also written several chapters and articles on various aspects of Mexican foreign policy, gender, and popular culture during World War II. Dr. Rankin's current research examines popular culture, gender, and nationalism in twentieth-century Mexico as well as issues of U.S.–Latin American relations in the 1940s.

Other Titles in the Greenwood Histories of the Modern Nations
Frank W. Thackeray and John E. Findling, Series Editors

The History of Afghanistan
Meredith L. Runion

The History of Argentina
Daniel K. Lewis

The History of Australia
Frank G. Clarke

The History of the Baltic States
Kevin O'Connor

The History of Brazil
Robert M. Levine

The History of Bulgaria
Frederick B. Chary

The History of Cambodia
Justin Corfield

The History of Canada
Scott W. See

The History of Central America
Thomas Pearcy

The History of the Central
Asian Republics
Peter L. Roudik

The History of Chile
John L. Rector

The History of China,
Second Edition
David C. Wright

The History of Congo
Didier Gondola

The History of Cuba
Clifford L. Staten

The History of the Czech Republic
and Slovakia
William M. Mahoney

The History of Ecuador
George Lauderbaugh

The History of Egypt
Glenn E. Perry

The History of El Salvador
Christopher M. White

The History of Ethiopia
Saheed Adejumobi

The History of Finland
Jason Lavery

The History of France
W. Scott Haine

The History of Germany
Eleanor L. Turk

The History of Ghana
Roger S. Gocking

The History of Great Britain
Anne Baltz Rodrick

The History of Greece
Elaine Thomopoulos

The History of Haiti
Steeve Coupeau

The History of Holland
Mark T. Hooker

The History of Honduras
Thomas M. Leonard

The History of India
John McLeod

The History of Indonesia
Steven Drakeley

The History of Iran
Elton L. Daniel

The History of Iraq
Courtney Hunt

The History of Ireland
Daniel Webster Hollis III

The History of Israel
Arnold Blumberg

The History of Italy
Charles L. Killinger

The History of Japan,
Second Edition
Louis G. Perez

The History of Korea
Djun Kil Kim

The History of Kuwait
Michael S. Casey

The History of Mexico,
Second Edition
Burton Kirkwood

The History of New Zealand
Tom Brooking

The History of Nicaragua
Clifford L. Staten

The History of Nigeria
Toyin Falola

The History of Pakistan
Iftikhar H. Malik

The History of Panama
Robert C. Harding

The History of Peru
Daniel Masterson

The History of the Philippines
Kathleen M. Nadeau

The History of Poland
M. B. Biskupski

The History of Portugal
James M. Anderson

The History of Puerto Rico
Lisa Pierce Flores

The History of Russia,
Second Edition
Charles E. Ziegler

The History of Saudi
Arabia
Wayne H. Bowen

The History of Serbia
John K. Cox

The History of Singapore
Jean E. Abshire

The History of South Africa
Roger B. Beck

The History of Spain
Peter Pierson

The History of Sri Lanka
Patrick Peebles

The History of Sweden
Byron J. Nordstrom

The History of Thailand
Patit Paban Mishra

The History of Turkey
Douglas A. Howard

The History of Ukraine
Paul Kubicek

The History of Venezuela
*H. Micheal Tarver and
Julia C. Frederick*

The History of Vietnam
Justin Corfield